FREEDOM, FESTIVALS AND CASTE IN TRINIDAD AFTER SLAVERY

FREEDOM, FESTIVALS AND CASTE IN TRINIDAD AFTER SLAVERY

A Society in Transition

Neil A. Sookdeo

To order additional copies of this book, contact:
Xlibris Corporation
1-888-7-XLIBRIS
www.Xlibris.com
Orders@Xlibris.com

CONTENTS

INTRODUCTION

The present-day Republic of Trinidad and Tobago, and the Caribbean region generally, have been influenced by waves of voluntary and involuntary settlers since Europe's discovery of the New World. The fact of African slavery would incline one to believe that places like Guyana, Suriname and Trinidad would enjoy majority populations of Africans or African-Americans. In fact, these three countries today have moderate to sizeable Asian majorities. For outside of the Caribbean it is a little-known fact that men, women and children from British-controlled India were taken to far-flung plantations as bonded laborers—then labelled *coolies*— in the years after the British Slave Emancipation Act of 1833. While some of the impact of this Asian labor migration to the Americas have been assessed by scholars, the effort here by a descendant of indented Indian laborers—albeit from South Africa— is a holistic assessment as to why Indians, and not free Europeans or Africans, came to work the post-slavery plantations. The discipline essential to the exercise of such a study as this required a choice of a sample and Trinidad became our spatial focus for the period 1834-1888. The macroeconomic imperatives which turned South Asians into "East Indian indenteds" in Trinidad were also responsible for that Trinidad's—and the Caribbean region— relegation to a producer of agricultural staples ranging from tobacco to cocoa and sugar, even after slavery. An implicit case is made in this study for the microcosm of Trinidad helping one understand the larger imperial reality, especially for the years following slave abolition. This reality is one where the colonies enjoyed varying levels of control over their human resources versus imperial goals, though Britain might sometimes promote one colony over others for either cultural, geopolitical or even sentimental reasons. In other words, if one British colony might have outshone Trinidad's economy up to 1888, that fact will not diminish a reality where colonies did not choose their futures.

The uniqueness of our contribution lies not simply in our presentation of the human side of this Asian immigrant story, but also in correcting the imbalance where East Indians have generally been presented as "free" laborers who, by their own volition, replaced African slaves on British plantations across the globe in the nineteenth century. Previous studies on this topic have presented Indians as an "ethnic problem" in the Americas rather than part of Caribbean labor history. The nature of Indian labor—whether it was truly free or not—and Indian agency are central to the concerns of this work. We noted that the East Indian was not prepared for life on the plantations of Trinidad; in part because few women were recruited when able-bodied single men were the priority group sought by the plantation management and Britain. The largely celibate lifestyles of men who had believed they would be taken to other parts of India was a cultural response to a paucity of Indian women and few of them venturing to cohabit or marry black women. The social and moral concerns over the highly imbalanced Indian sex ratio are compounded when we look at other aspects of Indian community life pertaining to whether their children were allowed a childhood in nineteenth-century Trinidad. Questions that arose were: Could children of Indian plantation laborers choose to go to school as opposed to working alongside their parents? When Indian children worked on plantations, could they be jailed for "labor offenses" like the adults? This study will show that it was the exception when children of Indian indenteds attended school or were treated differently than were adult contract laborers. A valid question here is whether Indians signed their labor contracts in India before arriving in the plantation colonies.

We also focussed on the world of leisure among the largely Hindu laborers. This world of the Indians included a sphere that planters and employers rarely penetrated, a world where the laboring man or woman could maintain cultural and personal autonomy, and where non-Indian influences were minimal. We succeeded in juxtaposing the worlds of labor and leisure, which culminates in our final chapter on street festivals, and asked questions about how these "worlds" informed each other. The fact that the East Indian in Trinidad remains approximately "Indian" rather than Anglo-or Afro-Trinidadian means that the Indian world of the migrant laborer survived this other middle passage and remains functional in Trinidad. Yet Indian parents did begin to opt for Presbyterian mission schools for their children as Chapter Four demonstrates with statistics on education.

In the world outside the communal barracks, makeshift homes and cultural repertoire, the Indian was just a laborer, just a package of sinew, tissue and muscle. This fact did influence the material conditions of Indian life. But did the nineteenth-century Indian sub-culture explain why Indians were the preferred replacement for African slaves? Long-standing, established cultures and sub-cultures nevertheless adjust, learn from and also influence their environment. Chapter Five, which also found evidence that East Indian culture influenced the broader Trinidad culture and was equally influenced by colonial life, might have been a starting point for this study because its climax is a massacre of scores of indented and non-indented Indians at their popular annual Muhurram festival. The infamous Trinidad massacre of 30 October 1884 appears to have had a tone of inevitability, if only to the extent that two equally self-confident cultures cannot coexist harmoniously before the advent of a democratic form of government. Ultimately, the organization of chapters adopted here had the advantage of focussing on broad social issues such as whether opportunities arose in the nineteenth century for building a free society and a national culture and establishing better race relations. This question might be asked of other volatile regions of the world such as the Middle East.

India's racial and social impact in the Caribbean is a consequence of the British as well as the French and Dutch

Caribbean turning to non-economic forces to prolong the life of their plantations, so that labor—initially, of all races—would negotiate with planter-employers from a weaker position than labor had generally won at the Emancipation of slaves in the 1830s. The imperial decision to allow indenture represents a complex twist in the history of free labor. The understandable chagrin of the freed slaves at a continuous stream of Indian migrants which weakened their post-emancipation clout within Trinidad ought not to cloud the reality: East Indians and Afro-Trinidadians were weak negotiators for their separate or joint causes with Britain and its planters. Our emphasis fell on British decision-making, not local politics *per se*, as Britain alone could have avoided sanctioning indented labor. While India may have been the jewel in the British Crown, in matters of post-emancipation labor Britain's economic and other interests moved away from India toward the planters in its overseas colonies.

In early colonial America British interests had converged with those of its tobacco and other planters because labor was at a premium before African slavery had become acceptable; the preferred solution had thus been European indenture. The movement of migrants out of India and Asia more generally—which shares characteristics with the migration of white servants[1] and sometimes with convicts sent to Australia, South Africa and the United States—is a useful background for studying the post-slavery return to indenture when post-emancipation complaints of sugar, coffee and cocoa planters were echoed in Britain. East Indian servitude was ultimately different than colonial servitude in the United States and these differences are discussed in the chapters that follow.

The nature of East Indian labor migration is, at first glance, self evident. This apparently voluntary emigration has influenced the tone if not the substance of Indo-Trinidadian history. East Indians appeared to have been free individuals exercising rights of free labor and movement in the years after the abolition of slavery within the British Empire. Laborers apparently agreed to contracts to work for a certain number of years in a plantation colony before returning to their families in India. A closer examination of the phenomenon posed questions about whether would-be laborers knew the distances between, say Mauritius and India and between Trinidad and India, and how free were their choices about the destination. An equally crucial question concerned timing: why were Indians not encouraged to migrate to places like Trinidad before the nineteenth century? The first arrivals in Trinidad on ships such as the 1845 vessel *Fateh Rozack* came soon after the African slaves were freed from bondage to employers in the British Empire.

The historiography has generally eschewed any careful analysis of the ever-changing rules of indenture, both at the recruiting end in India and at the assigning to plantations in each colony. Rules which applied to East Indian migrants in the 1840s cannot, in conscience, be used to explain what indenture in Trinidad entailed in 1876 or 1890. The conundrum is that after the abolition of African slavery, Indian indenteds were gradually coerced into longer and longer contracts in conjunction with fewer and fewer rights and redress for labor grievances; yet they were free persons. Those who came on the 1845 vessels were *not* compelled to enter into contracts and were *not* bound to specific employers, and were promised repatriation to India after five years.[2] Subsequent Indian migrants were bound by ten-year contracts of "industrial residence" in Trinidad and to specific plantations and employers with *criminal* sanctions for leaving the workplace without passes. This policy of passes turned Indians into the largest group imprisoned by British colonial Trinidad by the 1870s. Crucially, too, Indian "immigrants" could not end their obligations promptly. Repatriation of individual Indians could be delayed for years when the authorities failed to charter return ships, or when the ex-indented were asked to pay for their return fares, and when employers demanded that "the coolie" compensate them for all the days lost through bad weather, work deemed slovenly, and days spent in prison.

Indian indenture thus evolved into something worse than the free wage labor it was advertized to be for nineteenth-century Indians. After the first years of slave Emancipation in 1834 plantations began turning back the clock as far as freedom of labor went, transforming free workers into virtual debt-peons or underpaid, seasonal laborers.[3] Migrants from Madeira, Germany and France in the 1830s and 1840s fit into this framework; often Venezuelans called peons would travel to Trinidad for seasonal work; and there was immigration from places further afield.

Although critics of Indian indenture saw it as a modified system of slavery throughout its duration, we prefer placing indenture within a continuum where slavery and free wage labor are at either end. This helps us see that indenture shared features common to both regimes. Britain's best intentions with regards to its Indian subjects could be undermined in colonies once the sanction for this "coolie trade" had been given. In asking about how well a colonized and largely illiterate people understood the geographical and other details of their contracts, and how free they were in the cultural aspects of their lives during this post-slavery era, we see the practical interface between freedom and servitude, and from time to time, between imperial decision-making and policy-making in the colonies. Where Britain might have sought to promote free wage labor, the recruiting agent from the receiving colony and the validity of the information or propaganda could become critical in the decision of would-be East Indian labor migrants.

The rules governing the contracts of indenture were modified by the local government in Trinidad throughout the entire period of our study, and to describe the Indian experience in terms only of hindsight or in an inadequate shorthand may exacerbate distortions of national and global history. An overly simplified assessment of indenture appears in the following example:

All immigrants were given the option of repatriation after completing their five years of indenture, but the majority elected to remain and turn the West Indies into a racial hot pot. To add flavour, after 1850 Chinese were brought in, the majority going to Guiana, a considerable number to Jamaica and others to Trinidad.[4]

How does one assess whether Indian labor migrants *elected* to *remain* in a colony as opposed to opting for repatriation? Especially when there were logistical ambiguities and delays in chartering return ships, even as some planters enticed Indians to remain with rewards in cash and kind? What is the significance of a story which clarifies the nature of the ordeal of free labor as it applied to laborers from India? The process which turned East Indians into objects of employers and subjects of ethnological curiosity did not begin with them; 193 Chinese had come on indenture to Trinidad in 1806 already. The island consistently comprised 40-50 percent immigrants throughout the nineteenth century.[5] We have presented a part of world history and global population movements— voluntary and involuntary—as they played out in Trinidad. This is part of the story of labor and *freedom*, which is also about free labor, the right to negotiate wages and to unionize.

After many governments, organizations and peoples had fought valiantly to abolish African slave labor, it is important to know if and how their victory was rendered pyrrhic when new victims, even if not chattel, were found by Britain and its colonial planters. If Indians were rendered harlots of the British Empire, the strategies employed by the enemies of free labor hold lessons for other times and actors. So too do the successes and survival strategies resorted to by the victims, some of which is to be found in lower class festivals and leisure pursuits. Indenture of Asians also helped make the world a smaller place by bringing distant peoples together in new places under the aegis of the plantation (See Appendices 1 and 2 on Population changes in Trinidad). In this sense too Trinidad's legacy is an international legacy; several overseas Indians quietly endure the consequences of indenture today.

Until the publication of Walton Look Lai's study, *Indentured Labor, Caribbean Sugar: Chinese and Indian Migrants to the British West Indies, 1838-1918*[6] and David Northrup's *Indentured Labor in the Age of Imperialism, 1834-1922*[7] the study of British-sponsored indenture was shaped by the mining of ethnic and ethnological veins in the richly polyglot Caribbean. One consequence has been the politicization of differences, both apparent and real. Another consequence has been distinct or segregated discussions, even on labor.[8] We are impelled by a deeper search which, in the first instance, must explain the abrupt loss of clout by free workers in Trinidad between Emancipation and 1844. We might then comprehend the nature of the ordeal of East Indian labor migrants, so as to compare it with that of others in Trinidad as well as elsewhere.[9]

Our work falls within the domain of the new historiography of indented labor as described by David Northrup, a "feature" of which is a concern with "relating indentured labor to the changing historical circumstances in capital markets, ideas, and technology" which has shaped our world.[10] Although we see the East Indian story as integral to the story of Emancipation and free labor, the larger context is that of the democratization of the new world, especially in view of the bold experiments of 1776 in North America. It would have been useful to have located Trinidad's 1834-1888 experiments with indenture within the dialectic of struggle between capital and labor, as Walter Rodney has done for Guyanese history. The use of non-economic influences to transport a foreign people to labor on Trinidad's estates for less monetary value than the recently freed slaves were commanding is but the deployment of the colonial state to grant a longer life to agrarian capital or the plantocracy, thereby delaying socio-economic progress for all. We were also tempted by one scholar's use of a *trialectical* approach in understanding Trinidad.[11] Our preference eventually came down on the side of social transitions, such as that from slavery to free labor, and we have been mindful of of "globalization" throughout our study.

Currently, new perspectives and syntheses are making us more aware of backward *and* forward linkages in time thereby aiding our understanding of what has been happening to the global tribe as a whole a la the phenomenon of "globalization." For instance the United States may have ended slavery during its Civil War (1861-65) but the tradition of freedom enshrined in that nation's founding asserted itself both before and since the 1863 Emancipation Proclamation of President Abraham Lincoln. The rise of abolitionism and the earlier contribution of the Quakers in United States history are but evidence of this. Another is the outlawing of "voluntary and involuntary servitude" in the Anti-Peonage Act of 1867. Thus when Hawaii was absorbed into the United States in 1900, the prohibition of contracts of indenture came into effect there. In terms of global history, therefore, the USA may have been an early beacon of freedom which came late to slave Emancipation, but has led the way in embodying all kinds of freedom at several junctures on the global arena.

We who increasingly employ the term "globalization" on the threshold of the third millennium often forget that the origins of globalization lie further back in time, perhaps it has been the predominant trend in our recorded histories. Indian indenture has had unintended consequences in this apparent inexorable trend towards more interactions, more openness in commerce, democracy and world-views, not only in an Indian diaspora, but also in being a grievance used by M.K. Gandhi, Gopal Krishna Gokhale and the Rev. C.F. Andrews to fight for political freedom in the Indian subcontinent.[12] In a real sense, labor migration before and since slavery and Emancipation have been part of the imperative of globalization, which occasionally becomes obfuscated by inherited terminology embodied in such terms as "discovery," "Indians;" "Emancipation;" "development;" "civilized." At its most concise, globalization involves centripetal forces on the world stage virtually nullifying distance between peoples, places and economies through such developments as in transport and technology, and the transmission of ideas. Mass transportation on sailing-and steam-ships did bridge the distances between Asian peoples and western plantations; once in places like Trinidad, the newcomers wanted rights and freedoms similar to those enjoyed by their new compatriots.

The efforts to understand the motives among the various race groups in Trinidad, to understand colonizer and colonized, is but to humanize our study. Without the *agency* of the various groups we might imply that these amoral beings lived entirely at the mercy of all-powerful, economic forces.[13] In this study we have presented East Indians as complex human beings, not simply as units of labor deployed against free laborers of erstwhile slave colonies. We came to understand the frustrations of a people who left mostly anecdotal accounts of their abuse.[14] We also learned something of the difficulties and the motives of planters and other non-Indians in Trinidad. We remained mindful of the contest between capital and labor, without having resorted to crude reductionism.

Our formal hypothesis may be stated thus: Indian indenture is integral to Trinidad's colonial and labor histories, and the Indian experience in Trinidad did not entail a progression from harshness to mildness during the period 1845-1888. Indenture is also larger than its ethnic features, especially because it helps us view human institutions in transition. Chapter Four on Education turns out to be the most optimistic one and ironically so, because Indo-Trinidadians boasted only one school in 1857[15]—and that an orphanage—but 42 schools by 1885, the majority of these being Canadian Presbyterian establishments. As with the convoluted and segregated educational experience, indenture in Trinidad did not follow a linear path of progress towards freedom or the post-war (1914-18) market system.[16]

Scholars such as David Northrup betray a bias which insists on seeing a linear progress in human affairs and have avoided dealing with Trinidad's atypical experience. Progress can and does arrive via convoluted paths, with gains but setbacks and losses, too. We also differ with Northrup insofar as Indian indenture may not have been sufficiently exposed in its separate locations to parallel the recent direction of slavery studies which no longer focus on the harsh or mild features of that system.[17] The holocaust of Jews may have been an atypical German response after World War I, but that will never allow us to sweep that horror under the global carpet.[18]

Our choice of Trinidad and its social history during 1834-1888 was promoted partly for its atypicality in the trend toward greater freedom for indented labor, even at the close of the nineteenth century. This contradicted the concurrent experience of other indented workers, for instance the Portuguese and Africans, in the same island. Also, these 54 years allow one to view external influences—such as the colonial occupation of India by 1860; contemporary notions concerning race and democracy, free trade, and land—across the transition from slavery to freedom. Together they allow us to comprehend this aspect of globalization and its contradictions. Had this study begun in 1845 when British Indians first came to Trinidad, it might have repeated the practice of discussing Indo-Trinidadian indenture separately from that of other similarly placed groups in Trinidad. Our discussion will remain mindful of the imperatives of the plantation and of workers' many struggles against inhumane conditions. Such concerns are not absent in our own era, on the threshold of a new millennium.

The non-European character of indenture in the nineteenth century, the scale on which it went to plantation societies and its survival through 1916-21, slowed down the commoditization of labor more generally. At the end of slavery when land and capital were losing their preeminence as the most important factors of production in colonies such as Natal/South Africa, Hawaii, Peru and Trinidad, so wage labor could share the stage and limelight, the propinquity between African slavery and Asian indenture halted the process almost to the point of reversal. The sentimental attraction for calling Chinese indenture in Peru or Indian indenture in Natal and Trinidad "new forms of slavery" is less important than making the point that when free Asian labor was tied for years to distant plantations, all free labor bore the consequences of that defeat. Truly free labor ought to command its price and exercise freedom of movement among places of work and employers.

Although Indian indenteds may have shared the motives of earlier European indenteds in seeking to improve their lives, Indian migrants came to labor for non-Indians in alien social and disease environments. White servants did not come from colonized countries and they usually shared a common race and elements of European culture with employers. However, like the Indians, they too had to adjust to new diseases. When we look beyond the details of the first arrangements which brought Indians to the Caribbean we see that again, like white servants, they have become integral parts of the nations or territories which both during their servitude and since offered them opportunities to redeem their years of bondage through free enterprise. In Trinidad the work of the Canadian Presbyterian Church from about 1870 onward helped socialize greater numbers of Indians so that they were able to move to middle class status faster, than if that task had been left in the hands of colonial Trinidad. In our overall analysis, however, the differences between Indian and non-Indian migrants are critical. We arrive at these conclusions *inter alia* in Chapter Two after which the implications of these differences will be explained in terms of the options for Indians, both in their work lives and in terms of cultural freedom in Trinidad during 1845-1888.

A NOTE ON TERMS AND THE INDIAN BACKGROUND

An indenture refers to an agreement between a laborer and an agent or employer, with the latter usually paying the costs of transporting the laborer to the site of work. Those who serve indentures are referred to as indenteds, although the contract—"indenture"—has also given us a less elegant synonym, "indentureds" for this species of migrant workers. We will avoid the use of indentureds, except where meaning is added for earlier historical periods, as per eighteenth-century "indentured servants." Those who completed their indentures are called "indenture-free" Indians, although sources may use non-indented or ex-indentured.

An acceptable formal definition of what is meant by indenture is that employed by Ralph Shlomowitz: "The distinctive feature of indenture, as compared to free labor was . . . that the employer was given a criminal remedy for what were otherwise civil offenses. In free labour systems, workers who broke their contracts could be brought before the courts on a civil charge and were subject to a civil penalty (damages); in indentured labour systems, workers who broke their contracts could be brought before the courts on a criminal charge and were subject to a criminal penalty (imprisonment or fine)."[19]

Creolisation is used in this study to convey that persons from British India were setting down local, Trinidadian, roots, whether in speech, in fetes, in flexibility with their mores, and so on. In fact, indented workers ceased being Indians when they left India, even though they remained largely Hindu or Muslim as well as British subjects. After 1870, many Indians had begun to compromise on religious sentiments so as to send their children to Christian mission schools and improve their chances in Trinidad. This date is also significant for the reason that thenceforth Indians could exchange return passages to India for land in Trinidad, whenever the colony was willing to make grants, as in the 1869-1880 experiment.

"Trinidad" refers only to the larger island of today's twin island group, the Republic of Trinidad and Tobago. Until 1888—the endpoint of this study—the two islands were administered separately. Archival data in Britain are similarly separated. We are concerned, therefore, with Trinidad proper in this study.

My preference for "Afro-Trinidadians" to refer to people who in the nineteenth century were called "Negroes", "coloureds," and "freedmen" may appear anachronistic, and it is. Therefore, when differentiation between the communities is required I use "blacks" to mean generally all who had some African ancestry. "African" which had been used to refer to those ex-slaves and ex-indenteds who as far as the society went were unmixed Africans, today approximates "Black" as used in the United States. "Coloureds" is used here in the specific colonial reference to mixed-race persons; at times, this group will be subsumed within "African" or "black" or creoles.

"India" is used broadly to refer to both independent and annexed territories under the control of British East India Company (BEIC) and/or Britain during the nineteenth century. Until the Indian Mutiny or colonial rebellion of 1856-8, that massive territory called India was ruled by the BEIC. This raises interesting questions about the degree to which Britain could control, regulate and protect from abuse the allegedly voluntary emigration of people over whom a trading company had rights of supervision and government. I have used "British Indians", "migrant Indians", and after 1868, "East Indians"—when the Canadian Presbyterian Church began to substitute it for "coolie"—to refer to this conglomeration of peoples from the subcontinent (unless documents use alternate terminology). "Settler Indians" were migrants who gave up their rights to a free return passage in exchange for offers of land or money after 1869.

It is nevertheless correct to treat the people of India as colonial subjects of Britain long before the Company's demise. British army officers, not the BEIC, subdued Afghanistan and seized the Sikh capital of Lahore (in Pakistan) between 1838 and 1848, while ever since 1765 the Company's actions in India had been constrained by parliamentary statutes. According to P. Knupland:

India formed a part of the British empire even in the days of 'John Company.' . . . When British merchants suffered indignities at Rangoon [Burma], Lord Dalhousie, governor general of India, declared war. Theoretically the conquest came under the control of the East India Company, although a member of its court of directors declared before a select committee of the house of commons, 'The Court of Directors have no knowledge whatever of the origin, progress, or present state of war in Burmah.' 'John Company' and India were mere tools of Britain.[20]

Questions about the justice of exporting Indian people overseas were, if only in a limited way, cause and consequence of the "Sepoy Mutiny" or the great Indian Rebellion. In fact, some of those who had participated in that rebellion subsequently sought to put distance between themselves and the British authorities. Mutineers among warrior and other classes did make their way to Trinidad.[21]

"Caste" is discussed in some detail, especially at the end of Chapter Two. Since there is no equivalent to "caste" in Indian languages, the term will appear within inverted commas. Rather than an indulgence, this is a method by which one might redirect the focus to a more accurate understanding of the pan-Indian social system, so nonchalantly and conveniently termed "caste". One has only to read beyond the standard texts on Indian culture and religion to recognize that Muslims, Jews and Christians in India have retained "caste" even after conversions.[22]

The complex milieu in which the establishment of Indian

communities outside the subcontinent occurred, was impacted by
the labor and financial crisis in plantation economies (Mauritius
and the Caribbean), and the paradoxical place India held in the
British Empire. At the same time as unassimilated Indian tribal
groups (the Dhangurs[23], for instance) were being lured to
Mauritius and British Guiana, British Indian skills were coveted
in East Africa (civil servants and financiers) and in Aden (mainly
business professionals). Interestingly, Aden and the then East
African Protectorate respectively, were administered from India and
used Indian institutions and currency. Aden was administered by
the Government of India from 1839 to 1937, which facilitated
the free entry of Indians as artisans, clerks and supervisors. It was
the least English-literate—and therefore the most vulnerable—
Indians who suffered the worst abuses. As accounts of abuses
especially those which women[24] emigrants endured were filtered
through the press in an increasingly restless and nationalistic India,
the Indian Government agitated against "Indian slavery."[25] The
1916 wartime prohibition on labor migration was reinforced with
an Indian Act of 1922. This Indian Emigration Act gave India
rights of supervision with labor migrants already in places like
Ceylon, and also entirely prohibited labor migration to the West
Indies and Mauritius.[26]

"One can only wonder today," wrote Eric Williams, "how it
was possible for any country that had abolished slavery on the
ground that it was inhuman to justify Indian indenture with its
25 cents a day wage and its jails."[27] We will answer those issues
raised by Williams, but with the hope that our analysis will be at
least equal to any passion. Yet the full story of the East Indians of
Trinidad must be told. It is not only an historiographical necessity;
it has relevance to continuing struggles between capital and labor,
and between freedom and unfreedom, in our global village.

CHAPTER ONE

EMERGENCE OF A PLANTATION AND IMMIGRANT CULTURE (1808-1838)

Eighteen-hundred-and-eight was in many ways a momentous year for Trinidad. The indigenous Indian population, slowly increasing after the severe losses following contact with Europeans, began an irreversible decline. Small local events like a town fire in March 1808 also loomed large on the Trinidad landscape, reminding one that all politics may be seen as local. Napoleon Bonaparte's ambitions for France impinged upon the Americas, especially since Trinidad was a colony of France's archrival, Britain.

The year 1808 can thus be seen as a turning point for Trinidad's economic choices and destiny. For the island which had experienced slavery, the most momentous event was the abolition of the slave trade by the colonial master, Britain. Labor shortages or the claim that ex-slave laborers had become lazy and insolent would pave the way for many new immigrants, white, black as well as Asian (Chinese and East Indian for the most part).

Napoleon's ambitions helped reorient Trinidad's economic choices. The rivalry between Britain and France under Napoleon modified the British impulse to use Trinidad simply to attack and weaken Spain on mainland South America. British policy now focussed on making the island an economic success. In this era, economic success meant plantations, notably sugar plantations. This new goal of developing Trinidad was to dovetail with the planters' slow but insistent demand that Britain supply them with completely new workers from its population-rich colonies. In any other era or place, the logical impulse would have been to work out new employer-employee relations within the country.

This chapter will show that Trinidad did not have a developed slave economy before Abolition in 1808, nor did the plantations reach their zenith of production when Emancipation followed in 1834. Had the situation been otherwise, Trinidad would *not* have had a need for non-Caribbean labor immigrants when slaves became free men and women. Barbados, Jamaica and those islands acquired by Britain before the nineteenth century were sufficiently populated with African slaves at Abolition to present land:people ratios in favor of the planters. That is, in colonies where most of the land was already occupied or cultivated, squatting (or not working on the estates of former slavemasters) was not an option for Afro-Caribbean people. *They*, rather than new immigrants, continued to do most of the work on the estates and plantations. Elsewhere in Spanish America, Amerindians (Maya, Inca, Aztec) had performed plantation-type labor on the *encomienda* and *mita* systems, and were replaced by local mixed-race *mestizos* and relatively few African slaves. British Trinidad did not follow this pattern: the indigenous or first Trinidadians barely survived into the nineteenth century. The year 1808 was a somber one for Amerindian numbers. The small gain since 1797 was reversed.

Amerindians now numbered 1,635 individuals whereas three years earlier they had boasted a total of 1,733 people.[28] When slavery itself was abolished, Amerindians had lost more than half their 1808 population. The few Caribs who survive in Arima in present-day Trinidad, are of mixed Amerindian-African ancestry, underscored by the term "Black Caribs," because blacks had been accepted as partners and spouses by these first Trinidadians.

Trinidad, as one of Britain's newest possessions, was to have a different experience from Jamaica and the older sugar colonies. A long view of history reveals that once the indigenous Indians were on a one-way street toward extinction, Trinidad's "development" would depend upon immigration. Trinidad's first colonial master,

Spain, and afterwards the British too, enticed planters to come to the island with their slaves. Persons of color who wanted to settle as "freemen" had that opportunity tp leave other colonies for Trinidad. Even before the demise of slavery, free blacks from the United States, and other Americans who retired from the British armed forces, were settled in Trinidad. In fact, in 1806 Trinidad had sought Chinese laborers, in part to avoid the problems of the abolition in 1807. A few hundred Chinese had arrived, but within a year all but 23 had returned to China; subsequent efforts showed the near impossibility of conducting *free* emigration from an independent non-western country.[29]

Trinidad, therefore, has no post-Columbian history outside of voluntary and involuntary immigration, a trend which continued with the post-emancipation reliance upon African, European and East Indian indenture.

1.1 BAPTISM IN FIRE AND UNIQUENESS OF SLAVERY IN TRINIDAD

When Napoleon's 1808 invasion of Spain led Britain to abandon fomenting colonial revolutions in Spanish America, Trinidad took a new turn in the history of the region. The island had been retained after the Treaty of Amiens (1802) not because Britain intended extending the slave plantations there, but because of its strategic location (less than 20 miles from Venezuela) on the edge of Spain's mainland empire. Trinidad seemed to be an excellent base from which to supply men and materiel to anti-Spanish revolutionaries. Napoleon's invasion of Spain meant that its colonies were rudderless and potentially useful to the French occupiers. This forced the British to think about Trinidad's economic development. After 1808 Britons were encouraged to invest in plantations, including sugar, a long-term investment.

As fate would have it, a great conflagration in Trinidad also destroyed the "clothing, arms and ammunition" which Francisco Miranda—probably Spanish America's best known exile-revolutionary—had stored in the capital, Port of Spain.[30] It was at this late hour that British Trinidad took its decisive steps toward a plantation economy. In a sense, therefore, the 1808 fire attested to a terminus on the "destabilization" route for Trinidad. Now Britain was indicating it would remain for the long-term and invest in Trinidad. It had been moving rather slowly in the direction of a plantation economy under Spain but this was abruptly interrupted by the British conquest of 1797 and Trinidad appealed to Britain as a base from which to conquer the richer parts of Spain's empire. Now the ambitions of France and Napoleon forced Briatin into a grudging alliance with Spain, an end to attacks mounted from Trinidad, and a focus on economic activity after 1808.

A year of remarkable coincidences was thus accentuated by what may be described as a ritual cleansing in the Port of Spain fire. A blaze which began at about 10 pm on 24 March 1808, rapidly swept through the heart of the capital. The fire had originated in the main street of Port of Spain: By 11-o-clock Frederick Street was consumed and before 12 the whole front of the town was burnt . . . excepting the Commissary General's house and stores and Mckintosh's and Cipriani's brick buildings. . . . [31]

An estimated 10,000 people or a third of the population were adversely affected by the fire. Many lessons for the future were read into the 1808 fire. The most obvious lesson was that the capital had to opt for more durable, preferably brick, structures. In the years ahead, regulations outlawing the building of wooden houses would receive greater urgency after another fire devastated Trinidad's second town, San Fernando, in 1818.[32] Many of the surviving historical structures in Trinidad today owe their happy fate to the fires of 1808 and 1814.

The metaphor of ritual cleansing in fire for the sins of slavery, if at all valid elsewhere, appears quite unjust for Trinidad. The island had a mere 310 slaves prior to 1783, the year when a Spanish *cedula de poblacion* offered Catholics and other subjects of friendly nations generous land grants in Trinidad.[33] Newcomers per the cedula individually received 32 acres (even if they came in families) and an additional 16 acres for each slave they might bring along. The 1783 cedula therefore inaugurated plantation slavery in Trinidad. Persons of color—many runaways qualified—entering Trinidad were offered 16 acres each for themselves and the same for every slave they brought. Until 1789, "many slaves [who had] fled independently from the Antilles" to Trinidad were able to obtain "concessions as freemen."[34] Immigrants and slave dealers would help to double Trinidad's slave population between its conquest from Spain (1797) to a total of 21,895 by the year 1808. In contrast Spanish Trinidad, with a loan of a million pesos for the years 1790-97, had marginally increased its slave numbers from 6,396 to 10,009.[35]

Slavery itself had a peculiar character in Trinidad. An Englishman, Claud Hollis, had commented that the 1793 Slave Code in Spanish Trinidad, remarkable for its "mildness and equity" was also "faithfully executed." The change during British rule consisted in many Britons becoming absentee planters, whose estates managed by overseers and attorneys were more exacting on the slaves; and "whereas to Protestants, slaves were merely property," the Catholic planters more consistently viewed their slaves as humans worthy of being Christianized.[36] It appears callous that "mildness" and "slavery" are juxtaposed, but the least controversial way to assess this is to recall that Trinidad was a less developed slave economy than many of its neighbors. These kinds of comparison implicitly recall planters' cruelty and high slave mortality in the older sugar colonies[37], and the less exacting existence of slaves in Trinidad.[38] Was this because an infant plantation colony like Trinidad could afford to have a "paternal slavery" regime?[39]

While the specifics of Trinidadian slavery will follow, the few observations about slavery in Trinidad made here must be placed in the context of slave registration and amelioration measures as they were required by law in Trinidad, a crown colony. A Crown Colony was ruled directly from London, that is, without a locally elected planter legislature. Trinidad thus offered more latitude for concessions to abolitionists in Britain and America.

Scholars have emphasized the unusually large numbers of urban slaves in Trinidad, and the relatively small proportion of slaves vis a vis total population: about 67 per cent in 1810.[40] Even by 1813, only about one-half of all slaves or 12,256 persons labored on 221 sugar plantations (the corresponding figures for non-sugar estates were: 1,146 slaves on 165 coffee plantations; 1,040 on 75 cocoa establishments; and 605 and 779 slaves respectively for 51 cotton and 87 provisions estates.[41]) This was, nevertheless, a significant increase over the bare third of estates which Spanish Trinidad had devoted to sugar.[42]

Free laborers and slaves were often employed alongside each other. "Life for the non-plantation slave was in fact little different from that of the free African," said C.R. Ottley. He also thought, perhaps incorrectly, that Trinidad slavery was unique for having not only coloured landlords and slave-owners, but where Robert Mitchell could report:

I am the owner of a slave, George Ireland, who was himself in possession of a slave purchased with his own money. He bought also the freedom of his two children and died himself a slave in my service.[43]

Carl Campbell more accurately captured the uniqueness of Trinidad in this period by noting that its colonization was accomplished by "whites, free coloureds and even free blacks simultaneously, with the free coloureds being from the start numerous enough to constitute a separate group."[44] Unlike older British colonies in the region, Trinidad was not tied to slave-grown sugar.[45]

It seems entirely probable that had Britain acquired Trinidad even a quarter century before 1797, it would have been deployed as a sugar colony to contest with France, a century-old struggle for supremacy in the world sugar market. Just before the French

Revolution, however, a committee of the Privy Council had virtually granted victory to France on the strength of its colony of Saint Domingue, "superior in value to all the British West Indian colonies combined."[46] In the period since Trinidad's conquest (confirmed five years later at the Treaty of Amiens), the influence of British abolitionists had grown in Parliament; the new colony became their chosen battlefield. When on 25 March 1807 the British Government had passed the Act abolishing trade in slaves within the Empire, plantation slavery in Trinidad was in its infancy—just 25 years of combined British and Spanish rule. British entrepreneurs had had only a decade (1797-1807) in which to propel the subsistence economy of Trinidad towards "development" before the first crucial blow to slave-based economies was struck.[47] The Port of Spain fire on the night of 24 March 1808, through an incredible coincidence, occurred exactly on the first anniversary of the Act of Abolition.

The fire destroyed material property, and left the population, free and slave, virtually unscathed. Government scurried out of its recess and sought to comfort the afflicted and limit damage. This alacrity and efficiency sharply contrasted with earlier complaints about corruption and personality conflicts in Governor Hislop's tenure.[48]

The March 1808 destruction of the official meetingplace did not prevent the governor and the Council of Government arranging a meeting at the residence of the Attorney General, John Nihell.[49] The other members of the Council—Beggorat, Black, Gloster, Rigby and Smith—added their support for the idea both of proclaiming martial law, and of hiring vessels to "send off Express to Headquarters [Barbados] and the neighboring islands and also to the Spanish Main" for help.[50] It was necessary to open all Trinidadian ports to neutral vessels for supplies of food and building materials. As an added incentive to the crews of the vessels, "such transports would be permitted to take in exchange and export colonial produce of every species, cotton only excepted."[51]

There remains to this day a controversy concerning the number of persons left destitute by the conflagration. The contemporary correspondent already referred to calculated that homes destroyed, along with furniture and "stores of merchandise, supposed to be of the value of one million and half sterling; and that 10,000 people are without houses, beds, clothes and food."[52] Carmichael estimated 4,500 were left homeless. Michael Anthony points to an even lower range of 3,000 homeless souls. Nonetheless, he concedes that the 1808 fire was of "crippling proportions."[53]

As is often the case with everyday life, a single incident such as this occurrence may encompass elements of tragedy, politics and comedy. On the humorous side, the fire having incinerated the general printing office and equipment, the proclamations issuing from the emergency session of the Council was "published by Beat of Drum . . . by the Provost Marshal." On the more urgent issue, the United States was requested, through its ambassador, for lumber and assistance in the shipment of supplies.[54]

Joseph, the diarist and historian who witnessed the 1808 fire, describes the ungenerous behavior of certain groups of persons in the midst of the tragedy. All was pandemonium but for the deliberate method in "breaking open and robbing grog shops on the part of the soldiers of the garrison, who in general behaved disgracefully." Joseph expresses similar resentment towards "the slaves in general . . . [who were busy] robbing rather than aiding the distressed." With respect to specifying the cause of the blaze, Joseph opined it may have been Dr. Schaw, an apothecary who was intoxicated on that fateful night; he added that "one Mr. Sand[e]s, vendue-master" and neighbor to Dr. Schaw, confessed later (too late perhaps, because he was on his death-bed) that it was he, on account of an inconvenient debt, who had started the blaze, but only to destroy his own house and property.[55]

On the second day, the Council met to set up a special committee "to receive subscriptions Foreign and Domestic" for all forms of relief and assistance. Along with those on the Council, the additional members of the relief committee reflected an effort to unite most of the white groups: Col. Grant of the Royal Trinidad Militia; the Baron de Montalembert; the Rev. Mr. Clapham; the Spanish Curate, Bellarin; Don Manuel Sorzano; Messrs Edwin Gardiner and Francis Robson; last but not least, the alcaldes in ordinary.[56] Persons who had suffered losses in the conflagration were required to file affidavits showing property damage including "Negroes, furniture, specie goods or other effects." General and public losses were to be recorded by the Surveyor-General and Alcaldes de Barrio.[57]

The members (or regidores) of the *Cabildo* of Port of Spain met on 28 March to assess how best to help the victims of the tragedy. The institution, often accompanied with the adjective "Illustrious" was the most enduring of Spanish institutions; Thomas Picton, the first British Governor had restricted its activities to the capital in 1800[8] The Cabildo discovered that merchants and storekeepers had had taken out insurance policies; "the principal loss [thus] fell on the humble industrious order of society." As the stored food supplies had been destroyed in the fire, the threat of famine was very real. That scourge was obviated by strict rationing carried out by the Cabildo, with the help especially of the Governor and other members of government. The lack of financial means within Trinidad for purposes of rebuilding led the British Parliament to vote L50,000 sterling both for individual cases of relief and for rebuilding of the Royal Gaol.[59] The fire clearly revealed serious weaknesses in Trinidad's development—dependence on imported food and lack of capital.[60] As late as 1828 and 1829, Trinidad was importing more than its income: L478,870 and L451,628 for imports in these years as against L447,109 in exports for 1828 and L438,830 for 1829.[61]

While several writers of this period claim that Spain had not developed Trinidad, none of them appear to say what "development" means. For this writer, development entails quantitative *and* *qualitative* changes in the material conditions of life; in general talk of development is so contradictory that one might portray former plantation colonies as having progressed from "undeveloped" to "developed" to "developing."[62] P.D. Curtin may have been mindful of this when he qualified "development" in seventeenth century Barbados and Jamaica thus: "Since the serious development of the plantation system in Jamaica began in the late 1660s", and that of Barbados by about twenty years before, "the general course of economic . . . history in Jamaica over 1673-1702 should be roughly comparable to that of Barbados over 1645-72."[63]

1.2 THE NATURE OF TRINIDAD SLAVERY

Human fatalities in the 1808 fire were minimal, one slave and a grenadier of the 37th Regiment. The latter died of burns subsequent to his rescue of a child from the fire. In view of Dr. Schaw's possible innocence in instigating the blaze, the death of the slave may also have been the real culprit's way of deflecting blame. Gertrude Carmichael writes that the slave was "a Negro servant of Mr Sandes, the Vendue Master, who was trapped in a house near the seat of the fire."[64] Ill-usage of slaves did not always escape the courts in Trinidad. In 1809 already, a surgeon-planter was in court for having flogged his slave to death. Known as the Monsieur Le Bis case, this 1809 episode saw the doctor receive a fine of L50 because British laws had not replaced Spanish ones; and the relevant legislation in this case had not been confirmed by an Audiencia (which, prior to 1797, had been Caracas).[65]

Le Bis' light sentence was more the result of conflicting legal traditions operating parallel to each other in a newly conquered colony, rather than a reflection purely of slave abuse. None other than Sir Thomas Picton was recalled and tried in London for permitting the imprisonment and torture of an alleged thief, Luisa Calderon, a coloured girl whose age was given as "forty" by herself, and as low as fourteen by witnesses.[66] Both these cases became useful ammunition in London—the one for those who sought the abolition of slavery, the other for those who wanted to abolish Spanish laws and institutions.[67] It may be apposite to recall other examples where penalties were exacted for abuse of slaves. On 10 December 1816, a soldier of the third West India Regiment was executed "for the murder of a negress slave of whom he was jealous;"[68] and during the 1820s a Madame Closier was fined $200 for punishing her cook, Vargas, who frequently allowed the (food) callalou to get burnt.[69]

These anecdotes of slavery in Trinidad are corroborated by the story of the Lopinots of Aouca,[70] and by the planter, Carmichael. A.C. Carmichael, wife to a planter who had lived in several Caribbean territories over 30 years, had herself joined her husband only in St. Vincent and Trinidad. This was just prior to Emancipation, and their related decision to return to England. Though several of her recollections of "the domestic mannerisms" and private lives of slaves are flushed with paternalism, her book appeared after emancipation was a fact in the Empire.[71]

C.R. Ottley spoke of an "almost total equality both in numbers and in freedom" between domestic slaves and free Negroes, and that this was "a factor of no mean force in the unsettled social fabric" of the island at that time. "There were too many free Negroes milling about" for slavery "to break the spirit of the average Trinidadian." He added that since the early Spanish and French planters had encouraged fruit trees virtually all over the estates, these and the plentiful wildlife supplemented the diets and purses of all who expended a little effort.[72] Carmichael not only corroborates this but recalls fascinating individuals as well, like "B.W., a free American negro, and a rich man, with fine grounds on Laurel-Hill." There was also "C., a female, [who] was a personage next to impossible to manage . . . [and] a clever superior person." She charged half a dollar for dances given at her house and at which she provided "supper, liquor, and music," and subsequent to the departure of the Carmichaels, bought out her freedom. By the 1820s, Mrs Carmichael recalled, "Finding latterly that the respect formerly paid to the wishes of the master, though not given as commands, was entirely withdrawn, we were at a loss how to act. Sunday dances were now given regularly [they had been restricted

to non-Sabbath days], and it was of no use to interfere: whenever
we spoke by way of enforcing respect, there was some quotation
from 'Massa Buston;' [Buxton] for latterly Massa King George was
not even allowed the dignity of a copartnership with Massa Buston.
Though when any law was ordered to be put in force, which the
negroes did not like, then they used to say, 'I wish dat Massa
Buston would come and see a' we nigger, and no send out *dat
law*.'"[73]

Of course, it is unlikely that such freedoms would have been
regularly enjoyed on a mature slave colony like Jamaica. However,
natural increases and declines in the slave population, and total
manumissions, might be better indices of slavery in Trinidad. In
this period when the illegal slave trade was almost irrelevant[74] as a
means of increasing Trinidad slaveholdings, the difference between
deaths and births moved from a ratio 2:1 in 1819 to an equivalence,
especially for females. Manumissions of more than 130 slaves per
year (on average) while not remarkable, is not insignificant either,
for a growing plantation economy. At least 70 more female slaves
than males were freed for each of the three-year periods since 1819.

A.C. Carmichael anticipated her observation—"I never saw a
whip once used" (Volume 1 p.4) and that planters' wives were
painstakingly wonderful nurses to all the slaves (Volume 2 pp.13-
14)—might bring the rejoinder, that if slaves were generally so
well treated, "their population would *increase*, not *decrease*. But it
appears to me that much more natural grounds than the over-
working of the negro may be brought to account for this. I took
some pains to inquire into this matter."[75]

Among the reasons Carmichael discovered for slave population
decreases were the unequal sex ratios, the oft-recalled reluctance of
the slaves to marry, the late hours kept by some, and "the frequent
manumissions of negroes." While some of these reasons are less
convincing than others, the author's first-hand account cannot be
totally dismissed. Indeed, Sheridan attests that laws calling for
"suitable" slave hospitals were enacted in the 1790s in the
Caribbean, and that for Trinidad, even where Spanish medical

licensing laws may have been neglected since 1797 the island was first among British colonies to require licenses for practitioners in 1814. While "[c]ritics of the planters gave a dismal picture of the treatment of sick slaves[,]" slaves themselves, says Sheridan, "often objected to being confined to hospitals" during illnesses.[76] Carmichael's work attests, at the very least, to what Genovese and others have asserted, that the slave universe was not one created by masters only; it was also a world the slaves made.[77]

Scholars have recognized that slaves met exceptionally cruel masters and exceptionally humane ones, and one might add, several permutations of good and bad types. Even unfeeling masters could not always ignore the fact their slaves were human. "Two very important consequences" of these contradictory views about slaves as chattel and as people, "were the emergence and growth of the population of 'free black and coloured people' and the small scale agricultural and marketing enterprises of the slaves themselves."[78] Some of the pecuniary manifestations of this "confusion" has been ably summarized by O. Nigel Bolland.[79] In a paper given at a conference in London, Bolland argued that slaves frequently received money payments. He cited at least three ways in which slaves were "paid" for the work they did, including overwork and certain slave-hiring arrangements which approximated "labor market" negotiations. Arguing that the "custom of slaves receiving payments . . . [was] widespread in the Americas,"—bolstering his case with examples of slave bank accounts,[80] Boland's basic message is "[T]he comparative study of this transition should encourage us to reject the simplistic antinomy of slavery and freedom."

Scholars agree (outside of Trinidad's particularism) that sugar and slavery have a long association, and that sugar plantations exacted the most from slaves, especially in terms of mortality.[81] If it can be shown that Trinidad's economy was not dominated by sugar until after 1826, a case might begin to be made for conditions of a special nature on Trinidad's plantations vis a vis older sugar colonies.

Despite the lure of sugar, British Trinidad moved only hesitantly into sugar's orbit. The challenge from cotton and coffee (and their higher market prices) was repulsed gradually by the expansion of sugar. Yet, sugar's "peak of 1805 was not reached again until 1826," after which Trinidad was to remain under sugar's sway, until the cocoa boom at the turn of this century.[82] We have seen that sugar had been discouraged in Trinidad, (notably 1797-1802[83]) partly because abolitionists were determined to prevent Trinidad becoming the next site of the onward marching, successively soil-depleting sugar revolution. The corollary to the controlled expansion of sugar lay in the significance of cocoa as a viable second crop.

The steady increases in population, especially among the free sectors were perhaps related, because cocoa was cultivated mainly by "the considerable [numbers of] free colored and free black" Trinidadians, and unlike sugar, was not tied to slavery. Another contention (Barry Higman's) that the "cocoa industry expanded even more rapidly than sugar" is less convincing; moreover Higman's graph on productivity omitted sugar.[84]

When we recall that in 1797 (British arrival in Trinidad), a total of 96,000 lbs. of cocoa was produced, the increases from 1799 become striking. Meanwhile sugar doubled production in the five year period to 1803. Perhaps the crucial point is—and this may have been Higman's, too—the expansion of cocoa on its own terms was not insignificant both economically and socially. A visitor to the region in 1826 put it aptly:

"If I ever turn planter, as I have often had thoughts of doing, I shall buy a cocoa plantation in Trinidad. The Cane is, no doubt, a noble plant . . . [but] sugar can never be cultivated without negro labour."[85]

Except for the two years of relatively low production in 1802 and 1807, Trinidad's total cocoa output moved steadily to the million pound mark. This goal was reached in 1812; thereafter, cocoa remained above this level of production. Even in the difficult 1830s, Trinidad produced 2,571,915 lbs in 1838 and 2,914,061 lbs in 1839.[86] While it cannot be denied that sugar was a challenger akin to a bush fire, cocoa enjoyed advantages both of price and contribution to British imports. Prices in the latter half of 1811 for instance, were greater than 1:2 to the advantage of cocoa. Prices obtaining on Trinidad Exports during November 1811 were: Sugar, per cwt., L 1. 16. 0 (L representing British currency); Cocoa, per cwt. L 3. 12. 0; Cotton, per cwt. L 8. 2. 0; Coffee, per cwt. L 3. 12. 0; Rum (improved) per gallon at L 0. 9. 0.

While cotton enjoyed healthy market prices, production went through a precipitous decline (6,800 lbs in 1831) not able to improve on its 1808 total for 1808-1831. Coffee did not display spectacular shifts (until 1831 when it almost reached the million pound mark) the island's coffee matched the market price of cocoa for the second half of 1811.[87]

The production and export of cocoa as compiled by L. Ragatz show that among regional producers, Trinidad almost doubled the combined imports from Berbice, Jamaica and St. Vincent in 1812, more than quintupling its own exports to the mother country in 1814. Jamaica and Berbice had little more than double the 1812 totals in 1814. Trinidad exported 1,755,144 lbs. of cocoa to Britain by 1834, the figures for the next best producers, Jamaica and St. Vincent, were 2,713 pounds and 2,355 pounds respectively.

Such production data are important for an understanding of the kinds of lives and work regimes the slaves endured, as well as the strength of the sugar planters. Following Higman, one can assert that after almost three decades of British occupation and immigration, Trinidad's plantocracy was not the political force it continued to be in the older sugar colonies like Barbados.[88] Moreover, Trinidad in 1808 was not a monocrop (sugar) plantation but a diversified agricultural and cosmopolitan island.[89] In order to assess the nature of Trinidad slavery, we might also examine the interaction of "contrasting physical environments with phases of settlement."[90] It is analytically useful to differentiate among slave-dependent plantations on the basis of size, crop and maturity through space and time.

Richard Sheridan's delineation of three stages in the operation of slave plantations—"depending on the mix of demographic and economic factors"—show that the second stage of "near monoculture

slavery" was the most exacting on slaves. The "early slavery" era saw
"fairly balanced sex ratios and natural increases" among the slave
community. Although white indenteds were employed at this time,
the more valuable slaves got the lighter tasks. Planters set aside
time and land to meet plantation food needs; in the second phase
it was cheaper both to import food (leading to less healthy diets)
and to purchase fewer female slaves. The third phase was "slave
amelioration" which, for Barbados, came as early as "the 1760s
and 1770s."[91] Trinidad's unusual experience might be described
as one where phases one and three occurred simultaneously, while
the "near monoculture" phase came after emancipation. This period
was to coincide with the era of British Indian labor and will be
elaborated in the next two chapters.

In contrast to older colonies, Trinidad continued to enjoy
equivalent numbers for male and female slaves. At any time during
the heyday of Trinidadian slavery, a quarter of the slaves were urban
dwellers, while of the remainder, about 20 per cent worked with
coffee, cocoa or provisions, so that only about 50 per cent were sugar
slaves. Slave artisans and hirelings as well as migrant Spanish-American
peons were an integral part of the economy. Slave family stability
was more common than previously assumed by scholars; in 1813
for instance, 60 per cent of Trinidad slaves lived in units of under
fifty slaves (the corresponding figure was 27 per cent in Jamaica).[92]

If one looks at the population growth generally in Trinidad
and the increases in slave numbers vis a vis other islands, Trinidad
was remarkable for its relatively "huge" proportions of white and
coloured groups, and not for that fateful duo, sugar and slaves.
Most "near monoculture" colonies comprised at least 90 per cent
slaves in total population,[93] while Trinidad had a free population
of 33 per cent in 1810.

By 1802 (formal ceding of Trinidad by Spain), slave numbers
had been virtually doubled to 19,709—a figure close to the island's
highest slave total through Emancipation in 1834. The fact that
this five-year period in which servile numbers first doubled came
before Abolition, and that Britain had been a supplier of slaves,

even to the Spaniards and French, must be seen as contributory factors. Compared to the rest of the region (Table 1.1), Trinidad was a marginal slave economy. Additionally, years of crucial international and local events influenced some coloureds into leaving Trinidad (1803; 1809)-and many possessed slaves themselves— thus reducing slave numbers and expansion.

TABLE 1.1 BRITISH COLONIES: CHARACTERISITICS IN 1812

COLONY	1000s ACRES	WHITE	COLOURED	SLAVE	EXPORTS in L
Trinidad	1,527	2,896	*8,102*	21,831	384,117
Jamaica	2,724	30,000	10,000	350,000	7,269,661
B. Guiana#	1,100	5,000	3,100	95,000	1,569,990
Barbados	106	15,000	3,000	59,506	548,803
Antigua	60	3,200	1,400	36,000	492,220
Grenada	80	800	1,600	32,603	565,782
St. Kitts	44	1,200	500	30,000	436,528
St. Vincent	104	1,280	1,170	27,156	516,001
Dominica	186	800	1,500	24,000	258,858
Nevis	21	500	250	15,000	217,682
Montserrat	21	444	200	10,000	104,720
Virgin Is	21	444	200	10,000	94,122
TOTALS	5,994	61,224	31,679	771,096	12,458,484

* Statistics used are for 1813.1
# For British Guiana these are totals of cultivated acreage.
Source: R. Sheridan, Doctors and Slaves (p.7)
: texts consulted; I avoided Sheridan s 1812
population estimate

In the period before East Indians arrived in Trinidad, therefore, the island was unique not for producing spectacular quantities of sugar, but for having a "paternalistic" slave system and one of the largest free coloured populations in the Caribbean. Trinidad boasted the highest proportion (in total population) of coloureds, several of whom were assertive and acknowledged in status under Spanish rule. While this surely added to Trinidad's complexity in this period (see below), it also provided a challenge to foresighted whites. The slave population was mostly African, although 11,629 Creoles (Trinidad or Caribbean-born) was not much smaller than the African total of 13,980.[94] Of 11 colonies, Trinidad ranked with the lower half in the size of slave population, which, in comparison to Jamaica or Barbados was almost insignificant. The hey day of sugar lay in the 1830s and beyond—and the juxtaposition of sugar and slaves so familiar in the older islands would be replaced by the bondage of Indo-Trinidadians to the sweet malefactor of the West Indies. And it bears recalling that Trinidad became British at a time of growing abolitionist influence within the British Parliament as much as outside of government.

1.3 EARLY BRITISH RULE AND IMMIGRATION

In its forms of government, Trinidad was a long time in transition from ad hoc military regimes (since 1797) to an effective colonial government. Brigadier-General Sir Thomas Picton, (who had learnt his Spanish in Gibraltar) was made Commander-in-Chief and Governor of the erstwhile Spanish colony. "At first," H. Wooding writes, "he ruled as a military autocrat." In 1801, he received an appointment directly from Britain, as Civil and Military Governor. (The first Civilian Governor was still three governors away.) Symbolically, if not for practical purposes, Picton set up a Council of Government, with five leading Trinidadians, all nominated by himself. Renamed the "Council of Advice" in 1803, it was not replaced until 1831 with a nominated Legislative Council.[95] Picton is notorious too for having promulgated Trinidad's first British Slave Code (of 1800).

Although Slave Codes are only a general index of the actual conditions of slavery, the Ordinance of 30 June 1800 in Trinidad was issued at a time when abolitionists were close to achieving the ban on slave trading. Neither was Britain wooing sugar planters at this time in anticipation of the day when Trinidad would be returned to Spain. The instructions preceding Picton's Ordinance made apparent the experimental role of Trinidad in ameliorating and/or abolishing slavery: "[I]t is important," the preamble said, that everybody in Trinidad "mitigate the situation of their slaves, by rendering their servitude as limited and as easy as possible. . . ." Anticipating registration and amelioration measures just ahead, the ordinance went on, "and by promoting their natural increase, so that in course of time the importation of slaves from Africa may be considerably diminished, if not totally dispensed with; and whereas, those desirable ends cannot be more effectually attained, than by compelling owners of slaves to lodge, clothe, and maintain them sufficiently . . . in health [and] . . . sickness, age and infirmity."[96]

It is sufficiently enlightened, in the heyday of slavery, that a slave code expressed the hope that continuous inflow of slaves would become unnecessary. At no time during Indian indenture were measures as generous and as detailed as this Ordinance issued to, or by, Trinidad's planters. Housing provisions such as the Code's Article 1 which called on plantation operators to provide "well wattled and thatched . . . wind and watertight houses" for slaves; the "head or chief of every family" to be given a separate house with at least two apartments, did not obtain for indenteds several decades later. Orphans were to be accommodated in groups of three per house; beds for all slaves were to be raised "at least 18 inches" from the floor "to preserve them from . . . the moist ground." Slaves could fence off their provision grounds; a year's notice was to precede eviction and payment was provided for improvements made by slaves.

The 1800 Code may not have been fully implemented, as Meredith John argues; the context of slave amelioration does point to some level of altruism or planter self-interest for preserving new slaves. John himself demonstrates that planters enjoyed flexibility within the rules for feeding and keeping slaves fully occupied; for instance, when he writes that "Catholic owners [were] more benign in their treatment of slaves than were Protestant owners," usually because the former had smaller estates, and continued to allow slaves opportunities to greatly "vary their diets" (usually protein supplements) by granting additional free time in place of the salted fish stipulated.[97] Article 3 allowed for commuting plantains and cassava meal with money. A respected Trinidadian, J. Millette found Picton's Code, in general terms, an improvement over the Spanish Code.[98]

It is the context of amelioration which informs our assessment of the Picton Code, which is reiterated by Sheridan. These generous slave measures, he says, were possible because of the extraordinary powers reposed in the hands of the British governor during 1797-1801, in a colony without a planter's Assembly.[99] While in 1802 and every few years since, there was one petition or another for representative institutions for Trinidad, the trajectory after Amiens was in an opposite direction. The lessons of Grenada,[100] the United States, and the pressure of the abolitionists moved Trinidad imperceptibly, and even a little incoherently, toward Crown Colony government. Because Britain had not sanctioned a Planters' Assembly in Trinidad (as it had previously granted Jamaica), the colony was ruled directly from London—hence, a Crown colony. Agitation from prominent Trinidadians against unrepresentative government only tightened this noose. Although, in the intial phases of reform agitation, coloureds and whites fought separately, we shall see a degree of coalescing and cooperation among these rival groups during the 1880s (Chapter Five).

J.B. Philip, the spokesman for coloured rights said that between 1797 and 1808 "the tranquility of the Colony was continually disturbed by [a] small but active faction of English settlers," who sought to equate Trinidad's constitutional status with that of other British Caribbean colonies.[101] One of the prime movers in the English Party in 1802, John Sanderson, declared "it was impossible" to expect two legal systems to work efficiently unless one or the other was completely accepted or rejected.[102] It was George Canning who first expressed the idea that Trinidad was a place for noble experiments. In 1802, he had warned the House of

Commons that Trinidad was being threatened with a deluge of slaves because its fertile soils (unexploited by Spain) promised irresistible profits to planters who moved there. James Stephen, the abolitionist and relative of Wilberforce, expressed Canning's idea more fully in *The Crisis of the Sugar Colonies* (1802). Sale of land, or granting to all who would cultivate "by the labour of *free Negroes*" part of "that rich and unopened soil" would be an experiment of "unspeakable importance to mankind." In order to do this, direct rule from London-"parliamentary legislation"—was necessary.[103]

The lack of a representative government, however, was felt most acutely by the large free coloured population of Trinidad, notwithstanding military or civilian governors. This was true under Woodford, the first civilian governor of Trinidad, though he is celebrated in place names as well as by some of the historians already mentioned.[104] Woodford is remembered for a significant addition of "American" and other disbanded black soldiers to Trinidad's population, for stimulating communications and economic development, as well as for a stricter demarcation of racial lines: "The soldier governors were content to dominate the conquest society of moving frontiers. Woodford wished to put an end to it. Complaining that the people were reluctant to fulfil the terms on which land had been granted to them . . . [he sought] to check the exuberance of the society . . . by demand[ing] that land already granted be cultivated, and generally to sell, not give away, Crown land . . . Woodford wished to establish a settled society, institutionally fixed, racially defined and graduated in terms of social ranks [he created two categories of whites as well," 1st class and 2nd class"] In respect to the free coloureds he could be said to have . . . institutionalised racial prejudice."[105]

In this transition from a conquest society to one of settlement and "economic development," Campbell noted that lack of capital, not labor, was the "crucial weakness." Lack of capital continued to be more important than labor shortage in the whole debate leading to Indian indenture (See Chapter Two). In the first decades of the nineteenth century, it made sense for Woodford to use land as the means of incentive, reward and stimulus. Where the last Spanish Governor, Don Jose Chacon, had allowed the coloureds to benefit from land grants according to the 1783 Cedula (and overlook legislation which sought to relegate them to an inferior status), the arrival of Britain turned them into the group which received a premium in resentment from other petitioners for representative institutions, and in being regarded as their nemesis (as vanguard of non-Europeans).

Coloureds were still the most numerous group among incoming settlers during 1814-1817. Between November and January of those years, 3,823 free persons were allowed into Trinidad; many more may have entered illegally. These were refugees from the Spanish American revolutions as well as settlers originally from Grenada, Gaudeloupe, Dominica, St. Vincent, and Martinique. They included "whites, free coloured and blacks, and '*peons*'" (the last "a new kind of man of Spanish, Negro, and Amerindian blood who had been in the making in the Latin American tropics for 300 years.")[106]

It seems to me that Campbell and Wood are in agreement that in terms of economic as opposed to status privileges, there was no noticeable worsening in the coloured position despite Woodford's personal biases. While the increase in "legacy duty on property" inherited by illegitimate children "affected coloureds more than whites," writes Campbell, "It cannot be said that the land policy of Woodford was devised specifically to divest free coloureds of the land[,] which formed the material base of their economic strength . . . But he wished to restrict their ownership of land and all government institutions and agencies worked against their interest . . . For instance, all 'poor settlers, peons, and free men of colour' who had less than 5 quarrees could *not* dispose of their land without first obtaining permission from the governor."[107]

Some of Woodford's proposed measures were rejected by London, but it was in the arena which might be termed petty apartheid that the governor had his way. Segregation between whites and coloureds obtained in theaters, in the Steamer which sailed between the capital and San Fernando, in the differentiated fee scales for doctors who served whites and coloureds, as well as in the Protestant Church of Port of Spain, where segregation pursued the dead (separate burial grounds) as much as the living.

For our study, the Woodford years represent an era of assisted immigration, that of United States slaves who had fought for Britain in the War of 1812 and other disbanded regiments. The first settlement comprised North American "refugees" who arrived in a group of 61 men, 18 women and 7 children in May 1815. They were offered plots of land, or, an apprenticeship option with local planters (which was turned down with energy). Another group of settlers arrived in July from the U.S. and included 15 men, 14 women and 29 children.[108] These arrivals challenged Woodford to make order out of Trinidad's amorphous land settlement pattern.

The first two groups of "refugees" were settled near the capital, to allow the Governor to assess the situation readily; after the arrival of "Americans" from Bermuda (32 men, 14 women and 17 children in November 1815) and a group of 574 settlers in 1816 (when the Corps of Colonial Marines was disbanded), settlement spread north and south to remoter parts of the island. K.O. Laurence discovered that where women were few, especially when the soldiers of the West India Regiments were settled over the next few years, women were recruited from Nova Scotia, Africa and the United States for Trinidad's newest immigrants. Woodford's allocation of land concealed a sophisticated pattern:

"From the outset Woodford had planned the location of the settlements with a view to economic advantage. He intended not only that they should be used to open up areas which were unpopulated and, in the case of the American refugee settlements in Naparima especially fertile, but also that they should be so spaced out as to facilitate the construction and maintenance of roads. Just as the West India Regiment settlements were used to spearhead a road across northern Trinidad to the East Coast, so the American refugee settlements were intended to assist the building of roads connecting the South and east Coasts of the island with San Fernando."[109]

There were unexpected consequences which accompanied the new settlers (as was to be the case after 1845). Early in 1816 the governor established a fleet of Government carts employing the first American refugee-settlers: this brought cheaper rates and greater efficiency. "The normal charge for hiring carts was $3 a day, but the American refugees . . . were paid 30c a day plus clothing and medical attention." The Governor was thrilled at the success, believing that only the "'intelligent Americans'" had made this possible.[110] Such thoughts and praise would also interpenetrate considerations as to which group best suited Trinidad's post-emancipation plantation regime.

A development which lay ahead was that coloureds, whose numbers assured them prominence in Trinidad, would be quickly outnumbered by Asian immigrants who sometimes mutually exchanged cultural ideas with black creoles, the expected allies and partners of coloureds. There may have been more frustration in this coloured experience than has been recognized; just when emancipation increased their leverage within the society, a new "Asian" element entered the political equation. Coloureds were, subsequently, in the forefront of efforts to halt Indian immigration.

The Great Fire in Port of Spain had revealed many areas in public and private life where various socio-political cinders might ignite other sorts of troublesome fires. The effort to include the conquered Spanish and French Trinidadians in important public positions had not been a concerted one; resentment flared into the open each time petitions drawn up by Anglophiles—"The English Party"—sought the extinction of Spanish institutions. A much needed rapproachment between Catholics and Protestants took place in the Woodford years, when the governor seemed to cherish groups who might neutralize the coloureds.

In terms of regulations for new buildings, there was an immediate move to remedy problems of omission and commission.[111] The inability of Trinidad to feed itself in 1808 would, if anything, become worse as sugar gained ascendancy in this new colony, and also as new foods had to be imported (rice, *dhal* and ghee for British Indians). The problem of land titles "granted" by Spain, along with the competing Spanish, French and British traditions, including legal ones, would endure for most of the century.

Trinidad, however, was not a gloomy, pessimistic place in the decades before emancipation. An observer, who wrote about the Woodford years had the following to say: "To Sir Ralph Woodford who arrived in the colony shortly after the devastating fire of 1808, is due all praise for the admirable manner in which he organised the laying out of the streets and squares in the town. The former are broad and well kept, running north and south, and east and west, thus crossing at right angles. Sir Ralph's great aim was not that of building up a beautiful, well laid and planned city, but that he might at all costs assure the health of its many inhabitants."[112]

Another contemporary observer, F.W. Bayley, spent 1826 through 1829 in the region, and left us this portrait: the "women of Trinidad are most superb creatures . . . The coloured women all look innocent in Trinidad; then they have more of the olive, and less of the burnt umber stuff on their skins than those of the other islands that lie between Cancer and Capricorn . . . All creoles love dress, but I think the creoles of Trinidad are more tasty than others. French fashions are more in vogue here than our English ones . . . [without affecting] love towards Old England . . . the best feeling exists between the Protestants and the Catholics, [but] the English influence is predominant: the good Governor has gained the hearts of the inhabitants . . . The men love their sovereign, the women their sweethearts, and the children their sweetmeats. So love, loyalty, and lollypops are thriving in Trinidad."[113]

Without destroying some of the enchantment of this account in order to promote a metaphor of smoldering fires, we shall see that Protestant-Catholic harmony was a temporary marriage of convenience at a time when free coloureds were being "taught to "keep . . . their places."[114] In the 1840s, the fires of controversy over education along denominational lines would destroy even the semblance of cooperation between Protestant and Catholic whites; in the 1850s and 1860s French planters had to subsidize British Indian indenture though they relied more upon free laborers and peons for their cocoa and coffee estates. The comments of Bayley which appear superficial are understandable even today, when beneath the tropical serenity of Trinidad, embers of social tensions flare up and produce the occasional states of emergency (1970; July 1990).[115]

CHAPTER TWO

UNFREEING THE LABOR MARKET:

THE LURE OF INDENTURE

"[Question No.] 656. The labourer lives in much more comfort than he did in slavery, does he not?

"[Witness, W.H. Burnley]—There can be no comparison. The labourer is in a better state as to comfort, and luxuries of every description, than in any part of the world, or than ever existed in any part of the world; for it can only arise from such an artificial state of things, as has been produced by emancipation."[116]

We mentioned already how centripetal forces like that of economic imperialism or integration were bringing peoples of distant lands together into new relationships on colonial plantations, but that this aspect of globalization had several unanticipated consequences. One of these was Britain's gradual acceptance, then active promotion, of free trade principles. Starting in the 1840s Britain began to equalize tariffs on all sugar entering London, that is, equal access for sugar to its market including the slave-grown sugar of competitors. The move toward free trade had begun within the Empire itself in 1825. Free trade and a desire not to revive an African engage system, may have influenced Britain to conclude European treaties whereby its Indian subjects could work in the

French Mascarenes, the French Caribbean and in Dutch Guiana/ Surinam.[117]

While British planters argued that free trade principles behooved Britain to allow West Indian colonies to recruit Indian workers as Mauritius had done, they were not prepared for that privilege being extended to non-British colonies.[118] Moreover, they were vehemently opposed to the equalization of British tariffs. Mauritius, one of the Mascarenes, was relinquished to Britain by France only in 1810; Demerara or British Guiana was ceded to the British by Holland four years later. It is noteworthy that these colonies had been the first to seek Indian labor, and years before slave emancipation in 1833. What one colonial entity saw going on in another colonial territory, it was anxious to imitate, economic data usually being ignored.

In the long view of history (globalization), planters were bound to be chastened by the very forces which gave them access to an indented or semi-free workforce. For the immediate successors of the slave workers, however, global integration was occurring in an age of imperialism which favored the interests of Europeans, planters and non-planters, over those of others. The first losers in Trinidad during 1845-1888 were the Indians.

For the slaves, the same process which had aided their liberation in the 1830s would also blunt the promise of free labor. It was tempting for planters in particular to argue that with freedom, slaves would flee into the relatively limitless and fertile interior of Trinidad in a great refusal to continue as plantation drudges.[119] At some point in recent history, there was a somewhat parallel belief that non-Protestants lacked an ethic of steady work.[120] But just as Catholics took the lead in Europe's discovery and settlement of old and new worlds, the ex-slaves displayed several systems of ethics ranging the gamut from communalism to individual enterprise. At freedom, some Afro-Trinidadians acquired lands through pooled resources or through squatting far away from plantations where they set up *free villages*. Among those who continued to labor on plantations were many who felt tied to lands upon which ancestors were buried, but they demanded terms consonant with their new freedom.[121] Then as now, employers sought to reduce remuneration and the options of workers to a minimum, and were too free with their calumnies.[122] The claim that freed blacks would not work half as well as before was useful in planter petitions for bonded or foreign labor.

It is this constant tension between workers wanting more rights and compensation and employers offering less and less, which destroyed those conditions which for a few years after Emancipation made ex-slave workers equal players with planters and capital in the colonial marketplace.[123] Yet it was not a free market and the dependence upon, and vulnerability of planters and capital to ex-slave labor was terminated by Trinidad's turn to new workers on bounty arrangements and under indenture.

Had these newer workers been allowed their freedom—with rights to negotiate wage rates and prosecute employers who failed to keep their end of agreements—the leverage of ex-slaves and new laborers would have become entrenched. What in fact happened was that Britain gradually lessened its resolve to disallow planters new forms of unfree labor. The compromise arrangements were variously labelled following emancipation, but they were sometimes little removed from the spirit of slavery: "It took time to change employers' entrenched attitudes and labor practices and to establish new [rules] governing recruitment and employment."[124] Hence the radical change from Indians having entered Trinidad as free migrants without indentures in May 1845, but subsequent arrivals from India being tied down by increasingly longer indentures. Should the indenteds have disatisfied managers in any way, they were disqualified for the passage back home to India.

The British had ended slavery, but failed to set the tone for a free society where market forces and freedoms could flourish. At the simplest level, this was racialism, or the reality that planters as a group were connected to the British by race or politics, or both. In fact the planters enjoyed a lobby in London which promoted their interests. Without Britain's role as umpire or honest broker, planters would indulge their human weakness of greed, admittedly a useful, rational economic force. Britain was placed in highly compromising positions after slave emancipation. These compromises came in its response to West Indian planters' difficulties and European diplomacy, which brought charges of hypocrisy from rivals such as France. For instance, the subject of "liberated African labour emigration" was controversial because Britain had allowed Caribbean planters to indent West Africans in the 1840s. These Africans were recruited in Sierra Leone and St. Helena, where slaves who had been "confiscated" by the Royal Navy from the now illegal slave trade were initially resettled in, but gradually persuaded to seek paid employment outside of, Sierra Leone.

Britain's opponents also charged that Britain had allowed her colonies to stock up on slaves prior to the official abolition of that trade in 1807. This activity had given its planters a moral and economic advantage. Some 100,000 ostensibly free African laborers emigrated to the West Indies after 1838. This influx redounded to the advantage of the estates in Trinidad, a new sugar colony where the land:population ratio had allowed squatting or peasant farming on vast Crown lands by those who, for sometimes valid reasons, refused to work for their former masters.[125] But in the short-term the new immigrants helped weaken—simulataneously with the planters coordinating their wage and other policies—the power of freed slaves as well as their own clout.[126] Britain had failed to persuade other Europeans to accede to universal abolition in 1838 so that British planter hopes for the "great advantage over their rivals," gave way to chagrin and recrimination.[127]

It was for this and related reasons that Britain aided Trinidad planters through the transition to free labor by allowing in laborers on a scale at the wages suggested by the former slaveowners. As indentures became longer, and as return ships for out-of-indenture Indians were delayed again and again, beginning in 1862, Indians had to pay part of their repatriation costs to India.[128] Thus, ostensibly free workers became captive laborers in a distant island unless thay found the energy to complete their indentures and the fare to return to India.

A minimum daily wage of 25 cents, though much less than the 30 cents then being earned by free Trinidadians in 1841, was set for Indians only in 1872. This situation gave free reign to planter manipulation of the labor market and of the length of each Indian's sojourn in Trinidad.

Let us analyze how planters gradually won the upper hand during the first decade of the transition from slavery to free labor, and why Trinidad was not satisfied with the thousands of indented workers who preceded the Indians. The final decision had less to do with India and its poverty than with planter strategy and British imperial economics: the metropole and its people needed sugar and the success of the plantations as much as the planters needed workers with minimal rights. Britain and its colonies like India and Trinidad were linked in a chain of economic disruption, dislocations and simultaneously, a subservience to the political economy of the Empire. By one estimate, world trade increased tenfold between 1850 and 1913; sugar and related confectionary raised living standards in the West with per capita British sugar consumption increasing fivefold during the century.[129] The colonies and its peoples accommodated as best they could to policies and plans decided on their behalf in London.

It was British policy or assent to planter lobbies and concomitant decisions which gradually eroded the freedmen's bargaining position in Trinidad. At its most basic, planters were allowed a large reservoir of laborers, free and semi-free. Northrup points out that the apparent population explosion in colonial India is under scholarly attack and review, and that while individual Indians could and sometimes did exercise their freedom to choose, "the influence of the Raj was pervasive," especially as a network of railroads both encircled India and opened up its interior to Europe. He concludes, "Overseas migration was not spontaneous; an army of labor recruiters persuaded Indians to leave home and escorted them to the coastal depots" where Caribbean-bound ships lay in wait.[130]

Even after thousands of West Indian or creole labor migrants and many hundreds of North American and European workers, many of whom were on indenture, had entered Trinidad its planters complained they were short of labor. Notwithstanding waves of new indented Africans and Asians, cries of "labor shortage" did not subside. But Trinidad quietly resigned itself to this insufficiency of labor when India finally banned the exportation of indented laborers in 1917. Our evidence suggests that Trinidad's planters may have had a need for indented workers rather than a shortage of workers per se.

2.1 SUGAR WITHOUT SLAVES;

WHAT IS TO BE DONE?

If the end of slavery had demanded readjustments from everyone in the former plantation colonies, the end of apprenticeship appears to have been traumatic for the planters and former slaveowners. From their complaints to Britain about the "sloth" and "indolence" of free blacks, and other frustrations in maintaining their plantations, one might believe that the problem was entirely one of labor shortage.[131] The planters' difficulty after 1838 was less the insufficiency of labor than of prejudice. This was a question of planters having to accommodate to workers' exercising their emergent rights consonant with free market principles during the aftermath of slavery. The Democratic Revolutions after 1776 may have set the stage for Emancipation and other freedoms yet the plantation became more widespread in the colonized areas of the world: "Technicians and managers from the Caribbean had their own mental image of what a plantation should be and how it should be run. Their model was the slave plantation, and their background included a belief in European racial superiority, ideas about labor discipline, and concepts of a proper social order."[132]

This was the order which indented Indians sailed into upon departing their homes in India. Per Burnley's comments at the top of this chapter regarding the "luxuries" and "comforts" accruing to Trinidad's laborers as compared with the harsh climate and greater competition for scarce resources among Europeans, the implication was that ex-slaves could quit the estates and walk into virgin forests and natural orchards. While there is evidence that some ex-slaves in Trinidad worked fewer hours daily than they had under slavery, there is evidence too that others worked just as many hours as previously. Those who worked fewer days made that decision for varying motivations: some had fewer needs;[133] some became part-time market gardeners; some refused labor at low wages in ideological resistance. But production of staples continued much as before. It was the question of wages especially on the more demanding sugar estates which had become the bone of contention.[134] Former slaves would not oblige the estates until they received a higher remuneration than planters or estate managers offered.

Planters had experimented with recruited laborers from other Caribbean islands, and from China, Europe, Fayal and Madeira, in part to demonstrate an independence from local labor. Later overtures to non-local labor betrayed the planters' discomfort with the new freedom of their erstwhile slaves and fears about the rise of a land-owning black population. Planters lacked "goodwill," according to Asiegbu. "They might, by forcing the hands of the mother country and returning to the old system of imported labour, forestall the growing politico-economic threats" posed by the free blacks who were becoming property-owners.[135]

A look at export production statistics for sugar, cocoa and coffee, do not show precipitous or unmitigated declines after emancipation. Indeed, even when sugar output declined, it was less than the decrease predicted: between 1831 and 1841 sugar did decline by about 25 percent, but coffee production increased by 31 percent

in the same decade. Between 1831 and 1832, coffee production
expanded by 55 percent and every year thereafter saw an
improvement over 1831 figures. Cocoa production was more
arresting: from 1,888,852 lbs. in 1831, cocoa expanded to
3,090,526 lbs. in 1833, and remained over 2,507,483 lbs. (yielded
in 1837) each successive year.[136] Sugar alone among Trinidad's
three main staples showed a decline after 1834, a decline reversed
in the 1850s when Indian labor began arriving continuously.[137]
The favorable fortunes of cocoa and coffee in Trinidad during the
decade or two immeediately following slave abolition demonstrate
that sugar—the product, its production and its price—may have
sowed the seeds of decline, independently of labor.[138]

Several sugar plantations had in fact been abandoned,
amalgamated or moved into cocoa or coconut production during
the 1830s in anticipation of labor and credit problems.[139] Against
the background of research conducted by scholars of slavery, one
can agree that sugar was the most demanding crop on laborers and
that coffee and cocoa plantations were generally preferred over sugar
estates both by slave and non-slave workers. Historical data confirm
to a certain extent that planters had difficulty in treating their
former bondsmen as equals, that is, as free workers with bargaining
rights. At the same time, there is a fair amount of evidence to
suggest that some, though not all, planters encountered problems
of access to cash and credit. On balance, employers needed to
coordinate wage policies and cooperate in not hiring workers who
absconded from other estates—which they achieved with indenture
but not with the freed slaves—before they could alter the balance
between free labor in general and employers. In such a context,
Indian immigration may have been superfluous.

In a word, therefore, the planters' problem was sugar. The
peculiarities of its manufacture needed unusual efforts such as
working continuously for about 16-18 hours at croptime. Free
persons would on occasion accede to such hours but only on terms
and wages which planters were unwilling to pay. Sugar planters in
Trinidad were not content with modest profits.[140] They looked

across at the Indian ocean island of Mauritius where great fortunes were being made with bonded Indian labor. Whereas the failure of Britain to persuade her European rivals to end slavery in 1838 angered the planters, they were more outraged that newly-acquired Mauritius was permitted to employ Indian indenteds. Planters were set on keeping up with Mauritius ever since 1825 when Britain equalized the duty which Mauritian sugar paid to enter Britain, thus threatening the long-established preference rate enjoyed by West Indian producers. Planters showed no concern that a blurry line between freedom and bondage might extend from the Mascarenes all the way to the Caribbean.[141]

Like their government itself, British abolitionists had not been clear or unanimous about the kind of societies they wanted to have replace the slave systems of the Caribbean. W.A. Green argued that humanitarians, like British imperialists and Wakefieldian economists, would not have countenanced the destruction of the plantation. "Plantations provided the only available institutional framework through which European culture could be maintained," and the sole reason for continued white settlement in the colonies. "Britons on all sides of the emancipation issue" were chilled by the Haitian example where the end of slavery did not bring "economic equality or individual liberty."[142] On the other hand, imperialists and abolitionists in general shared an unspoken alliance against a common enemy after 1838: the remaining slave economies of Cuba and Brazil.[143]

Regarding the slaves, abolitionists had hoped to inaugurate a smooth transition to freedom by allowing a period of "apprenticeship" to 1840. Ideally, the ex-slaves would learn as much about the responsibilities as about the privileges which accompanied freedom during 1834 to 1840. As it was, apprenticeship ended sooner, resistance by Trinidadian planters notwithstanding, and before long planters' relief at the disciplined celebration of Freedom on 1 August 1834, gave way to bitter complaints about arrogant and expensive labor, about the falling price of sugar, about the fickleness of the British authorities.

The Report of the Select Committee on the West India Colonies of 1842 which made a comprehensive survey of the plight of those colonies was both a sop to planter interests and a useful summary of the experiment in free labor up to that year. The Report explicitly called for a reduction in wage rates and implicitly aided in routing the former slave workers' advantage. The means to this end turned out to be immigration under British control.[144] The planters who so envied the success of Mauritius were jubilant.[145] With the aid of Britain they would be able to tap the same sources of *wealth* that geography had lavished upon the Indian Ocean.[146]

2.2 LIVING WITH SUGAR WITHOUT SLAVES

It is true that in 1806 Trinidad had already looked to the East for laborers, in part to nullify problems of the abolition in 1807. A few hundred Chinese had arrived, but within a year all but 23 had returned to China. Subsequent efforts showed the greater difficulty of British planters to secure indented labor in a country outside its full colonial authority.[147] In 1811, a successful Antigua planter, Barham, had suggested importing laborers from India to forestall the decline in slave numbers, but James Stephen would not hear of it.[148] After abolition had become law in 1808, immigration became a regular ghost in planter deliberations. The Trinidad planter, W.H. Burnley, promoted the idea of Indian immigration again in 1814. In view of this background, along with data in official documents, questions arise about the willingness of planters to arrive at a post-emancipation *modus operandi* with the ex-slaves.

The above data do not deny that a sizeable minority of planters were financially distressed after 1833; merchants had not only refused new loans but demanded quick repayment of previous ones.[149] The complex set of motivations which eventually converged upon Britain, evincing a reluctant acquiescence in the export of its Indian subjects to distant Caribbean islands, must include planter determination to "teach the negroes a lesson."[150] One ought to

consider whether desperate planters so resented their former
bondsmen's new freedom that they actually preferred a new labor
force altogether. While immigration of assisted and other laborers
have been common, especially for North American and Australian
settlement, it seems to us that non-western and therefore naive
laborers arriving in Trinidad as early as 1806 and increasingly after
1838, may have predisposed planters *not* to negotiate the best
arrangement with the freedmen.[151]

Trinidad had founded an Immigration and Agricultural Society
with objectives, possibly in that order, as early as 1839 and passed
an Immigration Encouragement Ordinance a year earlier. Possibly
due to the harshness of the latter, London requested a revision of
the Ordinance. Colonel J.A. Mein, then acting governor, made
the requisite adjustments but could not oblige London on "balanced
sex ratios." In defence of admitting more males than females into
the island Colonel Mein explained that "this climate" was more
detrimental to the male, and that females outnumbered males in
Port of Spain. "[T]here is a population according to the last census,
of 6,781 females to 4,912 males; and that in the country the
proportion of inhabitants is even greater in favour of the female
Sex."[152] It was the exception rather than the rule that all restrictions
on immigration would be violated, at first gingerly, then blatantly.
And the arguments could be chauvinistic and not necessarily logical.
Ultimately it did not matter whether equal numbers of men and
women were brought to labor on Trinidad's plantations, so long as
new laborers were arriving. Complaints that high wages were driving
planters to ruin had begun to win sympathy among decision-makers
in London. The 1842 "Report from the Select Committee on the
West India Colonies" acknowledged the material, moral and
educational progress being made by freedmen and women, but
also concurred with planters that wages had to come down.
Immigration was generally accepted as the way to erode high wages
which fell for the first time only in January 1841 due to planter
cooperation. During the British 1842 Select Committee on West
India Colonies investigation, the witness Robert Bushe, managing

attorney for absentee owners and a planter himself, was asked: "In your opinion, what would be the best remedy for the state of distress among Trinidad's planters?" He replied, "I cannot conceive any other remedy except immigration." At the time of this testimony 10,000 immigrants had already entered Trinidad, and L15,000 sterling had been "laid aside for immigration for this year," already.[153] The 10,000 newcomers were mostly West Indian creoles. Until 1845, not a single East Indian worker had arrived and they are therefore not part of this data.

Immigration made the issue of laborers' rights and wages more problematic, and every time planter estimates for new workers were realized, the total laborers required was revised upwards. In 1842, when 10,000 West Indians had already arrived, one planter estimated that another 8,000 immigrants would satisfy planter's needs; he added that only 5,000 might be enough if such immigrants would work 12 hours a day during crop.[154] Between 1842 and 1850, at least 8,010 indented Africans alone had arrived but planters did not ask for a halt to immigration.[155] During 1845-50, colonial India allowed 5,568 indented workers to go to Trinidad. These two sources of indenteds thus supplied 13,578 new workers but those who estimated the need for between 5,000 and 10,000 were not assuaged. Or, very silent about the excess of laborers supplied. In fact, never once during Indian labor migration did planters themselves suggest they had received the required number of workers from India, including years of depression as in the late 1850s and the early 1880s. By 1917, an unadjusted total of 144,000 Indians had entered Trinidad.[156]

The self-interest, mainly of absentee planters, left former colonies—Trinidad, but also independent Fiji, Guyana and Surinam—with a legacy of Indo-Caribbean majorities and problems of racial and cultural justice. In so readily and frequently revising their estimates upwards, some of which were given in committees by eminent Trinidadians, planters were probably anticipating the day when Britain might abolish Indian indenture as it had abolished slavery. This was a legitimate fear in the context of declining sugar profits in Trinidad, although the closest Britain got to prohibition of this new slavery was temporary suspension in 1838 for the pioneers in this odious commerce, Mauritius and Guyana. Reports of abuses suffered by Indians also briefly halted Indian indenture in Trinidad during 1849-51. Sugar prices, meanwhile, had been falling steadily since 1846.[157] When abolition of indenture came, it did so on the strength of the Nationalist Movement in India led by Mohandas K. Gandhi who had seen its indignities in South Africa,[158] then a lawyer himself and on business in that country.

Immigration extended further the variegated European and non-European sources of Trinidad's population. But throughout the nineteenth century, immigration whether of West Indian creoles, whites and Portuguese or of East Indians, never changed the proportion of native-born and immigrant Trinidadians. The immigrant population during 1844-1901 hovered between 42 percent and 46 percent throughout while the Trinidad-born always remained a majority. With 59,815 inhabitants in 1844, Trinidad had a population density of 32 persons per square mile and immigrants were 44.61 percent and the Trinidad-born constituted 55.38 percent; by 1891 there were 200,028 people in Trinidad with density having increased to 107, yet Trinidad natives constituted 55.78 percent as compared with immigrants contributing the minority of 44.21 percent.[159]

While observers point immediately to the largely non-Christian Indians who began arriving in 1845, it is a fact that Indians were not much larger than one-third of Trinidad's total population throughout the nineteenth century. It is also sometimes forgotten that the first indenteds in Trinidad were Africans, then Portuguese and European. Europeans from Portugal, Britain, Germany and France had sent indenteds to Trinidad about the time of Emancipation.[160] At first planters were desperate enough to exploit any laborer, black or white, but by the 1860s the vast majority of planters would petition only for British Indians. Beginning with Governor McLeod, Europeans were dissuaded from entering

Trinidad as laborers because, in terms of "their health and treatment," the worst apprehensions "have been realised."[161]

An unquestioning acceptance of the proposition that East Indians were the best laborers for Trinidad's sugar plantations is challenged by contrary evidence. What became apparent after the 1860s leads scholarly hindsight to label non-Indian laborers as numerically inadequate, too costly, "or unsuitable labourers." It then seems to follow that "It was India which proved satisfactory."[162] The task is to explain why only India "proved satisfactory," not see it as a self-evident fact.

It was not simply that white and creole immigrants could not or would not work or that they moved on to set up small-scale retail businesses that India and East Indians were pursued. Within a year of the arrival of 180 Sierra Leonians the Trinidad planter Robert Bushe spoke of them as "the best [laborers] we ever had."[163] The 1842 Select Committee heard that if more U.S. blacks could be had, planters "would rather have 20 of those people [than] 40 of the old negroes" or ex-slaves. L.A.A. de Verteuil's history of Trinidad published in 1858 when there were 500 Chinese in the colony, said of them: "those who have become acclimatised may be considered as the best labourers in the colony."[164] Good Chinese, Portuguese and African workers certainly made Trinidad their destination; East Indians may not have been exceptional laborers but the attraction of Indian as a source of cheap labor was that Britain could arrange their transportation to Trinidad with a high degree of predictability. Planters were not unsophisticated in the decades after 1834; they knew that a saturated labor market would drive down wages. They may have anticipated that quantity would, over time, lead to a better quality of laborers.

Part of the problem was that one of the most desirable sources of labor, Africa, was protected by the memory of the horrid slave trade while people-rich China was protected—when its rulers chose—by its quasi-independence and laws.[165] Somee Chinese had been recruited for Trinidad in 1806 already; exactly a century later South Africa was using Chinese and Indian indenteds concurrently.

Some scholars have pointed to the similarities in the indenture experiences of China and Africa: western recruiters were confined to a few coastal enclaves and had limited access to laborers, voluntary or involuntary.[166]

One may disagree with the view that the supply of potential African indenteds in West Africa was limited, and that rather like India, Chinese and African "enclaves" could have netted more recruits than they in fact did. However, "The form compulsory labour takes will in the first place depend on the spirit of the times. Public opinion in the West would never have approved of the re-institution of slavery as such after abolition, no matter how acute the labour shortage. In these circumstances . . . other forms of compulsory labour were resorted to—often leaving the victims not much better off than before."[167]

It seems an accurate conclusion, therefore, that while planters in Trinidad declared their satisfaction with Chinese and Siera Leonian workers, it proved easier to tie British Indian subjects with indenture. Had Britain not taken up colonial government of India, it is unlikely that Indian indenture would have succeeded African slavery in the Caribbean. Other facets of the labor problem in Trinidad turn on how planters defined "best laborers" and what they perceived adequate profits to be. Good workers came to be defined in terms of how limited their options were in comparison with those of Trinidad-born and neighboring creoles, who could take the freedom of movement within Trinidad for granted. Hence, the option of squatting for Africans which, when it was tried by Indians, made them criminal vagrants.

West Indian creole immigrants targeted Trinidad in the years after Emancipation but planters were chagrined that 6,000 of some 10,000 arrivals were engaged in activities other than sugar.[168] Even the 100,000 Africans who came to the region after Emancipation could melt away in the population and spaces outside of the major towns. On the other hand, planters grumbled about labor even when they made decent profits. Burnley, whose name is so tied to nineteenth-century Trinidad, campaigned for immigration and justice to planters when his estates were profitable. Let us examine how Burnley's estate performed. In 1835, his plantations produced 399 hogsheads of sugar, his nett proceeds totalled L8,257 and Burnley's profits were L6,798. Only in 1837 did production fall below 300 hogsheads of sugar but his profits even then were L4,088. In 1840, Burnley produced 300 hogsheads of sugar and net proceeds totalled L10,463 with profits being L3,433. (These figures represent British pounds, shillings and pence).[169]

Upon examining these figures, it appeared "incredible" to observers that a planter retained, "as Burnley did in 1835, eighty percent. of his nett proceeds as profit." This share went down after total emancipation, to 40 percent in 1840, but "even that, I think, would not be regarded . . . as altogether unsatisfactory."[170] Indeed so. Herman Merivale was correct, therefore, when he said, "It is evident that in the new colonies . . . both profits and wages may be for a considerable time absolutely high; the condition of the labourer may be enviable," and yet the employers may "accumulate" quickly.[171]

Were planters so ill-equipped for the end of slavery that they expected to maintain the same levels of profits after 1838? Documents in the Public Record Office indicate that British "Guiana . . . has flourished greatly" in the period of apprenticeship," and in spite of the unexpected and "harsh drought" of 1839, the fair sugar prices yielded profits of about L2,000 "more than the average value of crops for the 13 years preceding." While details on Trinidad are sparse in the same document, we learn that "returns arrive regularly" from the stipendiary magistrates. It was a positive sign that most of these returns were blank where they would have given details on all "ejectments" of ex-slaves from estate houses for refusal to work, convictions "under the vagrancy law," and all contracts between employers and laborers as well as breaches of these contracts.[172] The planter, Robert Henry Church, told the 1842 Committee on 5 May 1842 that he neither "regulated [his] contracts with labourers" according to the "several" new labor ordinances nor had he ejected any ex-slave from Harmony Hall and Paradise Estates, which he managed for absentee planters.[173]

By 1842 planters had begun, grudgingly, to respect the new rights of ex-slave workers and had not used the ultimate leverage at their disposal, namely ejecting those who refused to work on their estates. Also in 1842, Governor McLeod had presented a mixed picture of the post-emancipation situation, in part because of incomplete reports. McLeod had found the situation "satisfactory, inasmuch as they shew improvements in many particulars," but he hadd not received full reports for areas under the Stipendiary Magistrates, "Messrs Cadiz, Guiseppi and Fernandez."[174]

McLeod's concern seemed justified because "it was notorious" that estates in the districts pertaining to the above-named magistrates could not get labor beyond three days a week. Their reports had merely stated that labor was "ample for the cultivation" without saying whether "the same quantity is now cultivated as during the Apprenticeship system." Planters and witnesses before the 1842 Select Committee testified that in 1842 Laborers "work far better now than they did" in the previous two years; owners and attorneys in London had decided "from January last[,] we would pay the wages, and no allowances." Allowances had included "a pint of flour," half a pound of pork, half a pound of fish, "and two glasses of rum a day besides." R. Bushe added, "When the present crop is over, we shall be able to reduce wages to 30 cents."[175]

McLeod also thought that daily wages of 60 cents was high: "The wages without allowances, may not to appearance be deemed to be excessive, but when Your Lordship is informed that two tasks can very easily be performed in one day, it will be apparent that the day's labour is not in fact sufficient for the price paid,—and I believe it would be more conducive to the good of this Colony if the task was encreased [sic] to a fair day's labor instead of diminishing the rate of wages. There are great difficulties to be met in this, however, for with the great scarcity of labour, the employer is much at the mercy of his labourer."[176]

McLeod's last paragraph painted a somewhat rosier picture: "I have much pleasure in bearing testimony to the general good conduct of the labouring class," adding specifically that during the current year labor has been "more continuous and steady" than previously. His concluding sentence speaks of "striking proof that the people are beginning to see their own interests. . . . "[177]

This is one of the most tantalizing documents for Trinidad's post-1833 labor history. Admittedly, McLeod had concerns; but neither he nor the magistrates pointed to specific impediments faced by planters or the colony. Much depends on what McLeod and the stipendiaries understood by words like "ample" and "own interests." The Governor did not consider paying cash wages at the prevalent rate a problem in itself: it were better for the "Colony" that the daily tasks be increased than wages decreased. In the testimony given to the 1842 Select Committee by planters themselves, the cause for concern was that a third of the estates were too poor to pay the current wages, a result of lower sugar prices. Robert Bushe had testified, "This year assuming sugar to remain at its present price, I do not think one third of them will pay their expenses." It was not a problem "for the rich," and perhaps those who employed "North American emigrants." They were found "more intelligent" than local workers and even when "not brought up to" agricultural work, "they always did more work," sometimes as many as 15 hours a day.[178]

As late as 1844 reports of the stipendiary magistrates sent in McLeod's despatch to London indicated that only remote parts of the country were experiencing labor shortages. This was the result of wage reductions and an attitude on the part of employers that labor ought to be had for six days in the week as under slavery. B.S. Fernandez wrote about the Eastern District, "the relation between the peasantry and the proprietor is not what could be desired," the latter wanting five or six days of work but getting only two and three. The reason for this, said the magistrate, was that the laborers' wants were too few, especially as the area was so remote. P.R. Rousseau reported for Toco (Northeast) that although very few immigrants had gone there, wages were down to about 40 cents per task, equivalent to 1s. 8d.[179]

In summary then, even if less than one-third of Trinidad's estates found adjusting to the cash wage economy onerous, the labor-intensive nature of these plantations reflects a vital facet of their difficulty. It is not absolutely true there was labor scarcity; cheap labor willing to wait months on end for payment on some estates, or to do the unpleasant work done quietly by slaves, turned Trinidad into a relatively labor-scarce and capital-scarce colony. The lost opportunities to mechanize and rationalize sugar production could not be regained when ex-slaves needed to be paid cash wages. In the period before the 1830s when slaves were chattel, planters had taken the easier route of producing the cheaper, less refined muscavado sugar. These kinds of choices had thus made Trinidad dependent upon cheap, continuous and ill-paid labor for up to 18-hour days during the harvest. Only a captive labor force, disallowed onto Trinidad's relatively vast, virgin interior where squatting was a rewarding option, would permit a continuation of the plantation society as well as the freedom granted the erstwhile slaves. British Indians came to play a similar role that Africans had played in colonial North America in replacing indigenous Amerindian slaves whose familiarity with the land allowed for escape, alliances with free tribes, etc.[180]

Moreover, the East Indian contribution in Trinidad and in the Caribbean region lie not in their arrival having led to wage reductions for the former slaves—because that had begun to happen well before 1845—but rather in allowing for the emergence of what may have been "the first modern multi-national corporations in the Caribbean."[181] This refers to the later nineteenth-century amalgamation and consolidation on sugar estates which permitted wide-scale mechanization. Having far fewer options than local laborers, because control over emigration was in British hands, India helped this development in yielding a cheap, continuous supply of its sons and daughters to cash-strapped estates especially in the crucial period of European beet sugar competition after

1870.[182] The down side of this phenomenon was the gradual dilution of creole political clout in Trinidad: in terms of the lowering of ex-slave wages, non-Indian groups were first upon the stage.

2.3 LIGHT AT LAST: POST-1838
EXPERIMENTS WITH INDENTURE

Before African indenture was inaugurated in Trinidad with the arrival of 180 Sierra Leone laborers in 1841,[183] two other events occurred which were to have significance for the future of free labor. Both of these took place in the first year of freedom, before the end of apprenticeship in 1838. First, on 12 February 1834 Trinidad's Governor Hill wrote Lord Stanley, the British Secretary of the Colonies, about the anticipated arrival of "cargoes of prize Negroes" from Havana. A total of 212 rescued slaves sailed on the schooner *Manuelita* from Havana on 16 January and arrived in Trinidad minus five who had died en route. The enthusiasm of planters for the laborers was evident in the applications for the new workers which "commenced to pour in."[184]

15 July 1834 marked the second important episode in the post-emancipation labor history of Trinidad with the arrival of the first supposedly voluntary indented workers. Forty-four Portuguese from Fayal in the Azores arrived on the *Watchful*. They, like the West Indian creoles from neighboring islands, had come on the bounty system. The details of their contracts are noteworthy: in exchange for the amount expended by private speculators or employers for their passage, "sixty dollars per head," the Fayal Portuguese were required to repay the amount at the end of an indenture of three years. At the same time they would receive six dollars per month, one-half of which would be retained as surety against non-payment of the initial cost of conveyance to Trinidad. The immigrants were to be provided "a piece of land for their own use and cultivation and to be provisioned like a Negro until their

lands [became] productive." It was widely believed that their experience with field labor in "sun heat" rendered them a "valuable acquisition" to Trinidad, "which only requires a sufficient laboring population" to make it "the most valuable" of Britain's West Indian colonies. Even as Governor Hill intimated to London the plans of other planters to procure more Portuguese workers, he sought assurance "whether any objections exist[ed]" about this in the British Government.[185]

The contrasting and chequered story of how newly arriving immigrants were indented, and under what conditions, tells us much about our global village. It validates Kloosterboer's assertion that the form compulsory labor takes is dependent first and foremost on the "spirit of the times." Stories about the horrors of Portuguese indenture rather quickly evoked sympathy in Trinidad. The corollary in action was a general laxity to enforce the contracts of the Portuguese indenteds.[186] Only a few years later, after the arrival of the first British Indians, their suffering and mortality did not lead to similar leniency. Rather it was argued by Governor Harris and planter-employers that Indian health and habits would improve if they could be bound by contracts.[187]

For the Indian who first entered Trinidad not under contract, but as free migrants, they were subsequently bound to indenture and a required absence from India for ten years before being added to a list of would-be repatriates to India.[188] What had happened in the rather fleeting decade from the arrival of the Fayal laborers on bounty in July 1834 until the arrival of the East Indian indenteds of May 1845, which denuded Trinidad hearts of sympathy? Indeed, individual employers stood to lose rather large amounts in investment with regards to bounty workers, whereas a less immedite agent—the colonial government—would absorb the losses of Indian labor. The facts are unclear; we can only attempt to uncover patterns or lack of them in Trinidad's responses to the many groups of migrants.

At thee very basic level, one might suggest that both black and white workers were known entities to would-be employers, if only in a general way, but that Indians were virtual aliens in labor, cultural and religious terms. The Trinidad government thus had to stand ready to engage surplus Indians each year after 1845 in public works projects whenever planters either rejected the new workers or took fewer than had arrived on ships. In contrast, there was a certain kind of alacrity among employers whenever black or white laborers arrived in Trinidad.

Upon the arrival of the *Manuelita* recaptives in Trinidad, planters made "immediate applications" for these potential laborers "to the amount of 938." This was many times more than the 207 recaptives landed alive. Governor Hill's decision to distribute the Africans in ten lots of twenty for the 200 adults left an impression of loot being divided. The children—"there were 7 little girls under 10 years of age"—were placed in the care of "respectable" families by the Governor. The adults went to 20 different estates, "in the capacity of free laborers pursuant to your instructions for 5 months." For the first 30 days the newcomers were to be fed, clothed and allowed to adjust. Hill had the employers sign agreements, copies of which were sent to the Commandants of the Quarters in the respective districts. The provision that employers would "lodge, medicate and give them an adequate supply of food, clothing and household furniture," along with the obligation to report each month to the Governor, were eminently fair. In an interesting harking to the recent slave past the Governor informed Lord Stanley, that both he and the Protector of Slaves would make "frequent" checks on the new African workers.[189]

Questions left open by these arrangements concerned the legal status of the Africans, especially once they had fulfilled the apprenticeship.[190] Hill queried whether the recaptives, if they were accepted as non-settlers, could be "corrected" in cases when they proved "refractory and disobedient."[191] Hill also suggested to the authorities in London that "control and regulation of these persons as free labourers" be the object of a local ordinance or an Order in Council.

Planters appeared highly satisfied with the arrangements concluded with the freed slave-immigrants and desired to engage another 5,000 recaptives on similar terms. They indicated that

10,000 could be employed by the island's estates if the authorities might permit employers to "apprentice them until 1840." Meanwhile the planters' lobby in London, the West India Committee, conveyed to Secretary Spring-Rice that liberated Africans ought to be engaged under regulations which made for their "efficient control." Spring-Rice's objections were countered with the argument that rescued Africans had come from "uncivilized" parts of Africa. As this was the period of apprenticeship and not full emancipation, the Colonial Secretary felt their indenture might be condoned.[192] The facts of how readily plantations were ready to indent and exploit African and Portuguese labor, and just four years before the formal end of slavery, did not augur well for any other group of nominally free workers. Planters' desire for "effective control" and to "apprentice" 10,000 Africans for six years—"until 1840"—were realised beyond their wildest expectations when indented Indians began arriving in Trinidad after 1845.

For the moment Trinidad passed an Ordinance on 19 March 1835 indenting or apprenticing liberated Africans for periods up to a maximum of three years. In return for a "reasonable" amount of work, the Africans would receive payment, food, housing, and medical attention.[193] In a foretaste of things to come, terms like reasonable, reliable, "vagrancy"[194] and absconding would bear the stamp of the planters' definition. When he came to the Colonial Office, Lord Glenelg voiced his apprehensions, for instance, that Hill had divided the Africans in "lots" as if they were "so much property."[195] Glenelg was wary about contracts concluded outside the colonies with Europeans *and* non-Europeans. His response to Guiana providing for up to seven-year indentures was illustrative. The Governor of Guiana had explained to Glenelg that many of the English apprentices "became habitual Drunkards," but "Your Lordship will perceive that, out of a total of 1,336 Individuals, only 15 are bound to serve for 7 years; 22 are engaged for only Six Months; 320 for One Year. . . . "[196] Glenelg specifically forbade labor recruitment in Africa and warned, "Whatever measures may be taken and whatever principles may be sanctioned . . . will necessarily form a Precedent for Imitation in any other" colony.[197] The history of the next few years demonstrated that long contracts of up to six years desired by planters had indeed become a precedent.

Lord Glenelg as head of the imperial department which oversaw the colonies wanted "special Magistrates" to protect the interests of all indenteds, and that the laborers be bound only as long as it took to work off the cost of their passages. With respect to West Indian immigrants, he observed that the "Negro in the Bahamas or Antigua, to whom Guiana is a remote and unknown . . . country," ought not to "fetter" himself because high wages might not materialize and he should be allowed to return to his island of origin. When it came to Indians, rather than indentures lasting only so long as it took migrants to work off their transportation to Trinidad or any other colony, employers gradually won the right to keep them from both their freedom and from India for a minimum of ten years at a time. Was it racial solidarity with the whites-on-bounty which made governors and even employers lenient with their agreements, and was it fear of potential accusations of disguised African slavery which seemed to also protect the new African indenteds in Trinidad?

It is important to note that any colony's ordinance, once passed, remained effective in that colony until the requests for revision came from London or a Colonial Office despatch for its abrogation arrived in the colony. In summary, the Colonial Office under Lord Glenelg "required that the contracts should be limited to three years (one year if concluded outside the Colony) and [excluding] immigrants from Africa," for the explicit fears of reviving a disguised slave trade. Guiana was quick in preparing a corresponding Ordinance. The Guianese law was confirmed by a British Order in Council on 1 March 1837. Once overcoming such legal hurdles at the Colonial Office, the laws and regulations of a colony were usually respected only when it was convenient for its public servants to do so. For instance, barely months after Guiana's immigration ordinance was accepted by the Colonial Office, the infamous planter in Guiana, John Gladstone, had a special Order passed in that colony to enable him to bring workers from India on contracts exceeeding the maximum by two years![198]

In the years after Emancipation, the colony of Trinidad appeared eager to accept black and white labor migrants who came to their attention, in part as a reaction to the uncertainty of the transition. When Lord John Russell wrote Trinidad's Governor McLeod on 9 June 1840 that Sierra Leone had potential emigrants for Trinidad, McLeod responded that he found "a great and general desire" among the planters to acquire them. An Enclosure by Governor Doherty mentioned that "many of the Maroon and settler population" had heard that immigration was being encouraged in the islands, and they were anxious to end their exile.[199] Thus began post-slavery free emigration from Africa during which the degree of voluntariness invloved would be, at best, ambiguous. Britain had cautiously allowed experiments with East Indian labor in Guiana and also overcame its earlier misgivings in sanctioning African indented migration to the region during 1838-1841.

All the scruples Britain had expressed in disallowing African indenteds per colonial ordinances, which explored various venues and avenues for potential laborers, were now discarded. In 1835 when Trinidad had sought to indent liberated Africans, it had met with a rebuff from Downing Street. "By 1840, however, necessity had begun to dominate scruple. . . . "[200] The ideas of Merivale, inter alia, that immigration would save the sugar colonies without recourse to protectionism gained currency, as did those who saw any collapse of the "sugar economy [as] vastly more pernicious to the welfare of Africans than the risks [of] the trans-Atlantic migration of liberated slaves."[201] By 1851, the complaints of Governor Macdonald of Sierra Leone that abuses in African recruitment threatened regular emigration, was testimony that employers do not change because laws do. In a foretaste of things to come, he could say with equanimity, "few, very few" of these Africans show any disinclination to leave Sierra Leone: "[T]hey emigrate of their own free will, or not at all."[202] It is possible, nay highly probable, that many Africans rescued from slave vessels succumbed to emigration because they felt a pressure to do so.

Guiana (Demerara) was the major recipient of African indenteds, but by only 342 workers over Trinidad's third best total of 3,460 arrivals. Authors Roberts and Byrnes' estimate that 26,827 Africans entered the Caribbean during 1841-50. Of these 26,827 newcomers to the Caribbean just 2,098 went to other than three recipients: Guiana, Jamaica and Trinidad, the big three which also took the lion's share of Indian indenteds. The governor added a caveat which confirms the raw status of data, thereby allowing for the inclusion of "periodic totals"—551 Africans for St. Lucia between 1846 and 1850, and for the period 1861-7, an additional 179 immigrants.

The available sources, including Governor Harris's report,[203] and statistics that planters presented to the 1842 Select Committee indicated that Trinidad had received some 9,000 African indenteds and 10,800 creole migrants from neighboring islands.[204] Some of this approximately 20,000 incoming workers were recruited simultaneously with East Indian indented migration.

The reality is that Trinidad's population for the years between Emancipation and 1900, remained virtually foreign-born by half. Indian indenture did not change this fact, which may have been more lopsided in favor of foreigners before Emancipation or Abolition of the Slave Trade in 1808. As only a few thousand Indians had entered Trinidad by 1850, the vast majority of the more than 40 percent foreign-born in the population of about 68,000 in that year would have been newcomers from Europe, neighboring islands and Africa.[205] Only by the late 1860s was India's place secured as the pre-eminent source for the West Indies' labor supply; until then, Indian immigrants were insignificant compared to other sources.

The supply of potential workers for the Caribbean became most predictable and reliable from sources in India, a populous British colony. The supply of island creoles and West Africans could and did exceed the totals from India in some years, but further research is needed to fully analyse the factors involved before meaningful comparisons can be made. For instance, in February 1853, a planter lobbyist, A. Colville, had reported that for the "six years" since 1848 some 46,000 immigrants entered Guiana, Jamaica, and Trinidad alone. Colville also expressed satisfaction with the continued "reduction in . . . wages."[206] Of Trinidad's share of this supply 18,000 of the newcomers entered Trinidad in just three years, 1848-50. East Indian migrants barely exceeded 5,000 for the years 1845-50.

The sanction for indenting Africans to post-slavery plantations in Trinidad had not come easily from London. We have already examined Lord Gleneelgs suggestions and prohibitions. Also, Colonial Secretaries Spring-Rice and Lord John Russell felt they had difficult choices to make, given that Freetown could not absorb all Africans freed from pirate slave-traders. In Jamaica, Alexander Barclay, commissioner general of immigration since 1840, exploited the ambivalence of the Colonial Office and of abolitionists so as to indent recaptives "settled" in Sierra Leone. Lord John Russell haad wavered between a total ban and "countenancing only one-year indentures." The insistence on short contracts would have ensured a "limited indenture" if free Africans were treated as slaves. He declared "that we [Britain] are not bound to maintain in the Colony of Sierra Leone," all the slaves rescued by the Royal Navy.

The overall problems and significance of African indented labor has been presented thus: "As a measure of economic salvation African immigration failed, for labor shortage was more a symptom than a cause of the sugar economy's decline." The situation with Indian indenture would prove similar, for Indian immigration was an artificially-directed movement of people to places like Trinidad. Monica Schuler pointed out that for African indenture, "after the first few years," planters paid Africans less than a living wage, thereby turning "the indentured labor system [into] . . . the equivalent of slavery rather than the humanitarian scheme that its British apologists claimed." Considerable tension resulted from planters' perception of Africans as units of labor to be managed and exploited like their slave predecessors, and the Africans' insistence that they were first and foremost an autonomous community.[207]

Researchers covering a wide-ranging area also bring evidence to bear on the above facts, as does Philip Curtin, who has shown that labor difficulties are a clue that several plantation economies were quite moribund at Emancipation. The decline of plantation eeconomies were related to the absence of economies of scale and because estate-based production precluded timely and efficient mechanization.[208] In the absence of decisions which required sacrifices from planters, Trinidad's labor-intensive sugar production masked severe structural problems. Failure to invest timeously in machinery for the attractive rewards of refining sugar for the higher market prices, made such investment even harder for planters after the 1830s. Where the local plantation economy had approximated a barter system in many respects, after 1833 labor needed to be paid in cash over and above continuing perquisites. Some estates were notorious for paying poorly or very late. Free labor willing to accept the planters' terms became increasingly difficult to find. The fate of Britain's Indian subjects showed how plantation Trinidad took several steps backward in the road to free labor, as in delaying their right to a minimum monetary payment for their work, and food rations and "lost time" turned Indian into virtual debt-peons of some of the harsher employers or plantation managers.

2.4 AN EARLY END TO APPRENTICESHIP: WHAT IS TO BE DONE?

While the experiments with immigrant labor had been underway, external developments again changed the equation between employers and laborers in Trinidad. This was the 1838 termination of apprenticeship, that arrangement whereby slaves would be freed after serving their owners until August 1840.

It was the Lord Henry Brougham who on 20 February 1838 proposed a speedier end to apprenticeship in the British House of Lords. He argued that "the final suppression of slavery" should take place by 1 August 1838, instead of 1840 as had been agreed upon in 1833. Guiana, Jamaica, Trinidad, Dominica, Barbados, and St. Lucia were persuaded to issue their virtual "emancipation" proclamations during June, July and August 1838. Mauritius resisted until 11 March 1839.[209]

By 6 November 1838, the Colonial Secretary was elated that full emancipation had proceeded so uneventfully. The worst fears of planters and imperialists alike were laid to rest. "The distinguishing feature above all of this progress is, that it has been accomplished without the smallest disturbance . . . without the overthrow of any social institution" and rather than seeking revenge, the ex-slaves felt tied to the British more now that "equal protection to the rights of all classes" had been assured.[210] London was clearly more enthusiastic about this transition to free labor than Trinidad's planters.

In the Original Correspondence files in the British Public Record Office, one uncovers a widespread reluctance among Trinidad's planters to "relinquish apprenticeship" ahead of 1840. On 28 June 1838, for instance, Governor Hill wrote to London that he had impressed upon the "proprietary body" that despite its late acquisition by Britain, Trinidad would not be allowed to continue with apprenticeship after other colonies announced full emancipation. Some planters were determined "to rely upon their apprentices for a cheerful continuation" of slavery until 1840. Hill decided to visit each estate to assess the situation: "no doubt the Apprentices are at present conducting themselves well and nothing should be said to excite them in any way. Reasoning and the high wages those who work for hire during their extra time receive may keep all steady, yet, when the praedials here learn from the Emigrants into this island that in the other Islands there has been a general discharge from Apprenticeship . . . I cannot but anticipate some stir among them."[211]

The governor then explained that in three meetings with the Council of Government, on the 1, 6 and 11 June, Apprentices were secured specific safeguards and benefits. If the Council agreed to these generous terms in the hopes that apprenticeship-slavery would be extended, they were to be disappointed. A Proclamation of 13 June 1838 had given to apprentices each Saturday for themselves to rest and to go to market; the period of daily labor had been revised to nine hours excluding meals; it further endorsed all "privileges, indulgences and allowances" which had been the practice over the three years previous to Emancipation. Mothers received an additional hour to suckle children under a year old, and for those with three or more children, "a reduction of working hours." Finally, there was to be a "grant of a dollar a year for each child."[212] The chagrin of planters that generous regulations had not persuaded London to allow slavery beyond 1838 was tempered by the fear that a servile revolt was possible if Trinidad fell out of step with other colonies.

On 26 July 1838 Governor Hill reported to Glenelg, "With sincere pleasure I acquaint you that I have succeeded in the abrogation of Praedial Apprenticeship." The Proclamation to this effect "was at my suggeestion, brought forward by Dr. Philip—"he is the first coloured gentleman that ever sat at the Board of Council," and the motion was supported by Charles and Thornton Warner.[213] The "opposition was temperate," with one Mr. W. Fuller, unofficial member of the Legislature and a planter, making an "energetic" but ineffectual vote against the early demise of Apprenticeship.[214]

The above data reveals, *inter alia*, that apprentices worked a maximum of nine hours daily, which would have maintained pre-emancipation production levels or bettered them. After 1838 planters charged that ex-slaves refused to work more than single four-hour tasks daily.[215] Acting Governor Mein wrote to London on 18 May 1839 that "all . . . restraints upon their Conduct and free will" having been removed, the freedpersons worked for subsistence alone. He added it were better "if the Negro could be led to a spirit of forethought" to save "for it being received as true that a state of continuous occupation or habitual moderate labour" would certainly "improve the moral condition" of any people or group.[216]

Mein indicated that ex-slaves worked barely five days a week but he appreciated the they were not more troublesome. Although "from the nature of their character they do not express active insubordination to their Employers yet they are well aware that the Master is very much at their Mercy, that labour must be had, which is difficult to obtain and that in leaving One Employer, they have only to to turn round and apply to another, who from the same necessity for labour will instantly hire them—there is no competition and the wages are exceedingly high . . . it may fairly be said that there is no labouring Population in Europe, who are so well paid and in every respect so thoroughly Independent as the peasantry of this Island. The natural result . . . is, that the proprietor is the principal sufferer surrounded with difficulties, and shackled in many cases with accumulated debt."[217]

Burnley's testimony four years later would be similar, indeed remarkable for comparing the favorable circumstances of Trinidad's ex-slaves with Europe's downtrodden peasants. Also, both Mein and Burnley commented that freedpersons were very aware of their leverage—having planters "at their mercy." Average wages for "Agricultural Laborers" in 1839 were "1/2 dollar a day", according to Colonel Mein. Artisans and "mechanics" earned twice as much, or "a dollar a day equal to 4/2 Stg." Mein also informed "Your Lordship that the Crops would fall short one third this year, and many of the smaller Estates will be thrown out of Cultivation both of sugar and Cocoa." However, he was hopeful that it would take another, "Two or Three Years before the minds of the Black population become accustomed to a state of freedom, and to the responsibility" which came with liberty. At the time, though, "[m]any of the evils" of slavery seemed, in Mein's view, to be falling upon the planter: "he cannot get the necessary labour . . . and his labourers are as much independent of him, as they were before obliged to be submissive."[218]

The one-third fall in production predicted by Mein was not

universal for export staples. Production figures for cocoa are given
in Table 2.1 for 1831 through 1856, which indicate that the
predictions of doom and gloom were rather exaggerated.

TABLE 2.1 TRINIDAD COCOA PRODUCTION IN lbs. (1831-1856)

1831	===	1,888,852	1844	===	3,303,715
1832	===	1,530,990	1845	===	2,528,482
1833	===	3,090,526	1846	===	4,021,198
1834	===	3,363,630	1847	===	3,738,376
1835	===	2,744,643	1848	===	2,956,704
1836	===	3,188,870	1849	===	4,728,185
1837	===	2,507,483	1850	===	3,816,728
1838	===	2,571,915	1851	===	5,008,920
1839	===	2,914,061	1852	===	4,246,851
1840	===	3,237,905	1853	===	4,842,875
1841	===	3,122,220	1854	===	3,761,057
1842	===	3,141,550	1855	===	5,427,351
1843	===	2,803,295	1856	===	4,905,796

Sources:
PP Volume XIII: Burnley's testimony on 2 May 1842;
HST Publ #260: "Exports of Cocoa from Trinidad."

While it is true that cocoa might have expanded slightly more
rapidly under slave labor arrangements, the apparent decline after
1834 was not consistent: the production of 3,188,870 lbs. in 1836
lifted cocoa above the c.2 million lb. mark achieved for the rest of
the 1830s. Indeed there were other years, as far removed from the
post-emancipation year as 1848, when labor may not have been
the cause of a production decline to 2,956,704 lbs. In the years
after 1848 cocoa production would not fall below 3 million lbs.
per annum; at the end of the period of this study, cocoa doubled
in output from 11,927,067 lbs. in 1887 to 21,352,312 lbs. in

1888. Output may have been influenced by the number of trees maturing and by the fact that independent cocoa farmers, including East Indians, were cocoa producers by the end of the nineteenth century.[219]

If it were to be counter-argued that sugar production more accurately reflected the post-emancipation labor situation, the data cannot support that argument. As we have seen, production declines ranged from one-quarter (per contemporary reports) to one-fifth (argued by Eric Williams). For the periods 1831-34 and 1839-42 which Williams examined, sugar production declined by 20 per cent. When compared with other West Indian colonies, Trinidad's production remained highest. Decline in Jamaica had been "one-half," in British Guiana "three-fifths" and in St. Vincent "two-fifths," when compared with 1831-34.[220]

Burnley's overall production averages calculated for the decade 1831 to 1841 also show increases for each period: 1831, '32, and '33: 2,170,122 lbs.; 1835, '36, and '37: 2,813,665 lbs.; and in the period of complete freedom a remarkable growth averaged for 1839, '40 and '41 at 3,091,101 lbs. Nevertheless, the frailty of averages—that they hide as much as they reveal—is true. The average production for sugar, molasses and coffee respectively were 24,143 hogsheads 9,746 hogsheads and 182,639 pounds for 1831-33; 23,108 hhds. 9,287 hhds. and 172,480 lbs. for 1835-37; and 18,641 hhds., 7,044 hhds. and 238,648 lbs for 1839 through 1841.[221]

At first few complaints were heard from post-slavery Trinidad. Governor Hill's account of the state of the society and economy more than a week after 1 August 1838 had been similar in spirit to his previous reassuring despatches. However, the growing focus on the need for better policing of the country especially per "An Ordinance to Establish a System of Rural Police," showed a concern among the elites and planters to control the excess energies of the freed men and women. On the labor question, Hill was his cheerful self: "Already considerable progress has been made on many of the Sugar Estates in settling their terms" of work with laborers. The wages, generally, "are 8 dollars per month and 3 pounds and half of Salt Fish per week with house and Cultivable Ground." It was those estates which had treated slaves and apprentices harshly which experienced insufficient laborers after Freedom Day. Some estates had difficulties because the planters "had published an offer of 12 dollars a month to negroes from Grenada," but did not offer the same to locals.[222] Nowhere in his reports did Hill suggest that laborers were averse to work. He was to change his opinion following this report. Yet, when examined against production figures for Trinidad as given to the 1842 Select Committee on 2 May by Burnley, Hill's about-face appears odd.

The averages given by Burnley for the decade—cleverly calculated so as to leave out abolition in 1834 and abrogation of apprenticeship in 1838—show that sugar production fell by 25 percent between the last years of slavery and the first three years of freedom. The year 1834 reportedly saw a good harvest, and were it to have been included might have improved Burnley's overall averages; in any event, there was not the 33 percent fall in production predicted by Mein. Coffee jumped from 182,639 lbs. by about 31 percent in the same period. Between 1831 and the next year, coffee expanded by 55 percent, 150 percent between 1832 and 1833; and even though 1834 showed a decline vis a vis 1833, it was still 755 percent more than the production of 1831. The decline in molasses yields over 1831-33 was perhaps proportionate to the fall in sugar production.

Burnley's averages omit certain facts. First, the highest sugar output for the decade came in 1834; if the assumption is that the soon-to-be-free slaves worked with enthusiasm after 1 August 1838, it is difficult to account for its dissipation by 1835. Secondly, the reality was not one of an irreversible decline in production: 1836 was an improvement over 1835 and 1831 as well, and the 18,641 hogsheads of sugar produced in 1841 was an increase over 1840 figures. As for the checkered fate of coffee, every year after 1831 maintained the increases of at least 500 percent over 19,994 lbs. produced in 1831, that is, during slavery. It was in 1835 alone when production was not greater than six times what it had been in 1831. Labor was just one variable affecting Trinidad's agricultural output.

Planters may have been more severely affected by falling sugar prices—an external factor—than by the arrogance of free labor. Falling prices combined with equalization measures made planters regard London as the source of their difficulties. A detectable strategy, once they realized the futility of attacking the mother-country incessantly, was an appeal to the British sense of fairness in allowing planters the respite they needed to get their profits up again. The key to implementing this strategy was utilising their London lobby and newspapers.

The Trinidad Standard and West India Journal ran an article in February 1839 with the ominous lead, "Is it too late to do anything for the West Indies?" This sense of alarm appeared to call for some deliberate plan to be adopted by West Indian planters. The newspaper tried to put on the best face: "Is it because a man has lost his right arm, that he should make no efforts to preserve his left?" However, from a laborer's perspective, "right arm" could be read as labor itself; in this analogy, then, the left arm was yet to be found in immigration. The Journal thought that planters were now morally stronger: "They can say, 'The policy of England, and the interests of her merchants, compelled us to employ slave instead of free labour. We were not free agents.'" The British Government had instructed "our forefathers" when they patented land in the Caribbean, that "for every 100 acres of land you must have 10 slaves, otherwise you shall not settle there." They brought ginger and coffee from the "Orientals" and multiplied the luxuries of life. In all their efforts, "they asked little and gave much . . . [but] we were deceived."[223] Trinidad planters would, in this vein, blame Britain for their financial and labor woes, which was much in evidence in testimonies given to the 1842 Select Committee.

Appeal for fairness toward the poor as well as toward those enriched by their parents' investments was made very effectively by the West Indian Committee in London. The planters deserved, the Journal had suggested, having acquiesced in the demands of abolitionists and having "absolved our labourers from the two remaining years of the apprenticeship," fairness and justice. "We are sure that every right-minded Englishman will respond to our complaint" and "will pity our wives and children, reduced from affluence to a bare competence, and now about to have that competence taken from them." The one pillar of their material salvation lay in the call, "reduce the duty upon our products; the reduction will benefit every man in Britain, and afford us a trifling relief." Should relief not be immediately forthcoming, the course of action was clear: "This is the language—these are the words—which the West Indian [planter]s should employ . . . should repeat, day by day till they become household words in the mouths of your wives and children . . . until these demands are met."[224]

Until 1825 West Indian sugar had enjoyed guaranteed access to the British muscavado market at the lowest rates among foreign and other British producers. In that year, Mauritius first reared up as the nemesis of the West Indies when its sugar entered London at the lower West Indian tariff rate. In 1835, Britain's East Indian colonial sugar was allowed into Britain at the West Indian preference rate. In 1844, all non-slave grown muscavado sugar was allowed into the British market at only 6s. higher than the imperial preference tariff of 24s. The infamous 1846 Sugar Duty Act announced that all sugar of a similar quality, regardless of what labor produced it, would enter London on an equal rate.[225] One sees planter success in obtaining a stay in equalizing duties on all imported sugars from 1846 to 1854, and a corresponding decline in the watchfulness in London over the rights of free labor as tantamount to a second pillar of salvation for the planters. Did the planters also succeed in winning over Governor Hill to their cause, a governor who had so eagerly worked in the spirit of Lord Brougham's motion for a speedy end to apprenticeship in 1838 rather than in 1840?

A few months after his jubilant despatch to Glenelg in July 1838 Hill appeared convinced that laborers were giving "way to their natural disposition of sloth and repose." He converted to the idea that it was "expedient"—more convenient?—to seek immigrant laborers from elsewhere than to negotiate the best settlement with the freedmen and women in Trinidad. In December 1838, an anxious Hill wrote that neither higher wages nor medical and other benefits had persuaded ex-slaves "to take off the ensuing crop." Unless an immediate remedy were adopted, "a large amount of existing Capital will be lost and the Prosperity of the Colony materially and permanently injured."[226]

The substantive policy for which Hill sought Colonial Office approval was "to provide at the Public expense" new laborers accustomed to agricultural work and "inured to labour in a tropical climate." The plan entailed appointing Immigration Agents in appropriate "places" with an "allowance in lieu of a salary of 12 shillings sterling for each effective field labourer of good character" they introduced into Trinidad. At the apex of the structure would be an Emigration Office and Officer who would receive incoming laborers and oversee relevant arrangements. Hill enclosed the amended Immigration Ordinance dated 19 November 1838 with certain provisoes which London had insisted upon; it emphasized that "the free choice" of potential immigrants would be jealously protected. One wonders how such a promise would be honored were newcomers to show similar human responses to employers as had the ex-slaves: "There is a mischievous agency at work which from time to time imposes belief upon the suspicious character of the negroes that their freedom is not perfectly secured and causes them to be unsettled in their minds and dispositions and when two days wages will maintain one of these laborers for a week they [work as little] . . . The introduction of laborers from other places would evidently assist towards *curing* this disinclination to work . . . [emphases added]."[227]

The focus upon immigration as the panacea for the ills of the colony appears boringly predictable. It is evident too, so soon after Emancipation, that when the interest of proprietors are threatened, those concerned about the political economy seldom observe their own contradictory reasoning. For instance, in Hill's December 1838 despatch in which he appears frustrated with the apparent "sloth" of Trinidad's freed population and sought Colonial Office sanction for immigration, he also piously defended the right of creole laborers to do as they pleased. It amounted to a call for creoles to abscond from neighboring plantations: "The Ordinances passed by many of the Old Colonies to chain the Negroes as it were to those Islands," made a mockery of Freedom. Hill explained that this rendered absurd the very "idea of the Negro Population having obtained perfect freedom" and that London would "not sanction the exercise of such unjustifiable power."[228]

It is a recorded fact that the end of apprenticeship saw a bitter rivalry among West Indian colonies for laborers, and that Trinidad emerged with the biggest slice of this immigrant pie: 10,800 to the end of 1849.[229] Also, in a paradox yet to unfold, Hill approved of the Colonial Office stipulation that private shipowners—a special kind of bounty-hunters—should withdraw and leave the job of transporting immigrant-laborers to officers of government. London would not tolerate any restrictions on free laborers, Hill advised, and even if the immigrant laborers refused to work for those who had paid their bounties, the Colonial Office would support the *freedom* of the laborer. The adherence to this principle on the part of Hill and officials in Trinidad would prove transient. When colonial revenues had been expended on immigrants who opted for jobs other than estate labor upon arrival in Trinidad, the Council would succumb to pressures for long-term labor contracts to show a return on investments. The planters were also strengthened after December 1838 by realignments between planters and merchants which had been at work in the four years since 1834, years in which the West India Committee had appeared to languish.[230] The planters argued "persuasively" for immigration to Trinidad and a few years before the 1842 Select Committee Investigation, Burnley had become the colony's Agent in Britain and the United States. One of Burnley's first acts as Agent was a visit to his native United States in July 1839 to procure free black immigrants. By

June 1847 over a thousand North Americans of color had been welcomed to Trinidad.[231] Beyond this Burnley had to contend with delays due to weather such as ice in the harbor, and opposition from American planters who saw "considerable numbers of laborers" going off to Trinidad. They counter-campaigned and warned intending emigrants: "they would get nothing to eat 'except monkeys, lizards and parrots'!"[232]

Some 1,333 North Americans entered Trinidad through Agent Burnley's efforts. Dwindling African-American interest in the island was impacted by reports that Guiana was a better prospect. Free Blacks of Baltimore in Maryland were astute enough to send out their own *scouts* who surveyed conditions in the region for American immigrants.[233] But what United States planters considerd the loss of a "considerable number" of laborers was a drop in the ocean in the estimates of the plantation colony of Trinidad.

Planters and the West India Lobby were also aided by a quiet, non-Caribbean force: Liverpool. Hall pointed out the role of Liverpool interests in furthering colonial immigration. The fact that in 1840, the Liverpool chapter—a center of mercantile interest—was ahead of all the other West India bodies in "encouraging emigration" of laborers "best fitted for tropical labour" to the sugar colonies was connected with replacing the lost profits for transporting slaves with profits via transporting Indians.[234] Be that as it may, following the 1842 Select Committee Report into the West India Colonies, the dice were loaded decidedly against all laborers.

Trinidad planters had complained that no group of employers ever contended with their unique fate: a revolutionary increment in the "power" of their labor force when the island remained chronically short of labor.[235] From the ex-slaves point of view, this transformation in their situation could not have been otherwise if emancipation were to have any meaning for them. Planters insisted that the entire post-1838 situation was an "artificial" one in terms of the leverage of laborers, between the benefits which Trinidad offered former slaves and the disadvantages endured by European peasants.[236]

An African-American, W.G. Sewell, who visited Trinidad two decades after Emancipation also thought the creoles were better off than Europe's peasantry. He estimated that, as late as 1860, 4,000 of the "11,000 field negroes" still worked on the estates although intermittently; of the remaining 7,000 workers five-sixths became owners of land ranging from one to ten acres each. When ex-slaves became small provisions' suppliers, they would become "casual labor" that worked only when they had extra time. Sewell was as unpredictable in his assessment of the ex-slaves as he was eager to defend indenture, in spite of the facts.[237] Any sample of laborers arriving from India show, with infants excepted, that families were *not* kept together on the same estates as Sewell wrote. In one random sample this author examined, siblings were separated in every case after arrival in Trinidad. "Caste" groups, too, were parcelled out so as not to have too many of pre-existing groups on individual estates.[238]

The idea that Trinidad's laborers were faring better than Europe's peasants was especially evident in testimony presented to the 1842 Committee by the planter-merchant, Burnley, quoted at the top of this chapter. Burnley disclosed in his 28 April 1842 testimony that he had lived in Trinidad for forty years, absences occasioned in London apart; he was "a merchant orginally, and latterly a proprietor of several sugar estates." He then testified that wages jumped from 15d. sterling per four-hour tasks to 2s. 2d. by May 1841: "Subsequently, the price of sugar fell considerably in the English market, and proprietors' of estates in Trinidad found that they could not pay so high a rate. In November . . . a meeting of the Agricultural [Society] took place, and they determined to reduce wages to 1s. 3d. a task; but the Labourers having more power than the employers would not accede to those terms; a struggle ensued, and I find by my last accounts, that on the 4th of February, a task was precisely the same as before, 2s. 2d., throughout the island generally, and in the district of Tacarigua, 2s. 6d., as stated by one of the members at the board of council."[239]

The Immigration and Agricultural Society had been born at a meeting in 1839 chaired by James Lamont, and at which Burnley was "appointed first Chairman."[240] Burnley also complained about the high cost of providing ex-slaves with rent-free houses;[241] but let us examine sugar prices briefly. Deerr argues that there was a rise in sugar prices through the Napoleonic era to 97s. per cwt. until a decline which dropped sugar prices to 23s. per cwt. began in 1831.[242] According to Carmichael, prices per cwt. were still 23s. 13/4d. in 1835, after which it rose only slightly,[243] until the slow and sure decline beginning around 1840. In testimony before an 1848 "Select Committee on Sugar and Coffee Planting," a witness with plantations in two islands, gave revealing statistics.[244] While costs of labor had more than doubled for each of the colonies between the first sample period, 1831-34, and the period of complete freedom after 1838, the disturbing tendency during the period of apprenticeship—with possible exceptions in Guiana and Tobago—had been to exploit labor at even lower costs than during slavery itself. For the period following complete emancipation, it would have been quite unnatural—in economic terms, irrational— had ex-slaves not sought to negotiate the best terms for their labor.

In this context of relative labor scarcity, there could have been nothing "unfair" in the laborers' demands for higher wages, though Burnley called it a wholly "artificial" context. Burnley saw nothing artificial in his 1814 idea of bringing laborers all the way from India into an alien environment, where planters succeeded in settling wages at 25 cents a day, maximum, reduced by prison terms for "slovenliness", "desertion," and arbitrary fines.[245] Again, in view of the planters never calling for an end to indented migration, then being demanded by blacks and coloureds, Trinidad's demand for Indian labor was itself *artificial*.

The early termination of apprenticeship may have persuaded some influential leaders in Britain to make concessions to the planters, both in a humane sense and in the practical concern for the West Indies not reverting to subsistence, so often described as the fate of independent Haiti.[246] The lax enforcement of Immigration rules regarding source and sex ratios were, clearly, concessions to the planters. A flow of semi-free migrants could begin in earnest. And it did.

2.6 SOLUTION AND STIGMA: RACE, RELIGION AND INDENTURE

In a reader on labor in the Caribbean which excluded Indian indented labor in its several chapters, one reads in passing: "In both [Guyana and Trinidad], the so-called East Indians were introduced in the years after slavery *specifically* to compete with the manumitted blacks. In both they came to supplant African labour in the sugar fields.[247]

It was not the Indians themselves who *specifically* introduced themselves as a Caribbean labor force. Of Trinidad's 28,000 new laborers, a mere 3,993 of some 5,162 East Indians were counted in 1851, yet neighboring creoles had comprised 39 percent of this incoming migration, a total of 11,000 if West Africans are listed separately.[248] It needs repeating that withdrawal from the estates by ex-slaves was a gradual process: in 1847 planters could "command" only 37.5 percent of the labor they controlled in 1838; however, three years after the first Indian arrivals almost 20 percent or 3,116 of the erstwhile field slaves still worked on the plantations.[249]

The 1834 arrival in Trinidad of "half-freed slaves,"[250] from Havana had inaugurated post-emancipation indented migration. Trinidad then received its first contingent of Africans from Sierra Leone in 1841, following the approval from the Colonial Office in London. A breakdown of immigrants through 1851 (using Harris' "African" number) yields: 11,000 West Indian Creoles (39 percent), 3,993 East Indian survivors (14-18 percent), 1,300

Portuguese immigrants (6 percent), 500 Chinese immigrants (1.7 percent), 1,333 African-Americans from the United States (4.7 percent), 8,010 African indentureds (28.6 percent).

West Indian creoles were the most numerous among the various immigrant groups, followed by Africans at 28.6 percent. The East Indians who entered the country totaled 5,162, but Comins noted 3,993 survivors in 1851: in either case the percentage does not change the fact that Indians were only the third largest group of immigrants by 1851. Wages were already in a fixed pattern and both in rhetorical and practical terms, if all other factors but immigration are considered in wage declines in Trinidad, West Indian creoles and Africans, not East Indians, played the key role in wage-reductions.

By the early 1860s, however, many West Indian planters as well as British officials saw India as the most convenient source of supplying additional laborers. Much of this thinking was in acknowledgement of the fact that a colonized people were easier to export overseas. After the 1856-58 Indian colonial revolt, British rule became direct and harsher within India, with some Indians seeking to escape from proximate British control. Africans rescued from slave ships were a temporary labor supply; and during the period up to 1851, recaptive Africans in Freetown had learned unpleasant details about plantation life, and that emigration declined. The governor's report made reference to former Maroon exiles and "others, actuated by a spirit of adventure" who had initially embraced the "experiment." [251]

Those Africans who had tried the experiment had returned "greatly dissatisfied," and while they did not volunteer details, "nothing would induce them to give it a second trial." Contemporary planters and some imperialists then looked to India which seemed to be a huge labor reservoir for the British colonies. With millions of people apparently living at the edge of poverty, they would jump at the chance of earning higher wages outside of their motherland. Yet, combined with all other immigrants who entered the West Indies since emancipation, the Indian stream was only about 2 percent of the immigrant deluge that left Europe during the same period.[252] The total number of Indians who entered Trinidad during 1845-88 was 79,522 or an average of 1,893 per year. Another 64,000 British Indians entered Trinidad before India's abolition of indenture Act of 1917. That almost as many migrants came in less than 30 years after 1888 as had come in the preceding 44, was due to planters cutting wages while competing with the European beet: plantation conditions drove Indo-Trinidadians off the plantation. Infusions of new migrants became the mainstay of indenture.

Clearly East Indians were a tiny part of "the total immigration into the Caribbean in the nineteenth century" of over one million people—"about 10,000 a year." In this total, all Asians (Chinese, Javanese and Indians) together comprised about fifty percent, and that towards the second half of the century.[253] It may be that contemporary social, demographic and political complications arising from the majority status of Asians in parts of the region is reflected in exaggerating the eagerness, voluntariness and numbers of Asian labor migrants to the Caribbean. The scholar who contends that it was the arrival of the Indians which led to the reduction Trinidadian wages is seen to be treading on thin ice per our discussion thus far. But there is a myth too, that the Indians who left India for other colonies were literally the scum of the earth.

For instance, the historian Eric Williams, without any discussion of the cultural, religious, or geographical origins of the British Indians, nonetheless reiterated the view: "One of the most vigorous of the abolitionists, G. Thompson, said that the immigrants into Mauritius were indolent, mendicants, runaways, vagrants, filthy, diseased, dissolute, immoral, disgusting, covered with sores; some were priests, some jugglers, some barbers, some wrestlers, some cooks, some grooms, some buffoons, some herdsmen, some pedlars, some scullions, bakers, tailors, confectioners, instead of agricultural labourers. [Thompson] added 'It would be found wherever this system is scrutinised, whether in India, Africa or

Demerara, that these persons were a deeply demoralised class of human beings . . . '."[254]

That these adjectives might have been inapplicable and unfair to many migrants to Mauritius is left out. That the notorious list did not apply to most of the migrants to Trinidad is all but settled in the historiography. Our efforts in this regard are to emphasize that point and strengthen our argument. The sample ship registers bearing village and "caste" names of all immigrants analyzed by this author, and by Donald Wood and Comins, refute the assault on Indian origins made by Thompson. After looking at the origins of Indian migrants over two seasons, Comins' results for the 1879-80 period—and 3,108 individuals—reflected a cross section of most groups which obtain in Indian society itself. In the sample 175 or 5.6 percent of the Indians were *brahmins*, 294 or 9.5 percent were *kshatriyas*, the "warrior caste groups," while 648 or 20.85 percent were Muslim. If these numbers are subtracted from the total, almost 36 percent are thereby accounted for as belonging to India's two highest castes and the Islamic faith. The remaining 2,091 are not uniformly the social outcastes of India: only 274 of this total or 8.8 percent are *Chamar*, the cobblers and leatherworking caste known as lowly both in India and in the Caribbean;[255] only one is a *Chundul* from unassimilated forest dwelling tribes. The rest were from agrarian "castes" (255 Ahir and Satope: 8.2 percent), cowkeepers (31 or 1 percent), [256] oil-pressers (59 or 1.89 percent) and *Lohar* or ironmongers (0.6 percent). A few Christians were also listed, for not every conversion took place in the colony.[257]

In our analysis of the register of the 1873 ship, *Syria* whose passengers were sent to twenty different estates, we have a cross-section of India's highest and middling "castes," roughly proportional to the group sizes in India. There were 27 Muslim Indians on board. The 41 *brahmins* or priests and teachers were the third largest group on the ship; the warrior "caste" or "*chuttree*" (also Kshatriya) constituted the fourth most numerous Indian subgroup (19) on the *Syria*. The leather-working subgroup, *Chamar*, was most numerous with 126 persons, but the second largest "caste" was *Aheer*, a milk-dispensing people numbering 57. As already mentioned, these groups were not sent to the employers as intact units. The brahmins and *chuttrees*—groups from which many leaders came—were so distributed among twenty estates, that only two estates, Craignish and Paradise, did not receive members of India's two highest subcultures. There were 28 "castes" with fewer than ten members each, which experts may designate both high and low.[258]

India's *varna* system is complex, with status often defined by contradictory variables, so that easy conclusions are prone to bias and error. And there is always the difficulty of regional names for one "caste" which may not be understood elsewhere, as Comins' list and my own sample testify.[259]

Apart from the very first recruits for John Gladstone's estate in British Guiana who were tribal people called "Hill Coolies," subsequent Indians to the Caribbean came from settled communities in the Gangetic plains.[260] Indented migration of Britain's Indian nationals was not a movement of *outcastes*—those outside the four-fold "caste" system, and comprising forest peoples and others not yet assimilated—but involved a "fair cross section of rural India . . . a more complex process than has been realized."[261] At the time, India was as much a land of contradictions as it has remained. Its achievements aside, India also had its own version of slavery which, Noel Deerr points out, became an argument among the British to justify labor migration. Ironically, India had outlawed servitude in 1843 and twenty years later the United States similarly outlawed "voluntary and involuntary servitude," which was extended to Hawaii upon its annexation.[262] The familiar arguments made for African slavery were repeated: Indian slavery was more onerous compared with the opportunities available to these hapless victims in the colonies. In the next chapter we juxtapose these claims against the reality of sick and underpaid Indian workers, their frequenting the jail for labor-related offences, and in the worst cases, not receiving food or wages for months on end.[263]

The indenture experiment with British subjects from India went badly from its inception in the Caribbean. This initial chapter in Indo-Caribbean history may have begun in British Guiana, but its lessons were deliberately called to mind by Trinidadian officials at various times.[264] Both in Guiana and in Trinidad, the heart-rending reports of gallant whites failed to have the effect which similar accounts about Portuguese indenteds evinced in Trinidad, as in the case of the governors who intervened on their behalf. It also made a difference that apart from being non-Christians, most Indians were illiterate about writing petitions, and unable to hire such services. It still appears somewhat incomprehensible that the published indictments of the 1838 venture in Guiana as in the account of John Scoble, Secretary of the Anti-Slavery Society, would be obliterated from memory within four years.[265] Scoble's efforts led to the suspension of the first private efforts of John Gladstone's relatives and partners (Arbuthnot-Gillanders) for his Guiana estates, but Indian labor migrants were back in Guiana in 1845, this time under British arrangements. If anything, it would now be harder to abolish the system despite the severe abuses in Trinidad exposed by a Magistrate, Major Fagan, during 1846-48 as discussed below. In retrospect, the 1838 spirited opposition of Lord Brougham to halt Indian indenture in its tracks was nullified. He had opposed allowing an Order in Council in Guiana sanctioning long-term contracts, and condemned the plan as one which made "indentured apprentices" of British subjects alongside "the half-freed slaves." His words were strong and prophetic. "It is easy, indeed, for them,"—the Guiana planters—"and their West-Indian confederates to speak in soft language of bringing over free men— of introducing labourers—of increasing the number of hands employed—of enabling the owners of estates to find workmen as they wanted them. But I will tear away all these flimsy disguises— I will show you what it is that lurks under these fair words—I will demonstrate to you, and by facts, rather than by mere arguments, what every one of those whose acquaintance, with the slave-trade is the most enlarged and the most minute, who have for half a century and more been occupied in tracing it through all its forms, and pursuing it in each disguise which it unceasingly assumes— that nothing but slave trading can be, the meaning and the result of all that is thus doing."[266]

And in a speech which in its printed form constitutes 70 pages, Lord Brougham made his point eloquently, pleading against "extending" the "monstrous iniquity" of the slave trade "to coasts which hitherto it had spared."[267]

Even in the 1880s, the last decade for this study, Indians failed to see many opportunities outside of plantation drudgery in spite of what planter propaganda had made of Trinidad in comparison with colonial India. In 1881 2,731 immigrants left India for Trinidad but 85 never set foot on Trinidad soil, having died en route. Upon disembarkation 45 or 1.6 percent had to be sent to the hospital. Shipboard mortality was 3.1 percent. In 1891, mortality before landing in Trinidad was by no means improved: 3.5 percent or 114 out of 3,278 immigrants who departed India's shores perished on the way to Trinidad. In that year 37 persons went directly to hospital, and another 262 followed them or went to the convalescent depot: this constituted 9.1 percent of the immigrants, some of whom would die later.[268] If this disturbing state of affairs is explained away by conditions of the voyage, then conditions in Trinidad did not offer immigrants longer lives or the certainty of returning home either. As discussed already, of the 5,162 Indians who came to Trinidad through 1851, only 3,993 were accounted for five years later.

Another set of alarming statistics arises from estimating the numbers repatraited versus those who "dissappeared." The total number of Indians who had come to Trinidad through 1891 was 88,501 of which 11,885 returned to India. "[T]he actual number added to the population by cooly immigration . . . has been 76,616." The number "surviving on 5th April 1891 was 45,577."[269] This distressing decline of 40.5 percent might be lessened only slightly by Indians who fled plantation life for Venezuela.[270] It is thus not surprising that a planter, Henry Clarke, wrote from Jamaica to a friend that the indenture of Indians there was 'more unjust and inhuman than slavery. . . . '[271] Clarke may have been aware that no governor or leader rescued East Indians from abuse but Governor Harris had indeed rescued the Portuguese.[272]

In the years after emancipation, Caribbean planters exploited, often equally cruelly, European and non-European indenteds and mechanics. Guiana demonstrated that it was prepared to endorse seven-year indentures—as in early colonial North America—for British immigrants so as to prevent them becoming "drunkards." In Trinidad, the governors showed a different hue: they queried whether Britain had any objections to the colony indenting whites. Whether London objected is unclear, but local officials recognized the Portuguese, for example, as people not encumbered by a lack of "civilisation." This created an attitude among whites in Trinidad which allowed an uneven application of indenture rules to the Portuguese laborers so that employers could not always enforce the indentures.[273]

As mortality and demanding labor took their toll on the Portuguese white Trinidad demonstrated that it did not have an appetite for Portuguese suffering. None other than Governor Harris (1846-54) campaigned to end Portuguese labor migration. Within a year following their arrival the Fayal Portuguese had petitioned then Governor Hill. They alleged that they had been "induced by certain evil disposed persons under false pretenses," to leave their homes for a fate as "agricultural labourers." The petition spoke about the horrors of their "slavery," the high mortality, lack of food and shelter, and that upon dying, "the bodies of the miserable victims of avarice have been thrown into holes and ditches without Christian burial." By the petitioners' count, "one third" of their original number only were alive, or about 15 out of the first group of 44. The final plea to the Governor was for the survivors to be "transported back to their native country." The petition suggested many had, "fallen victims to the unhealthiness of the climate or to the cruelties of the slavery system to which we, equally with the unfortunate blacks have been subjected. For let speculators in human blood deny it as they will, the awful calamity which has occurred among our countrymen, in so short a period as ten months, must have resulted from one or the other of these fatal causes, or from both. . . . "[274]

There was a second Portuguese petition, this time from a widowed laborer. Josef da Costa's petition stated that he and 27 others had entered Trinidad clandestinely, having left Fayal on 31 October 1834. On Trinidad's northern coast they had encountered nine of their countrymen, four of whom had since died with neither doctor nor priest attending. da Costa sought work in Chaguanas on the estate of Mr. Graham, where he "worked for two months in the fields with the Negroes." Both he and his wife fell ill, and "through the kindness of Mr. Graham," they were taken to the capital's Marie Ursula Hospital. da Costa's wife did not survive. He remained in the capital in a state of grief and apathy, eventually taking up employment with Mr. Lock, who was abusive. da Costa fled Lock's property and appealed to Trinidad's Governor Harris for help.[275]

Where white Trinidad was generally moved to sympathy for the Portuguese, the idea that additional laborers *had* to be found might have led them to de-emphasize, if not ignore the suffering of other groups. The Trinidad Immigration and Agricultural Society in its first communication to London in 1839 had inquired whether "publicity" should be given to the "dangers incurred by European immigrants, especially from France and Germany?"[276]

Admittedly, the French and German laborers in 1839 like the East Indians who arrived after 1845, may not have been fully informed about conditions in Trinidad. Little of the concern shown towards Portuguese, French and German laborers would accrue to the Indians (Chapter Three). On the arrival of the European immigrants, Acting Governor Mein had shared his concerns about their welfare with Lord John Russell in 1839. After acknowledging the receipt of "the Queen's Order in Council confirming, with certain provisoes, an Ordinance passed here on the 19th April last

'For the encouragement of Immigration,'" he had noted that 295 "Foreigners" had arrived from Havre aboard the French ship *Elisabeth* on 29 October. In a situation where Trinidad was pleased with the royal assent to recruit immigrant-laborers it seems contradictory that its governor investigated how well-informed arriving immigrants were about Trinidad. "Although these people" had not come to Trinidad under provisions of the Immigration Ordinance, "I yet thought it necessary to direct the proper Officer of my government immediately on board the vessel," to examine conditions on board as well as "the understanding on which they had emigrated from their native country, and the expectations by which they had been induced to come to Trinidad".[277]

The report which the Acting governor received on the *Elisabeth* was "satisfactory" with respect to the treatment and health of the immigrants; Mein was not as satisfied with the "conditions which were exacted" from them by planters. These related to their short-term indenture as field laborers. Mein viewed "the introduction into this Colony of these people, most of whom are French or Germans with considerable apprehension."[278] In an era when Europeans were seeking their fortunes on every continent, with North America alone receiving 28 million immigrants between 1831-1913[279], one wonders if it was concern over the consequences of white laboring alongside black which raised so many detailed concerns on the part of British officials.

Eventually various nationalities were represented in Trinidad's post-slavery labor-force, including groups from the British Isles. From the United States came privately recruited black settlers and soldiers both before and after Governor Woodford; Africans came from St. Helena, the Kru Coast and Sierra Leone on one-or three-year indentures; and finally after 1845 came the significant wave of Asians from quasi-independent China, Dutch colonial Java and British India. While many exotic groups were able to melt into the island mosaic, the groups which had stuck out like sore thumbs in Guyana as much as in Trinidad were the Portuguese and East Indians. West Africans and creoles from the Caribbean became

immersed in the Afro-Trinidadian population by the thousands.[280]
East Indian and especially Chinese indenture studies are only now
reaching maturity.[281]

Despite the similarities in the plantation experiences of the
Portuguese from Fayal and Madeira, and of the British Indians,
race and religion favored the former. There was no equivalent of a
Governor Harris to halt Indian bondage, nor similar concern over
the fate of other immigrant whites as evinced by Governor Hill
and Acting Governor Mein.[282] Nor did the Queen hearken to the
Mandingo who petitioned for a return home to Africa.[283]

Notwithstanding the suffering of Portuguese settlers in
Trinidad, the persistence of individual entrepreneurs and the
continuing persecution of Protestant converts in Madeira, brought
several hundreds more to Trinidad. The newcomers had little success
in imbibing the knowledge of conditions from their compatriots.
New Fayal Portuguese had arrived in August and September 1834
making a combined total of 61 men, 15 women and 13 children.
Seale, an English merchant in Fayal, was reportedly responsible
for this migration on the bounty system and in late 1834 he had
already arranged to send 100 more laborers to Trinidad. In an
1838 report, Hill thought it desirable to introduce equal numbers
of Portuguese men and women to "ensure the growth of a white,
rather than a black, population in the colony."[284] Hill died in
Trinidad during 1839, and so did his idea.

More immigrants from Fayal had come in 1839, while from
Madeira came several hundreds over the next decade. If those from
Fayal came for economic reasons, the Madeira Portuguese were
mainly Protestant refugees.[285] There were Madeira Catholics in
Trinidad but an 1856 account called *The Madeira Persecutions* gives
the number of "refugees" at around 700. Their health concerns
and high mortality might shed some light on why the Fayal
immigrants had fared so badly: the complaints were generally about
intense humidity and tropical fevers. One group of Madeirans
apprenticed to an estate "in the neighborhood of marshy ground,"
were soon "prostrated" by an attack of fever; the governor speedily

removed the survivors "from the pestilential neighborhood" to the healthier, "more salubrious" Port of Spain environs. The urban setting allowed many to take up alternatives to field-labor, such as vending and domestic service but in 1847 their total, including children, included 50 cane-workers. While mortality decreased, Madeiran immigrants "were occasionally disabled" by dysentery or by intermittent fever even around Port of Spain;—"opthalmia likewise prevailed amongst them." The epitaph for these as for other migrants was that their numbers were too small or they had proven unreliable in resolving Trinidad's problems.[286] The relatively small number of Portuguese is part of the explanation. Yet religion and culture also emerged as important factors.

The religious community to which the Protestant Portuguese belonged spanned Britain, the Caribbean and the United States, and it must have made other alternatives available to them. Reverend Wilson has filled in the background to our understanding that many Portuguese who had migrated to Trinidad re-emigrated to the United States of America. Not only the British evangelists, Dr. Kalley—"a pious physician,"[287]—and Rev. W.H. Hewitson, both of whom had preached to the flock in Madeira, but the Madeirans' pastor in Trinidad, Senhor Arsenio da Silva, had British connections too. This and the contacts with the Rev. Gonsalves, a Madeiran-American, and the American Christian Union helped Portuguese Protestants re-emigrate to the US.

Before his 10 January 1849 death, Pastor da Silva succeeded in getting a promise of land from the American Protestant Society (APS). The offer was made good by the Rev. Mr. Norton and M. Domette, Esq. secretaries of the APS. Gonsalves, who went to Trinidad to arrange the removal of his countrymen and women later wrote that in his last days da Silva had worried no end about "the lambs of the flock who were mixed in Trinidad with a low, vicious, degraded Roman Catholic population," which was in some respects "worse" than "the rabble of Madeira."[288]

According to Wilson, between 600 and 700 Madeirans left Trinidad for the United States. This community was joined by others directly from Madeira during 1849-54. The United States then boasted a total of about "1000 souls, having a church, minister, schools" as well as "flourishing" in temporal things. Some 500 Madeirans remained in Trinidad, "with [their own] church, minister, and schools."[289] Roberts and Byrne's statistical tabulations show that Trinidad received 172 additional Portuguese from "Madeira, Cape Verde and Azores" between 1856 and 1860, perhaps the last years of sizeable Portuguese immigration during the nineteenth century. The grand total for this source of immigration to Trinidad is higher than their "897" because, among other things, it omits the 1834 Fayal immigrants and those who came during 1835-45.[290] In our estimates above, we use the generally acceptable total of 1,300 Portuguese newcomers, who, together with the smaller number of indented Europeans constituted around seven or eight percent of Trinidad's immigrants by 1851. In 1882, there were 709 Portuguese and 1,206 Chinese in Trinidad.[291]

Overall, the Portuguese experience in Trinidad was less onerous than either African or Asian indenture, whether they opted to leave for the United States or not. The Portuguese who arrived after 1850 were not compelled to sign indentures, and those with indentures were not held rigidly to them.[292]

We will delve now into the specific conditions in Trinidad which set Indians apart on its plantations so that their imprisonments, beatings, deprivations and under-payment, represented backward steps in the road away from slavery. The gains made at the end of slavery were reversed to such an extent that Indian indenteds inhabited a world apart when free labor was the perceived order of the day.

CHAPTER THREE

PLANTATIONS AND ASIANS:

VOYAGES TO PRISONS

"Breach of contract was treated as a criminal offence and all too often employers took legal action against Indians in order to punish them, maintain labour discipline, and secure docility. Since an immigrant could not give evidence on his own behalf, and friends were too afraid of reprisal by their employers to do so, the rest was a foregone conclusion since magistrates all too often sided with the employers. Punishment of immigrants took the form, separately or in combination, of fines, imprisonment, or an extension of the indenture period. . . . "[293]

In any account of employer-laborer relations, past or present, there will be humane and diligent persons on both sides. In nineteenth-century Trinidad, there were human plantation managers and staff but the overall pattern of management was as coercive as it had been under slavery.

East Indian indenture resembled, within a few years after its inception in Trinidad, a hybrid between unfree and free labor regimes. In this sense indenture straddled the past and the colonial present, a la the experiences of the early British American colonies and that of slavery-in-transition, or that period of apprenticeship between 1833 and 1 August 1838. The freedom of labor during 1838 and 1845 had been curtailed by the time British Indians came to Trinidad: the planters had rallied to exploit both free labor and the difficulties of the mother country, and in the process

blunting the promise of full freedom. After the first shiploads of
free men and women arrived from India, freedoms like that of free
movement, became severely curtailed and eventually prohibited.
The plantations pressured Britain into binding later Indian arrivals
to specific employers or plantations with harsher terms and for
much longer than it took to pay the cost of transportation, the
passage generally constituting the debt of most indented or contract
laborers. These harsh restrictions of movement generally, and of
Indian freedom of choice regarding specific employers represented
a major backward step for free labor, even when compared to
concurrent experiences of the Portuguese and indentured Africans
in the previous chapter. In spite of harsher and longer ordeals than
those of European and black apprentices, neither land grants nor
free passages to India were guaranteed the East Indians. The planters
or their managers made these the most unreliable parts of the East
Indian's faustian bargain.

Clearly therefore, Trinidad plantations coveted Indian labor
because it carried neither moral nor severe material obligations for
them. The Indian "transients" and their needs for recreation, schools
and wives were of little concern to those who fought tenaciously
and successfully to lengthen the Indian sojourn in plantation
colonies. Non-Indians came to decide when an Indian had
completed the "industrial residence" and if s/he might return home.
Once bound with indenture, the East Indian found it extremely
difficult to extricate himself or herself from the plantation. Labor
freedom continued to be curtailed in every way. The ordeal of free
labor during 1834-1845 was replaced by an ordeal of a ten-year
"industrial residences" for East Indians, until each one of them
had completed all the obligations placed on them by planters and
managers. It was then that an Indian, in theory at least, could
return home to India. But repatriation was constantly held hostage
to the needs, finances and politics of Trinidad or the profit motives
of the planters. The first Indians who entered Trinidad did so
without contracts; by 1854, every Indian was bound to employers
for three years, "during which time he could not change his

employer," or leave the plantation without a pass signed by the manager.[294] Indians were in effect a captive labor force.

Although Britain had promised the Indian government "a free return passage" for every migrant, Trinidad decided that this right could be claimed by Indians only after another five-year industrial residence plus an indenture for two periods of one year each. There was a bright side: migrants could avoid the industrial residence by paying five shillings a month "plus two pence half-penny per day" for each working day of their "contract". Those who avoided industrial residence in this way did so with loans from other migrants or shopkeepers, interest often at "150 p.c. per annum." A reform with consequences for Indian family life came in 1868 when Britain raised the ratio of women migrants "from 33 to 40 for every 100 males shipped."[295] The goal, a difficult one to realize, was often unmet, exceeded in some years, but its appearance represented an acknowledgement by the British that a consistent policy in this regard was both fair and helpful for promoting family values.[296]

There are, in accounts of harsh labor regimes, exceptional masters and employers who defy the harshness of the time. While Trinidad too had planters who were humane employers, overall labor management patterns were coercive—with indenteds being marched off to prisons and courts for leaving the plantation without passes, refusing to visit the makeshift hospitals when ill, for vagrancy, "negligence, carelessness and even an impertinent word or gesture to the manager or his overseers." While the employer "was never prosecuted" for breaking his part of the indenture contract, "almost every misconduct of the immigrant carried with it a criminal liability."[297] Under slavery the whip had enforced discipline with African and other slaves; after slavery, prisons imposed discipline on the East Indians.

In a recent study, David Northrup concluded that while indenture became a "trap" for some Indians, despite a process "intended" for their benefit, the idea of liberation through emigration was valid for other Indians, especially women. In this chapter, our data reveal that a migrant labor force which sought cash wages outside India became a poorly paid, virtually captive, and socially stigmatized group in Trinidad. Indented Indians were manipulated so as to spend time either in prisons, in hospitals or in extra fieldwork, reflecting in part, the propinquity between unfree and ostensibly free labor systems in Trinidad for the period under study. Imperial good intentions notwithstanding, the racial and imperial context in which a colonized people became laborers on a distant island which had just freed its slaves destined Indians to follow—at least part of the way—in directions which slavery had already taken.[298]

In another milieu, with different actors, indenture might have retained the essence of a free labor system. In the aftermath of slavery, Indians appeared too unlike Europeans or Christians to have been given the benefit of the doubt, either by the planters or the officers in charge of that peculiar emigration. Those who staffed the Emigration Department concluded that they were assured of monetary and social success only if they respected the planters, their objectives and their assessment of non-European laborers.[299]

Soon after Emancipation in 1834-38, planters were able to rally against all laborers. Within a decade labor was being extracted on sugar and to a lesser extent, cocoa estates, by criminalizing non-performance of work by a migrant labor force. It seldom mattered to the courts and prisons that Indians rarely saw the convoluted rules or read contracts in an English they barely understood.[300] If the period 1845-1888 was not one long prison-term for the Indo-Trinidadians, then it was akin to house-arrest, that is, isolation on plantations. That is true, *inter alia*, because once indented, it was unusual for a migrant to complete his or her servitude on time which in turn jeopardized his or her repatriation, an obligation generally avoided by plantations. Before leaving India's shores, the indented were not advised of potential jail-time for labor offenses in the colony, or that they would need permits to walk the public roads. Anyone, including black and brown creoles could stop a Indian and demand to see his or her pass; if the indented failed to produce one, he or she was taken to the nearest constable.[301] This right of making a citizen's arrest on matters relating to an Indian's freedom of movement suggests that creoles were freer than were the Indians. At the basis of this problem was the goal of the plantation to exploit the Indians as thoroughly as possible.[302]

British indenture regulations replaced the Protector of Slaves from the previous labor system with a Protector of Immigrants.[303] That the break with slavery was not abrupt or immediate was highlighted on those plantations where Indians and former slaves shared the same barracks, or arrived in Trinidad on the same ships.[304] Major Fagan, who became Protector in 1846, lost this position within a year because he had reprimanded a planter, Edward Walkinshaw, and the indented workers were removed from his estate, temporarily as it turned out. Governor Harris, who had supported Fagan, had to reconsider once the British authorities intervened. A Report on the "Inquiry into Walkinshaw's Abuses" found that Indian workers had indeed attacked Walkinshaw but because of Walkinshaw's "own ill-advised and impudent courses."[305] Still, Harris was advised to return the workers removed from Walkinshaw's estate. In retrospect, the Fagan-Walkinshaw contest was a sad watershed for the rights of free labor in post-slavery Trinidad.

In contrast to Portuguese indenture in Trinidad, Indian servitude developed into a system of retaining slavery without the whip where possible, but with jails where necessary. Few within Trinidad empathized with the alien, largely non-Christian Indians; the Fagans and Andre's (Andre was the first to protest the Hosay Massacre of 1884) were isolated or punished, and Harris himself did not argue principle with London.

Even as plantations reported that the first Indians proved "'more intelligent, more apt, more docile, more civil . . . devoid of the savage disposition of the African,'" these reports hinted that freedom of movement for Indians was not consistent with the planters' ideas of free labor: "One manager (of the Union Estate in Couva) agreed that the East Indians were 'docile, obedient and of a cheerful disposition,' but added that they needed a 'judicious but adequately stringent superintendence restricting them [from] the ruinous habit of wandering through the country.'"[306] It appears inconsistent that plantations which had begun to move away from the paternalism of slavery would demonstrate a logic which explicitly stated that if Indians were allowed freedom of movement, they would *ruin* their health. Herein lies the justification for the detested pass laws of East Indian indenture. From an Indian perspective, this "wandering" and "vagrancy" were pitiable efforts to find a way back to India. This perspective has been muted in the historiography but it reveals that while the migrants were anxious to return home to India, planters contested that right or alternatively their obligation to secure return ships for the Indians.[307]

The inclusion of a migrant's right to be allowed to return to India was the informal basis for allowing a resumption of indenture after the 1838 prohibition in the Caribbean. Non-Indians may find it difficult to appreciate this position: It was "a condition signifying the guarantee that he was not transported to life-long exile, a feature reminiscent of slavery days . . . This single contractual condition aroused the most anxious jealousy of the planters, for they believed that the emigrants claimed the return passage just when they had become skilled and most useful to the colony, and also because they carried back to India large sums of money causing 'a lamentable drain' of colonial wealth."[308]

J.P. Grant, a member of a Commission of Inquiry into the abuse of Indian labor set up on 1 August 1838 in Calcutta—and which saw the abuses as eminently preventable—submitted a separate minute in which he argued the Indian's right to repatriation was the best punishment for bad employers. "Repatriation" was emphasized by Lord Stanley in his despatches to Mauritius and the West Indies as a way of overcoming the 1838 suspension of migration.

Thus persuaded, the Government of India enacted Act XXI of 16 November 1844, stipulating that colonies grant the migrant a return passage on the expiry of their term of industrial residence.

But as more of the first indentures neared completion in Trinidad in 1851, and Mauritius persuaded India that repatriation was redundant after a five-year stay there, the West Indies "lost no time in claiming equal advantages." The Colonial Office suggested that the colonies would find repatriation rights more palatable were the period of industrial residence increased from five to ten years for every worker. Despite some spirited objection within the Indian government to this lengthening of the "exile" the compromise of longer residence in the colonies was the price plantations exacted for agreeing to chartering return vessels to India. Trinidad was averse to institutionalizing that right. In fact, Governor Harris tried to push the Government of India—by letter on 4 October 1853—into relieving Trinidad of financial and logistical responsibility for repatriation. The provincial authority in Bengal insisted that changes in the regulations be fully explained to those intending to go to the colonies. In fact, during September 1855, a virtual focus group of 154 men and 55 women promptly refused to go on the new conditions, except for a single male. By omission and commission, "repatriation at the completion of ten years residence in the West Indies" became the rule for Indians in Trinidad. This did not prevent individual planters in Trinidad from finding other ways of delaying the repatriation of indenture-free Indians, as per the 1869-1880 land-for-passages deal.[309] Trinidad had attempted both before and after that experiment, to have Indians pay a part of their passages.

The plantation proved adept at staking higher moral ground whenever a right or privilege was denied the Indian. There were situations where plantations reneged on providing boots or shoes, decent quarters and latrines,[310] or simply recruiting a reasonable number of female migrants. The management countered that these were not the obligations of the estates, although better all-round health might have been promoted by attention to such matters. "Yet, in accounting for the treatment received by the early indentured laborers . . . what mattered more than the dead hand of slavery was the vital state of employers' purses." Since these purses remained tight for one reason or another, and in the last quarter of the nineteenth century because of stiff beet sugar competition from Europe, plantations found it harder to secure capital for mechanization.[311] In this context, it is not surprising that for most Indian indenteds there was neither increases in wages nor improvements in their overall health.[312]

3.1 THE NATURE OF FREE INDIAN LABOR

Our documents revealed the daily reality of indenture in statistics communicated in reports of the Inspector of Prisons. But Indian indenteds were not part of the general prison data prior to 1874 and Lionel M. Fraser's becoming Inspector. First, a brief look at prison statistics from the immediate pre-and post-emancipation periods to allow a comparison with the East Indian experience.[313] The issue of penal sanctions against Indians was the achilles heel of the new "free labor" system.

No definite pattern of criminal behavior emerges for the last years of slavery in Trinidad, 1828-1835. If there was a trend, it was a mixed pattern with the various categories, including death in prison, fluctuating around a mean (53 per annum for male prisoners). For both 1832 and 1833 Trinidad jails had 54 prisoners each (48 and 45 males respectively) but the totals are higher for every other year during 1828-1835 (55, 68, 58, 89, 54, 54, 60). By the end of slavery (1835) imprisonment totals climbed from 54 to 60, not a spectacular increase. As is so often alleged by scholars such as Eric Williams, the years before Indian indenture allowed the extraction of labor power with the whip rather than prisons. When the whip became anachronistic, the courts and jails became the recourse, but not always in that order.

This brief examination of pre-indenture prisoner totals show that Trinidad under slavery did not have a criminal culture. The rulers and dominant elites relied on various combinations of rewards and punishments as per conditions for post-1833 apprentices discussed in the previous chapter. Totals of all punishable offenses rarely exceeded 100 per year. There is no explanation why a few prisoners died annually; by the 1870s, prison deaths had increased but by then a prison doctor offered explanations, usually illness or disease.

Anti-vagrancy and anti-squatting laws were passed in Trinidad immediately after Emancipation, not so much to imprison ex-slaves but to maintain a long-term leverage over the economy and society. A more immediate concern was the establishment of a police presence where it had been unnecessary before. The 1838 "Ordinance to Establish a System of Rural Police"[314] is one such example. D.V. Trotman has argued that the perpetuation of the plantations after 1833-38 made it necessary to tie free people to the estates, while the courts were most obliging in playing a coercive role with laborers. After 1854, when indenture laws tightened the lasso around Indian workers, they were frequently "guilty of breaches" of labor laws. Thenceforth, Indians were not free migrants but bound to individual plantations for three years; this was to be followed by a five-year industrial residence, and finally two one-year indentures, commutable by a monetary payment that was out of reach for most Indians.[315]

One "misdemeanor" that newspapers in the early post-Emancipation years focussed on was the "Killing and Maiming of Livestock." Had these "actions" been classified crimes, which they were not until 1839, totals in our brief analysis above might have increased slightly.

An article on the maiming of livestock appeared in the *Trinidad Standard and West India Journal* following "two communications upon the subject." The letters called upon the editor to aid in seeking effective legislation against this "kind of injury," which "in Great Britain is a felony, punishable by transportation for life, [yet] does not amount to a crime in Trinidad." The point about each country having a nuanced approach to defining what constitutes crime bears keeping in mind throughout this chapter. Courts in Trinidad required a planter to "*bring an action of damages against the offender*"—quite difficult to do—which gives "strangers" the idea that this "offence itself is unknown in this Island." The newspaper then summarized the letter-writers' suspicion that the "labouring class" was the source of the offenses, perhaps in avenging damage to their gardens by the planters' stock; cases of "malicious killing and maiming of livestock" were "not . . . few" in Trinidad. One case was recounted of workers on a Naparima estate having avenged themselves on a pair of oxen after a quarrel with the manager. While the paper was in press, the Legislative Council had reactivated an ordinance to deter anyone injuring the livestock of others, and sought London's approval of it.[316]

One of the most detailed pre-1874 accounts of Trinidad's imprisoned population is a despatch from Governor Longden which accompanied the Blue Books for 1870. The number of "prisoners committed" was 2,012, including 30 adjourned cases. Many more than 2,012 were incarcerated before trial although, the totals represented "a considerable decrease upon the numbers committed in the four preceding years." Most offenses were those "against immigration laws, breach of contract, &c." (727), larceny (257), debt (213) assaults (154) and "indecent behaviour and language" (116), labor offenses thus comprising a third of all cases.[317]

There were other interesting categories in this early yet detailed report, which may have reflected the society's hostility to the annual fetes of the laboring classes, as per "riotous conduct" involving 11 cases, three "committed for offence against fire ordinance," compared with seven cases of arson and 56 committals for such offenses as "furious driving, throwing stones, &." Five cases of murder were part of the total as were ten cases of attempted murder. Longden found that East Indian "offenses are of two kinds, breach of contract in not performing their allotted tasks, and contravening the Ordinance by quitting the estates to which they are indentured[,] without a pass," the punishment being seven days' to three months' imprisonment. But 1870 was noteworthy also for a marked increase in burglaries and "nocturnal robberies in Port of Spain, which were attributed by the public, in great measure, to the influx of a number of French convicts from the convict settlement of Cayenne."[318]

In 1874, *The Trinidad News* reported that a minimum of 43 arrests per week had been made between 27 June and 7 July. The categories "Fighting" and "Drunkenness" were conspicuous among the charges. Indians would have contributed to these "crimes," as well as to offenses in the category, "obscene language,"—a predictable and universal form of resistance. The same newspaper suggested that all Indians were stigmatized when Indians who were free settlers could be treated as the rest of the "coolies." The article cited the case of "A most respectable, free Coolie,—one of the first batch of Indian immigrants who arrived in the Island—was imprisoned for being without his pass," but who was released from prison soon after his case became known.[319]

We have already noted that prosecutions and prisons were not directed at employers, no matter how grievous their violation of indenture contracts. On the other hand, Indians swelled the prison population after the 1850s, not for violent crimes, but for being without passes or allegedly failing to please managers and planters. In other words, Trinidad's need for prisons increased with its dependence upon indented labor.

On 13 April 1874, when L. Fraser became Inspector, Annual Prison Reports became a requirement per "Clause 100 of the New Gaol Regulations." In 1873, nine Turnkeys had been dismissed, and three had resigned; and the fate of ordinary people—including children—was harsh. Council Paper 39 revealed 2,649 prisoners in the Royal Gaol for 1873: of these 282 were females.

The record was broken down into 2,504 "Felons and Misdemeanents" (2,239 males and 265 females) and 145 "Debtors" (128 of whom were male and 17, female).

Inspector Fraser was determined to inflict the severest punishment on prisoners and thought that the system had failed to embarrass prisoners toward improved behavior. He looked to Sir Joshua Jebb, "an admitted authority in matters of Prison discipline," who advised, "'The deterring elements of punishment are hard labour, hard fare, and a hard bed; and for the lowest class of prisoners . . . Hard sentences,'" which amounted to "labour at the treadwheel or the crank, or shot drill or stone breaking or some such work."[320] With immigrants from India, such "hard sentences" conveniently turned to the plantation advantage. Where prisons housed East Indians for parts of the year, the subsistence costs were not borne by plantations which had engaged these laborers. Sometimes the Government of Trinidad lowered its own requisition for indenteds when the work might be had free from East Indian prisoners.

It was a world which did not care much that Indians were not criminals, when material advantages flowed from such labelling. The migrants were involved, overwhelmingly, in civil disputes with infinitely more influential employers of another race. In the years 1872 and 1873, Indians without passes (354 and 476 respectively) comprised the largest category of offenses even when breaches of the labor ordinances are included. Over time Indian workers too began welcoming prison as a respite from the plantations. Trinidad then began a search for ways of rendering sentences more onerous.[321] The desired behavior could not be cultivated when jails, not schools, became closely connected with Indian servitude in general, and immigrant life in particular. The data adapted from Fraser, reflects poorly on the host society.[322]

The category "fighting" doubled between 1872 and 1873 from 68 to 141) and it may have been due to the frustration among the laboring classes, including perhaps inter-racial conflict or competition. "Exposing the person" increased from 12 to 17 and is similarly an index of sexual frustration in a predominantly male labor force, or less likely, an index of increasing perversion. Other remarkable comparisons are, first, the doubling of "riotous and disorderly" conduct from 41 to 82; and secondly, a *decrease* from 356 to 332 of Indians imprisoned for not having passes or "tickets of absence" from their assigned plantations. At the same time, the number imprisoned for breach of contract had increased, thereby taking additional laborers out of the potential problem area of moving about without passes.

An occupational analysis of the prisoners also adapted from Inspector Fraser's report, is illuminating. Apart from 75 percent of these prisoners being "labourers," a merchant and 11 each of soldiers and planters were also imprisoned possibly for debt although more serious crimes may not be ruled out. No planter appears to have been imprisoned for violating their part of the indenture agreements. Most, if not all, of the seamstresses and washers were women. Certainly women were also hucksters and shopkeepers as well as bakers and "labourers." The proportion of women prisoners as given in the Council Paper is one in ten against men, or 10.6 percent (282) of the total.

Quite distinct from the predictably high proportion of labor offenses categorized as criminal, one unusual category was that of "harbouring immigrants." It could be facetiously argued that there was an increase of 300 percent from 1 to 3. This may have been due to the horrors of indenture, the sympathy which their situation evoked from those willing to risk harboring Indians or both of these developments. In terms of Isaac Dookhan's summary of indenture quoted at the top of this chapter, it would have required great courage for an Indian to help another against their common employer because of the fear of reprisals.

With regard to prostitution which was apparently increasing during the 1870s according to then Chief of Police, Fraser, we find that among the migrants—among whom males predominated—there existed an almost negligible number of prostitutes. In 1874 only two Indian sex-workers were discovered: Ninety were "Port of Spain women and 38 San Fernando women between the ages of 17 and 38. Another group of fifty-three San Fernando prostitutes include[d] two girls of about 11 years whose identity as prostitutes is debatable . . . Creoles dominated the 1874 list."[323] Sixty of the ninety prostitutes from the capital were Trinidad natives; 18 hailed from Barbados; ten from other West Indian islands; one 25-year old Calcutta woman. Of the women from Trinidad's second town,

San Fernando, 38 said they were born in Trinidad; of the non-natives just one came from Madras, India.

This list of 1874 also fails to support the notion that dangerous criminals or prostitutes predominated among Indians. This is not to deny that Indian men had sought the services of creole women nor that Indian women are conspicuous in the prostitution practice in present-day Trinidad.

Fraser also denoted religious and national affiliations of prisoners which is an aid in ascertaining the racial and ethnic composition of the prisoners. As might be expected, 39.9 percent or 1,059 of the total (2,649) were "Hindoos." Again, in proportion to their numbers, Muslim prisoners numbered 271, about 10 percent. In the country-by-country analysis, 51.2 percent or 1,357 persons originated in India. That gives us a figure which is only 27 short of the 1,357 committals from "India," since the sum 1,330 is arrived at by adding Muslims and Hindus. Categories such as "Jews," "Moravians," "Baptist," "Presbyterians," "Roman Catholic," and "Church of England" will have included at least a few Indians.[324] No one indicated they were atheists, and the 26 Chinese were listed without religious affiliation. In view of Trinidad's need for laborers who might be better controlled or exploited than the freedpersons, it is not surprising that the Indian-born category of prisoners was the most numerous.

The national origins of other prisoners are as fascinating and informative as they are elusive. Among those listed simply as "Trinidadians," one might assume that the number 535 comprise blacks and coloureds. From a breakdown of occupations of these prisoners one might conclude that an imprisoned planter, a printer or a debtor, even a baker might have been white. Those listed from European countries—49 French and 30 English—were probably white rather than persons of color. Sizeable numbers of creoles from other islands also contributed to the prison population in 1873: 139 Barbadians comprised 5.24 percent and Grenadians 1.7 percent.

The Fraser years also saw the introduction of age breakdown of prisoners. This data may help elucidate the nature of the society in terms of how it treated juveniles and children under eighteen years. As many as 154 children, four of them under ten years old, were incarcerated during 1873. This constituted 5.81 percent of all prisoners. Therefore one in twenty prisoners was a child. Of course contemporary ages at which youth are expected to work and the legal age for imprisonment are more humane today; yet Trinidad's treatment of Indian children was an index of how little Trinidad had moved from slavery and oppressive control of non-Europeans. Recruiters from plantation colonies had persuaded first parents in India that high wages were available them, and that children could earn nine Rupees. In view of this it was not unusual that Indian children labored in the canefields once in Trinidad; but it is surprising nevertheless that Indian children were jailed as adults.

As more than a third of all prisoners were indenteds who had displeased plantation personnel, a corresponding proportion of child prisoners were Indian. If we extend the category of young prisoners to include all those under 25, 789 or almost 30 percent of prisoners in 1873 were youthful violators of Trinidad's draconian labor ordinances. It is fair to say that there was not much of a childhood among laboring Indian children in Trinidad. In the age group 5-10, there were 4 prisoners, 47 prisoners between 10-15 years, for ages 15-18, 103 prisoners, for 18-20 years, 149; for ages 20-25, 486 prisoners, for ages 25-30, 782 prisoners, for ages 30-35, 370 prisoners, for ages 35-40, 431 prisoners, for ages 40-45, 107 prisoners, for ages 45-50, 112 prisoners, for ages 50-55, 19 prisoners, for ages 55-60, 27 prisoners, for ages 60-65, 5 prisoners, for ages 65-70, 4 prisoners, for ages 70-75, 1 prisoner, for ages 75-80, 2 persons were not spared from imprisonment.

The elderly East Indians, as with the children, were not spared severe plantation discipline either. Twelve persons over 60 were among the prisoners, two of them aged 75. The vast majority of those incarcerated (2,069) were adult male workers, exactly that group which was the primary target of recruitment.

The experiences of Indian migrants were not very different, or improved, a decade later. Trinidad continued to imprison too many Indians for civil offenses as per figures in the Blue Book for 1880. This source yields aggregate numbers of prisoners less frequently in preference for total *convictions*, which almost always is less than the number initially taken to prison. In 1880 the number of "serious offenses," according to the governor, was 242 as against 2,844 lesser crimes. India predominated among birthplaces of persons convicted: 1,547 of 3,092 or just over 50 percent, followed by 690 Trinidad-born prisoners, 216 Barbadians, 144 Grenadians and 92 St. Vincentians. The dubious category "Other countries" had the third largest percentage of convictions with 403 persons constituting 13 percent. The principal offenses when compared to 1879 had changed only slightly from 1872-73. "[I]ncreases over those for 1879 arise under the heads riot, breach of indenture, immigrants without pass, and larceny."[325]

The disproportionate ratio of 36,020 India-born persons and their 12,809 children born in Trinidad accounting for one-half of total prisoners in Trinidad's total of 153,128 people is borne out when we compare native-born and foreign-born inhabitants for the years 1881-82.[326] The India-born segment of 23 percent increases to 48,829 when ethnicity allows us to group all "East Indians" together, but the proportion rises to only 31 percent of Indians in the population that constituted half the prisoners of Trinidad in this era. All the other non-Indian foreigners together also made up a third of the population but did not constitute their proportionate share of prisoners.

Those Trinidadians of non-Indian nationalities born on the island constituted the single largest category in the population: 69,307 in a population of about 150,000, or 45 percent of the total. Other foreign nationals accounted for slightly more than 23 percent of the population, a similar proportion to East Indians born in India. We cannot decide if Indians had a higher reproduction in comparison to non-Indians in the island: we noted that Indo-Trinidadian children was 12,809 or 8.3 percent of the population, we do not know what proportion of the 69,307 Trinidad-born non-Indians were children. However, the varied and international character of nineteenth-century Trinidad becomes apparent when we closely examine national origin: Immigrants from other British Colonies—24,047; From the United Kingdom—1,062; From China—1,266; From Africa—3,035; From India—36,020; Portuguese—709; Italians—42; From Venezuela—2,227; from other foreign countries—2,083. There were 441 persons whose national origin was not described. In the last two categories we may note that Jews, Turks, Syrians and Lebanese did enter Trinidad and remain a recognizable minority today.

A quarter of all East Indians were children born in Trinidad (12,809 children and 36,020 directly from India). In the next chapter, we find that no schools were provided for these children because their parents were supposedly transients, but many of whom never went back to India. The argument of colonial Trinidad and the continuing neglect of more than 12,000 local children could not be condoned after 1869 when repatriation to India was discouraged in favor of settling small plots of land equivalent to the value of the return passage. Were Indian children better treated in Trinidad, one might easily justify the harsh plantation life of the adult Indians.

Indo-Trinidadian children were inordinately influenced by a life of prisons and plantations. It may be safe to venture that non-Indian children lived lives with more education, leisure and labor. Together with those born in Trinidad, the "Indians" comprised less than 32 percent of Trinidad's population. Immigrants from other "British Colonies" and non-Indians born in the colony constituted almost 61 percent of the total. It does not seem likely that the response to Indians and their locallly born children was out of fear of their numbers, at least not until the end of the century.

The Blue Book for 1881 reported that convictions for 1880 had represented only 18.64 percent of total cases going before the courts. For the year 1881 a total of 16,665 offenses were reported by police, which the Administrator of Trinidad found was "only

83 more than in 1880." The greatest number of offenses were "under the Masters and Servants Act, and breaches of the labour laws by Indian immigrants," followed in "numerical order" by "offenses against the person, common assaults, &c."[327] Throughout the period of indenture the situation remained virtually unchanged while improvements in East Indian life came slowly and grudgingly. The number of prison committals in 1886 was 4,363 "as against 4,411 in 1885, and the daily average number in custody [was] 586 as compared with 621." Some 16 percent of the total prisoners were women (678) as compared with 1.3 percent juveniles (53). Of the ten deaths in prison only one was by "judicial execution," the others having died from unspecified "natural causes."[328] A sign of improvement was that fewer children were incarcerated in 1886 whereas juvenile inmates had made up 5.81 percent of prisoners in 1873.

If this chapter were to strive to be fair to planters and indenteds, the daily average of about 600 persons in prison might be explained as the result of planters success in shifting the costs of indenture to the state during seasons when plantations needed fewer laborers. The indenteds continued to welcome the respite offered by prisons compared to life on some of the harsher plantations. Hard labor such as breaking stones was a common way to harshen prison-stays. Another strategy involved "the erection of a stone wall, separating the female from the male prisoners' labour yard," along with an increase in numbers of separate "working cells" for the females from 26 to 86.[329] To the extent that Indians were guilty not of crimes, but of "slighter offenses" relating to their position as a migrant labor force, one cannot assess the deterrent value of Trinidad's prisons. Prisons failed to deter the lesser "labor offenses."

A question which needs to be answered is whether laborers could benefit planters when they were sent to jail, that is, sent away from the site of work. The answer turns on the duration of prison terms which were usually short, from seven to 90 days. In that sense the imprisonment of Indians, free or indented, served both penal and control functions with the function of *control* being predominant. The usual deterrent function of prisons failed with the Indians, probably because the institution was for indenture what the *whip* had been under the system of slavery.

The case for a positive trend insofar as fewer child prisoners is strengthened by data outside of our study period. In 1898 children constituted 0.2 percent or nine prisoners between ages 12 and 16. One negative in this data is that six of the nine children imprisoned were girls. The oldest group, "60 years and above" listed 6 females and 29 males, but did not reveal the optimum age. The prisoners totalled 3,953 persons, of which 573 or 14.4 percent were females. Although "Hindoos" again constituted the largest single ethnic group among prisoners, that total of 1,294 or 32 percent was closely followed by 887 Anglicans, with some 227 "Musselmen" being the third largest category. Another positive sign was that 38.4 percent of "Misdemeanours" not "Breaches of Immigration Ordinance," at 26.5 percent, was the dominant offense in 1898. Indented Indians now constituted less than the established proportion of one-third to one-half of prisoners.[330]

We cannot dispute that "the nature and demands of the plantation system had a profound effect on the [high] rate, pattern, and characteristics of criminal activity" in post-slavery Trinidad. The study of crime does offer a fuller "understanding" of the "nature" of plantation life. The argument is not that without the plantation there would have been no crime; rather "that crime is essentially a social phenomenon and that societies produce crime rates and patterns peculiar to themselves."[331] Racism was a factor in the categorization and rates of criminal cases before the courts in Trinidad, as with what officials saw as repeat offenders turning prisons into boarding homes.[332] In essence, Trinidad was not a criminal's paradise and far too many Indian laborers were in and out of jail for non-criminal actions. The status quo was not helpful for building a stable post-emancipation community. After the relatively horrid experience of recruitment, the passage as illustrated in the *Poitiers* voyage (below) from Calcutta or Madras, the Indian sub-culture in Trinidad was almost rent asunder. A new, creole value system did take hold among Indians towards the end of the last century. As we look at bewildered British Indians on board ship headed to places unknown, as we follow the experiences of low wages and conflict experienced by the first arrivals at the Clydesdale Cottage Estate during 1846, we can assemble the pieces of the puzzle as to why Indians sometimes saw prisons as a welcome respite from plantations.

3.2 WHAT WAS SINGULAR ABOUT INDIAN INDENTURE?

Writers sometimes assume that readers know all the nuances that indenture experienced as it shifted from a bondage of Europeans to the bondage of Asians. For instance, B.C. Roberts writes simply that, "The essence of the indenture system was that laborers were recruited under a contract to work for a given period in exchange for the financing of their passages to [a] colony."[333] While this definition is not as useful in this study as is the one given by Ralph Schlomowitz, Roberts does alert us to the fact that the cost of transportation to a colony—where indenteds made a fresh start in life—was the benchmark for determining the length of service to potential employers. But he fails to delve into the reasons why Asians dominated this trade after 1860; some answers suggested in Chapter Two relate to race and religion generally, and in Trinidad, to the Indian migrants' lack of options in a plantation-culture complex.[334]

At a conference on "From Chattel Slavery to Wage Slavery," at the Institute of Commonwealth Studies in London,[335] one of the Caribbean scholar-presenters betrayed the commonplace but erroneous assumption that indenture in the Caribbean was a peculiarly "East Indian" experience, and that the subsistence and "medical provisions" for indenteds rendered their ordeal quite tolerable. Assumptions about generous medical, food and wage provisions of indenture are not borne out for any decade of the Indian ordeal in Trinidad. It is easy to become confused as to the exact nature of Indian bondage but all aspects of contrast among the experiments with non-slave labor in the Caribbean after 1834 ought to be kept in view, experiments which also included European and African indenture in Trinidad.

In comparing European and Indian indenture, Stanley Engerman points to racial differences as a critical variable explaining their contrasting destinies. While Europeans dominated the "first stream" in the seventeenth and eighteenth centuries, it was the general "absence of white contract labor in the second stream" which made it a "generally accepted" form of economic development.[336] We note further that while European servants usually worked for other Europeans and were meant to be settlers after their indentures, Indians were a powerless, colonized people who worked for non-Indians who promised to return them to India. Had they been recruited as settlers from the start the rules might have been more tolerable, especially in terms of what exactly was to be offered Indian settlers.

Respect for family life, sometimes an assumed contrast between Indian and African bondage in Trinidad, is profoundly discordant with the historical record of the experiences which Indian indenteds lived day-to-day.[337] For a start, few wives or women came in a lopsided male labor migration. In its earliest phase, there was much public outrage in India at the break-up of families entailed in this ill-informed labor agreement. One Calcutta Town Hall protest meeting ended with the petitioning of the President of the Council of India. The petitioners had publicized that fact that merely 100 women had emigrated with 6,000 men in five years: "3,000 families at least had been left without their natural protector and head."[338] More to the point, the family quarters for Indians in Trinidad were single rooms 10 feet by 12, partitioned by a low board from the family next to them. They offered no privacy, were "defective" and remained without toilets in the period 1845-88, until 1914.[339]

This chapter will now examine inherited assumptions and examine to the extent possible, conditions on board ship during the voyage from India; conditions on the plantations; and the extent to which medical and other provisions were forthcoming. The tardy attention displayed by Dr. Meikelham in this instance to indented Indian charges at Edward Walkinshaw's estate is supplemented by our knowledge that he too was a planter.[340] This caused a conflict of interest when time was of the essence rather than sadism by the doctor whose negligence caused the death, or at least the rapid expiry of Kundappa, from the malady of foot sores. This account of an emaciated, skeletal man near death being permitted to be transported to another estate by donkey cart, screeching to be left alone to die quietly when someone lifted the filthy blanket that covered him, is heart-rending.[341]

In 1909 George Fitzpatrick of Trinidad told the Sanderson Committee investigating abuses endured by Indians such as those on the Hermitage Estate where four overseers had beaten several Indians, including one woman who "being pregnant at the time, abortion immediately took place. . . ." The authorities "were satisfied to lay a charge" merely for assault and battery, with a fine of L2, and L3 compensation to the woman. The charges of the men against the accused and the other overseers were "withdrawn." The same Indian men were shortly thereafter accused of assaulting an overseer and sentenced to imprisonment with hard labor.[342]

The "indenture agreement" supposedly comprehended and voluntarily entered into by adult Indians,[343] is sometimes portrayed as the main watershed between the different systems of labor in colonial Trinidad. Eric Williams once declared that the contract signified that the Indian was a free person.[344] The only clear break with unfreedom was that the new laborers were *not* chattel;[345] beyond this, the issues of freedom of choice as well as of free wage labor were theoretical. It is in the actual operation of the system that the similarity in conditions between bonded and ostensibly free workers become apparent. This reiterates the point that unfree conditions in the Caribbean did not disappear simply because the plantations had turned to Asian labor. As Engerman expressed it, "The acceptance of contract labour might also be suggestive of

Ramasawmy, the 20 year old patient, "continued very ill" on 20 October and began to approach his end quickly. The surgeon recorded, and the immigrants witnessed on Monday, 25 October, "Ramasawmy becoming much weaker." The next morning's entry was, "Ramasawmy appears to be dying fast." Ramasawmy's journey ended the next day without his seeing Trinidad. The surgeon's notes bear out the fact that Indians brought money and muscle: "One *anna* and 10 *pie* found on his person. He was buried in the afternoon." Ramasawmy's body was very likely "buried" overboard as the survivors watched and wondered about their own fates. The record does not reveal whether Ramasawmy's next of kin were informed of his death.

The macabre play of the cycles of life was lightened somewhat by the terse news on the last day of October. "A woman, named Erloyen, gave birth to a living Female child at 4 p.m.," followed by the entry, "Child small [and] hardly mature." Subsequent entries show that the child did well, probably more eager for life on foreign plantations than the now pensive adults.

When inclement weather prevented cooking of food according to general Indian taste, the discomfort increased for a pre-industrial people who had to repast on biscuits and water. Such concerns appear again on 12 November: "Provisions unable to be cooked again today. Space between decks kept clean and dry. Sick seen as usual—and Emigrants daily asked as to their freedom from syphilitic or cutaneous disease." On Wednesday, 17 November, the Surgeon entered, "One man suffering from Pneumonia and appears dangerously ill," comes suddenly in the improving situation. On 23 November, we learn that "One man still dangerously ill." The person in question was Mootoverpen, and while others may have been sick his case was highlighted because he was near death. The Surgeon then recorded on 2 December, "Mootoverpen died this morning of Pneumonia and was buried during the day." Again, Mootoverpen must have followed Ramasawmy to a watery grave. No sooner was this done than a man named Erulanden became "dangerously ill." He was "still in danger" on 3 December. By the third day, Sunday morning, the doctor wrote, "Erulanden died this morning. Cooked food and water supplied. Space between decks clean, dry and well-ventilated." Thudding news of mundane chores, that life must go on, was probably the best preparation yet, for these recruits for the plantations.

On 12 December there was a scare as two men reported sick and were found to have contracted Vancella "or Chicken pock." The Surgeon next noted with relief, "No more cases of Vancella." Excluding minor injuries, fever and "itch" the *Poitiers* landed in Trinidad without further mortality at Christmas. By 28 December all passengers were finally allowed to land. Two persons went directly to the hospital, one Mohammed Saib, because of an eye injury. No details about his injury were recorded. The *Poitiers* voyage may have been horrendous for the Indians but it was an atypical voyage compared with devastating mortality on board other vessels.

Other voyages before and contemporaneous with the *Poitiers* experienced high and worrying levels of mortality. G.S. Arora is critical of shoddy or non-existent mortality data of the early years which was not completely remedied for later voyages. The East Indian "middle passage," he writes, held problems for the migrants with regard to "food, water, living space, medical care and the Officer's treatment [of] them." The Indian Government Act XIII of 1864 fixed the probable length of the voyage from Calcutta to the West Indies at 20 weeks; although most vessels reached Trinidad in 90-100 days, the Act was a guide as to provisions safeguards. Controversy over mortality led to the suspension of Indian labor migration between 1848 and 1851; efforts to introduce steamers for this trade bore fruit only in 1901.[351] Arora appears to have over-emphasized "middle passage" mortality in the first period for Trinidad, 1845-1848, which was probably light in comparison to the 1850s and 1870s.

We have seen that the mortality on the *Poitiers* was three from a total of 300 or 1 percent; Arora says that "no exact figures" are available for the ships which brought approximately 5 000 Indians to Trinidad before the suspension in 1848. He is able to ferret out two 1846 voyages which experienced one male death on the *London*, and three deaths on the *Cadet*. We incline towards a belief that officers and crew were more careful on these early voyages to the West Indies.

It remains accurate, however, that "the real trial of the emigrants began on the voyage." Surgeon Superintendants were responsible for the welfare of migrants upon boarding the ships, and Arora believes that it was one of their most "difficult and delicate duties . . . to protect the emigrants against the master of the ship." Average mortality after the resumption of labor migration in the period 1850-56 was 3.7 percent, but for the 1856-57 season mortality ranged from a low of 5.75 percent (on the *Wellesley*) to 31.17 percent (on the *Merchantman*). As a consequence of this the Government of Bengal appointed Dr Mouatt, Inspector of Jails in the Lower Provinces, to investigate the causes of the alarmingly high number of deaths.[352]

The British authorities appeared horrified by middle passage mortality in the 1850s. In a despatch dated 22 July 1857, the Court of Directors of the British East India Company drew the attention of the Indian Government to this question. Mortality rates approaching one out of five who embarked could not be ignored when officials had argued that the Indian would fare better outside India. It was inexcusable in view of British insistence that with the death of slavery, the only international traffic in human laborers was being conducted *officially* as well as voluntarily. In Trinidad itself, instead of mortality or other abuses being debated, the right of planters to apply free trade principles to potential laborers from Asia remained the focus. "The free movement of labor from one part of the empire to another became [a] manifestation of the idea of free trade that dominated the nineteenth century."[353] This in itself was not a bad thing, except that Indian emigration was not always informed or voluntary. The European counterpoint to this aspect of the free trade phenomenon ironically

saw laborers from Europe dissuaded from coming to Trinidad or
estate labor even as planters looked to India to supply their labor
"shortfall."[354] Dr Mouatt's August 1858 report on the reasons for
high mortality among migrants bound for the colonies "disproved"
the assertions and suspicions of some surgeons and British officials
"that the great sickness and mortality were due principally to the
primary selection of sickly and unfit subjects in Bengal." Dr Mouatt
placed most of the blame on "conditions obtaining on the ships,"
exacerbated by the increased proportion of women and children,"
by improper sanitary precautions on board," and in some cases by
the shipment of water of the river Hoogly" when it was polluted,
as well as by not practising informal or formal quarantining. Then
there was the inevitable "change in the diet of the emigrants, by
the absolute want of suitable food for young children and infants,
by the presence of grain cargoes," and occasionally by the
"inexperience of the medical officers," which was complicated
by language barriers between crew and Indians.[355]

Although mortality on voyages forced the Government to take
remedial actions, it would be towards the end of the nineteenth
century that deaths en route were no longer an urgent concern.
The 1860s and 1870s were underlined by the arresting mortality
on the ships *Tyburnia* and *Delharrie*, respectively. The *Tyburnia* left
India on 15 December 1959 and arrived in Trinidad on 4 March
1860 with 7.81 percent or 24 casualties out of a total of 327
souls. The proportion of women to men was 23 percent.

On 12 November 1860 an investigation into mortality on
board the *Tyburnia* revealed irregularities of standard procedures.
The violations ranged from "castes" being excluded in addition to
the religion of each migrant, ages of young and old were completely
omitted, the "death of a young man" was also omitted from the
pilot's register, 80 migrants were taken without certificates, the
minimum proportion of women was not met, as well as reports of
some would-be-migrants having deserted just before sailing. The
investigating committee found that the Emigration Agent, Mr
Johnstone, had been "repeatedly warned" about such irregularities

without much effect and the matter failed to reach "the notice of higher authority." The recommendations were that medical officers maintain a detailed diary, prohibit the migration of the very young, maintain a proportion of women at 25 percent or less, send one Indian cook for every 100 migrants, and allow equal space, milk and appropriate food for mothers and children and also increase the food of the rest of the migrants—that is two meals instead of just one. The Government of India rejected the proposal to lower the percentage of women below 25 percent of male migrants; but the suggestions of separating the Protector's Office in Calcutta from that of the Master Attendant, and the appointment of a Medical Inspector of Emigrants at each port, were accepted. The last change was salutary, as these officers thenceforth kept a watchful eye over Indians and the Immigration staff as well.[356]

Table 3.1 SHIPS AND MORTALITY EN ROUTE TO TRINIDAD

Name	Sailed on	#Died	% Died	Embarked	Surgeon
INDUS	12 Jan. 1872	6	1.4%	413	C.H. Graham
ATALANTA	17 Feb. 1872	6	1.4%	404	J. O'Donnell
WOODBURN	31 Jul. 1872	16	2.7%	˙577	R. Rivers
WILTSHIRE	21 Aug. 1872	19	3.3%	569	J. Carroll
RAJAH O'COCHIN	14 Sep. 1872	14	3.4%	413	M.A. Raheem
DELHARRIE	20 Sep. 1872	44	8.5%	516	A.O. Wiley
JOHN ALLEN	19 Oct. 1872	4	1.2%	324	J. Dimwiddie
COLMONELL	28 Oct. 1872	18	3.8%	473	H.Lyne
HOWRAH	30 Nov. 1872	13	2.8%	458	G.C. Jackson
JUMNA	12 Jan. 1873	10	2.2%	449	T. O'Donovan
ATALANTA	28 Feb. 1873	3	0.7%	395	J. Shircore
SYRIA	24 Aug. 1873	24	5.5%	438	P. Hughes
WINCHESTER	10 Oct. 1873	27	6.0%	444	W. Johnston
BROCKHAM	2 Nov. 1873	16	3.7%	422	W. Holman
JUMNA	23 Nov. 1873	16	3.6%	447	J.M. Barry
Total		236	3.5%	6,742	

NOTES:
a. J. Lowthar signed the above document (9 July 1874).
b. The births on these ships to Trinidad was 44 or 0.6 per cent of the total number of emigrants (6,742).
c. Total births for the period on ships to all of the West Indies during 1872-73 was 177 persons; total deaths were 1,163.
Trinidad's proportion of this figure is therefore 20.2 percent.

One of the worst mortality figures is that for 1872 on the *Delharrie*. Almost 9 percent of the "human cargo" died before landing. The sense of doom, of having made a mistake must have plagued not a few of the migrants. Survivors watched 44 would-be Trinidad workers succumb en route. In spite of British Indian migration assuming much too much importance in the Caribbean other migrants, and in some years in greater numbers than East Indians, continued to enter Trinidad into the 1860s.

As late as the 1860s non-Indian immigrants flowed into Trinidad and outnumbered the Indian stream in 1863, 1864, 1866 and 1868. The specific numbers follow with male-female proportions for East Indians only. In 1863 there were 2,850 black and white immigrants and 1,766 natives of India (1,390 males, 299 females, 48 boys and 29 girls). In 1864, black and white immigrants totalled 2,599 while India sent 920 labor migrants (685 males, 179 females, 48 boys and 29 girls). In 1865 non-Indian immigrants numbered 2,339 and Indian immigrants totalled 2,670 (1,830 males, 523 females, 185 boys and 132 girls). The following year black and white newcomers to Trinidad represented 75 percent of the arrvals and East Indians just 25 percent (329 males, 84 females, 32 boys and 14 girls). In 1867 Indians showed their best totals yet at 3,186 (1,860 males, 986 females, 12 boys and seven girls) while the significant total of 2,286 blacks and whites constituted 42 percent of all arrivals that year. In 1868, there were 2,352 black and white arrivals in Trinidad with the smaller Indian proportion of 36 percent (or 1,337 persons divided among 996 males, 293 females, 31 boys and 20 girls).[357]

The only whites in this migrant wave were Portuguese from "Fayall", whose exact numbers are difficult to determine as the total under "Others" in Table 3.8 include neighboring West Indian migrants. It is worth noting that when East Indian immigration had become established in Trinidad by the 1860s, there were years in which non-Indians still outnumbered Indian labor migrants. Portuguese and West Indian immigrants outnumbered Indians in four out of six years for which we have non-Indian figures. The

Fayal-West Indies percentage in the India-Fayal-West Indies total in 1864 and 1866 were 73 percent and 79 percent!

In 1862, a total of 467 Chinese—321 men and 126 women—arrived in Trinidad and another 1,386 more Chinese arrived in 1865, of whom 1,202 were males. In 1858, 32 Africans arrived—29 men and 3 women—and in 1860, another 561 men and 126 women. In virtually all of these cases, women were heavily outnumbered by their male counterparts, although a one-third proportion of females to males had been insisted on for African indenteds in the 1840s. The proportion of female migrants ranged from 23 percent in 1866 to a high of 36 percent in 1869, before adjustments for mortality. In 1868 the ratio had been increased to 40 percent as a means of promoting stable family life.

The numbers of Indian migrants who repatriated far outnumbered the Chinese who returned home during 1856-70. In 1858 and 1859, one and three Chinese returned to China, and a total of five during 1864. The total of nine returnees were all male. Indians who repatriated to India after completing their indentures ranged from 274 in 1856 (167 males, 38 females, 41 boys and 28 girls) to a high of 508 in 1865 (354 males, 87 females, 35 boys and 32 girls). As late as 1870, despite the incentive of converting the passage to India for small plots of land, 388 Indians went back (215 males, 98 females, 40 boys and 35 girls).[358]

These statistics demonstrate that opting to go back to India was on the rise between 1856 and 1858 and reached a highpoint in 1865, but despite decreasing numbers of returnees thereafter, some 300 Indians returned "home" each year throughout the 1860s and 1870. By 1895 at least 16,024 Indians had re-emigrated to India from Trinidad, most of them paying some of the costs.[359]

The rest of this chapter discusses the rhetorical issue raised by Eric Williams: "One can only wonder today how it was possible for any country that had abolished slavery on the ground that it was inhuman to justify Indian indenture with its 25 cents a day wage and its jails."[360]

3.4 MAKING AMENDS TO BRITISH

WEST INDIAN PLANTERS

Indian indenture was an onerous option which, following the Report of the 1842 Select Committee on the West India Colonies, was eventually accepted by Britain along with its attendant costs. This official basis of recruiting migrant laborers was a departure from the ad hoc and privately funded schemes which had characterized the decade 1834-1844. The huge sums Britain paid on behalf of the colonies, for recruiting agents; operating Immigration depots in India and the housing, feeding and transportation of the recruited migrants, were to be paid back by the colonies over five years. It was an intriguing development, all the same. Some of the intrigue is explained by Lord Stanley, in the following document where British-sponsored immigration is presented as a quid pro quo for the equalization of duties on all sugar entering Britain. Indians had truly become the means whereby principles of free trade could be implemented.

On 27 November 1843, before labor migration from India was sanctioned, Lord Stanley wrote Peel: "[T]he very favourable accounts which have been received of the extensive Immigration from India into Mauritius, under the new regulations . . . have brought upon me still more urgent and pressing entreaties from the West Indians for a relaxation of the prohibition in their favour: and this is the more urgent, because, as I always foresaw and told them, the supply from Sierra Leone proves very insufficient . . . The difficulty will be much increased if we take any step for reducing the amount of protection now enjoyed by the West Indians, without at the same time increasing their facilities for obtaining labour."[361]

Indian Immigration to the British Caribbean had begun as a shortlived private venture in Guiana in 1838, but Caribbean-wide British approval came only in July 1844. Britain agreed to pay the costs of transporting Indians to Trinidad and elsewhere and to reimburse the Treasury from the surplus funds of the colonies. "The Trinidad Government [was] to pay yearly into a Sinking Fund a sum equal to one-twentieth of the amount of the bonds issued" to finance the redemption of the loan at the end of five years, which translated into an annual interest of five percent. The total cost of the loan was to come from the 3.5 percent *ad valorem* export duty of the Colony which would continue for the life of the loan.[362]

Ordinance 19 which authorized the final arrangements for Indian immigration to Trinidad, in its Preamble, quoted "the Ordinance 18 of 1st February 1843 to raise funds for the cost of bringing immigrants from the coast of Africa and makes these available in regard to 'such ports of Asia as may be appointed by Her Majesty.'" Governor McLeod enclosed "certain rules I have established relative to the Coolys." The rate of wages which McLeod disclosed was a fraction of what free labor had been paid since 1834. Some planters had offered Grenadians $12 per month; most Trinidad creoles earned about $8 a month, but Portuguese indenteds had received $6 monthly; the lower than $6 a month offered to Indians was not always offset by the cost of provisioning them, quite apart from issues of quality and quantity of food, housing and medicine. Wages in Trinidad were on the way down since 1841 but Indian wages were even lower[363] as seen from official documents: "To each *Sirdar364*, per month $3.35; To each headman, per month $2.90; To each male labourer, per month $2.40; To each female labourer, per month $1.45; To each boy under 12 years," monthly $1.45."

It might be argued that wages of sirdars and headmen were higher than what Portuguese indenteds had received because half their $6 had been kept by the employer each month for having advanced the $60 bounty for their passages. These positions were ancillary to those of plantation personnel in that they enforced the managers' wishes, but were a small minority of the total Indian labor force. Regarding "wages-in-kind" such as food, clothing and medical aid which British Indians supposedly enjoyed we note firstly, that laborers in Trinidad had always received foods, gardens for their vegetable needs, and such medical attention as was available on the property or at public hospitals. Secondly, at soem point the reputation of managers and planters must be assessed in terms of the indenture agreements, and promises made to the immigrant plantation workers. Indeed, wages promised to Indians before they agreed to leave their homes had been attractive and "exorbitant."[365]

In 1844, before the first Indians had arrived, official Trinidad through its Governor McLeod had expressed dismay at the low level of remuneration which had been "fixed at a meeting of the Proprietary Body" via their organ, the Immigration and Agricultural Society. McLeod wrote to London: "I have found no guide for this in any of the papers printed by order of Parliament, for although Mr Anderson, the Agent sent from Mauritius says in his letter of instructions to the [Trinidad] Agent in Calcutta that he may without hesitation assure the labourers wishing to emigrate that they will receive immediate employment on their arrival in the Colony at the rate of five rupees per month etc., yet there is nothing to ensure to them the continuance of this."[366]

The untruths and unrealistic promises which Trinidad agents had made to African recruits in Sierra Leone were blatantly replicated in India.[367]

McLeod in his October 1844 despatch, addressed other wage-related issues before the first Indians arrived in May 1845. London sent no directives on McLeod's query nor any indication that officials in London shared his concern. Nor did the Colonial Office insist on officials being forthright with would-be immigrants and avoid untruths such as those noted by McLeod; unrealistic wages were still being promised by Trinidad agents during the 1864-65 recruiting season in India. McLeod had in fact gone further in his criticism of the experiment: "Looking to the possibility, nay the probability, that as labour becomes very plentiful the price of it may fall very considerably, it would seem necessary to guard against the contingency of an illiterate and, I believe, simple-minded people being induced to emigrate to the West Indies in the persuasion of bettering their condition and of taking back their earnings, finding themselves from circumstances they had no intellect to foresee, and over which they could have no control, compelled to labour at an immense distance from their Native Homes for a remuneration altogether inadequate to fulfil their expectations."[368]

Governor McLeod was reiterating the concern of the Secretary of State for the Colonies in the 1830s, Lord Glenelg, that were West Indian creole-immigrants to find wages lower than they had anticipated, they be allowed to return to their islands. But he also mentions the motives which generally brought Indians to Trinidad: "bettering their condition and of taking back their earnings." Migrant earnings which were taken back to India aroused consternation in the colony, and throughout the period of indenture Indians were cajoled into settling in Trinidad. McLeod in 1844 may have lacked the influence of his successor, Lord Harris, who according to Comins "stands Saul-like above the Governors [and who] overcame the obstacles to immigration from India."[369] Still, McLeod had sounded a warning bell and in his magnanimity suggested that Britain might provide for British Indians returning earlier if they should find wages lower than they were led to believe. To date we have not found a document which addressed these pre-*Fateh Rozack* concerns regarding the Indian labor scheme.

The wages decided upon for East Indians were an index of growing planter confidence and of Britain's collusion in finding a captive but ostensibly free labor force for its colonial plantations. Low wages must be placed in this context, unfolding since the 1842 Select Committee Report into the West India Colonies, and Merivale's ideas. Indians themselves were hardly responsible for the wage scale drawn up for them before their arrival, least of all because virtually none of the 1845 pioneers had any idea about Trinidad's location and its population.

That wages had been falling since 1842 could not be missed in 1845 when the *Fateh Rozack* arrived; planters and proprietors allowed the male Indians less than a third of what freed persons received in 1841. Indian women were not to receive more than 25 percent of that rate or $1.45 per month. Unwittingly, Trinidad reinforced chauvinism among Indian males by equating the labor of women to that of male children under 12 years of age. Later observers of Trinidad society would comment on the alleged Indian preference for male children. For instance, Graeme S. Mount wrote that even if women were not the equals of European men in North America, "few Canadian men would have thought like the one [East Indian] who referred to his son as his only 'child' when he also had a daughter."[370] Precisely to the point in this context is the fact that the labor of grown women, and boys less than age 12 were equated, while girls under 12 years were not mentioned as worthy of wage-labor. Yet at 12, girls could be imprisoned, as our earlier data for 1898 demonstrated. Western women were deprived of the franchise until the 1920s, and did not have a voice in religious bodies either as Mount himself admits with reference to the Presbyterian Council.[371] In this context, the authorities could easily offer more in wages to a boy of 13 than to a woman old enough to be his mother or grandmother. Other benefits which were intended to supplement Indian wages were certain food items and pieces of cloth.

These efforts to offer food and clothes suited to nineteeenth-century Indians entailed, at least on paper, giving each migrant worker "Rice 45 lbs per month; Peas [dried & split] 9 lbs per month; Ghee [clarified butter as shortening] 1/4 gallon per month; Salt 11/8 lbs. per month; Fish [cured or dried] 41/2 lbs. per month; Tamerinds 41/2 lbs. per month; Onions & Chillies [hot pepper] 11/8 lbs. per month. As for non-food items, each year, workers were to receive, two blankets, two *dhotis* [male waist cloth], one jacket and one cap, one wooden bowl "and medical attendance, house and garden rent free."[372]

As the planters of Trinidad were preparing a welcome for the first British Indian laborers, its politically astute coloureds were emphasizing the need for a more representative government, improved roads, better education and access to medical facilities for the masses. They appeared conscious of ethnic politics, or at least aware that Orientals would not melt as easily in the new society-in-formation. Leaders among black and brown creoles were also wary of continuing planter efforts to lower remuneration on their estates. East Indians were resented by Trinidad's coloureds as well as by a significant part of the eclipsed Catholic planters of French and Spanish ancestry.[373] Unlike British Guiana, where non-planting sectors of the population petitioned for the importation of Indian workers, Thomas Hinde and 140 co-signatories to a petition in Trinidad opposed the strategy of the Immigration and Agricultural Society, for a host of convincing reasons.

The Hinde "memorialists" expressed their concern over "the intended motion of one of the members of the Board to borrow 200,000 pounds sterling," in London for the intended project. The petitioners were antagonistic toward the Society of which Burnley was a distinguished member—

"We would ask the Trinidad Immigration Society (Agricultural Society we cannot style them, for they seem to have lost sight of the primary objects of such societies) would it not have been more prudent to have taken the hint of the Home Government and exerted themselves to find another remedy. Have they exerted themselves to extend the use of animal and mechanical power in agriculture? Have they ascertained to what extent the plough is employed in this Colony? If the plough was proportionately as extensively used in Trinidad as in the equally wild countries of Canada and the United States, the present extent of cultivation might be doubled with the same number of hands and salaries and wages remain the same. We are of the opinion that salaries and wages are not too high in Trinidad and that they afford a bare sufficiency of the necessaries and conveniences of life in this intemperate climate."[374]

While this petition failed—in view of Britain's larger imperial politics and economic thinking—it is possible that this detailed petition is the source of some later distortions in Trinidad's history. One might refer to that part of the petition concerning "combination" among planters to agree about lowering wages. The Hinde petitioners thought that the coming of Indians would allow the Immigration Society "to organize a close union of the Sugar Planters, and by these means to give the Sugar Planters full power to diminish the rate of salaries and wages." They had been cooperating on wages since 1841 before the Indians arrived.

The larger imperial strategy has been called upon to excuse missionaries who promoted both the status quo and the system of indenture. Mount argued "In all fairness . . . the economy of Trinidad depended upon sugar," and as late as 1909 John Morton, Canada's pioneer Presbyterian among the Indo-Trinidadians, defended this system which he argued was of "divine inspiration."[375] The next most important Presbyterian missionary, Kenneth Grant, implicitly criticized indenture when in testimony before a Labor Committee Investigation, he said an "improvement of wages and working conditions" would "attract free laborers."[376] This implied the Indians were not free workers.

The coloured petitioners against Indian immigration had offered an alternative. A better program of action was for Trinidad to imitate the ancient Romans by intersecting the island with good roads. From a more practical stand than the Reverend Morton, they argued that Blacks from the United States "excelled in roadmaking," and could be procured for Trinidad at less expense than immigrants from British India. They feared the imperial and/ or planter strategy would increase taxation and lower wages with this consequence: "few[er] immigrants will come from the old Islands and none from Sierra Leone" or the United States and even the "ignorant" Indians would find Trinidad more expensive, and would surely "discover their mistake."[377]

The first arrivals in Guiana had already borne out the truth of some of these dire predictions, at least in the non-existence of medical facilities on the estates and in East Indian mortality. Of the 414 who sailed to British Guiana in 1838, 18 had died en route. The number returning to India in 1843 at the end of five-year contracts totalled 236, barely 57 percent. Sixty were said to have "elected" to remain in the colony; two absconded, but 98 or 24 percent had died before qualifying for their return passages back to India. On the monetary savings which are referred to in an effort to water down the harshness of indenture, a paltry 180 rupees each over five years is what the survivors showed for their ordeal. Of course, as with all averages, those who received less than 180 rupees were equally hidden as those who made more than the average. Later, when the total length away from India was extended to ten years, savings of out-of-indenture Indians, upon having completed five years, increased during the five years of "industrial residence."[378]

The health of East Indians was precarious especially in the first 18 months after arrival, although there were always estates where sickness and mortality remained "disturbingly high." Malaria, hookworm and related debilitating illnesses contributed to a state of health which, "as late as 1907-12" produced sickness in Trinidad "seldom less than twice" the total Indian population. Data at the Public Record Office indicate that ankylostomiasis continued to be a major health hazard for Indians well into the twentieth century. Mortality in French colonies was worse as 11,944 of the 25,509 sent to Martinique died, as did 19,000 of 45,000 who went to Gaudeloupe, and half the 9,200 in French Guiana.[379]

The two biggest holes in the indenture system relate to the lack of medical facilities up to about 1870, and to the wages expected by the Indians being much lower than had been anticipated. More often than not wages were only goals to which the indented might aspire but which, at week's end, were reduced by a host of factors including bad weather and illnesses, for which the plantation mde the Indian liable. These costs thus fell on the Indians who had far fewer resources than planters.

The medical provision per indentures was another of its more poignant myths. For more than twenty years after the first arrivals from India in 1845, no sustained effort was made to live up to the generous promises of free medical care. In 1866, Trinidad at last began to taking the issue seriously and a new Ordinance was passed. Six employers ordered the construction of hospitals per this new ordinance so that in 1867, only 92 of the 155 estates in Trinidad

had their own hospitals. Indeed 13 plantations had chosen not to
employ Indians rather than fulfil their health-care obligations vis a
vis the Indians.[380]

This discrepancy between promise and plantation reality is
connected to the larger myth that British Indians traded their hell
for an island paradise. The right to hospital stays when laborers
fell ill sounded impressive on paper, but even makeshift estate clinics
were rare before the 1860s. Provisions of the Emigration Ordinances
pertaining to food, health and wages appeared generous in theory
but translated into little practical value for the daily reality of
indenture. That many survived indenture and a few even prospered,
was testimony to their stamina, or a combination of their efforts,
the anonymous planters who were good employers, and
opportunities within a proto-capitalist colony, for which many
Indians were prepared to wait and sacrifice. On the other hand,
the alleged advantages of Indian indenture were of powerful
propaganda value in Britain where poverty and suffering were the
order of the day for millions of working class people. Trinidad
whites were not spared from poverty and suffering either, as the
concern for destitute, orphans, and handicapped persons
attested.[381] The net result was diminishing activism or less empathy
for ex-slaves and other non-Europeans.[382] Here, the Church may
have been the exception, a subject for Chapters Four and Five,
below.

Indeed the missionaries of the Canadian Presbyterian Mission
to the East Indians of Trinidad (1867), especially the Reverends
Morton and Grant, at times wondered if they were "medical
missionaries." The need for medical treatment was so urgent among
Indians that evangelization was to some extent helped by the
planters' negligence. In 1870 Governor Arthur Gordon wrote that
the new medical Ordinances had made a difference but "the
dependence of medical doctors on planters for their income could
lead to the temptation to place the planters' interests" before that
of the needy patients.[383] Gordon noted that mortality rates were
not helped by the shortage of clean drinking water. As late as 1914,

water at the Woodford Lodge Estate was "found to be [unfiltered,] thick and muddy," while one Couva Estate refused Indians water on Sundays.[384]

During the 1870s, doctors were made Government functionaries and the indenture system was made to yield benefits to the entire populace as medical facilities were now opened to all and sundry.[385] The situation in the first decades following the eend of slavery had been dismal for all who belonged to the lower classes, the first among these being the East Indians.

3.5 VIOLENCE AT WALKINSHAW'S ESTATE

In this concluding section we examine the quality of the first impact which the free wage labor system in Trinidad had on new Indian migrants. The abuses at the Clydesdale Cottage Estate of Edward Walkinshaw which we examine here occured in 1846, a year after the start of Indian labor migration. In summary, the abuses spoke to an absence of humane conditions including the withholding of food rations, the paucity of medical attention and non-payment of wages for five to six weeks. This eventually resulted in violence and a subsequent investigations.

Officially the story begins when Walkinshaw alleged in court that he was assaulted by East Indians employed on his estate. The planter accused the authorities of having precipitated this incident by not having been severe enough with laborers he had earlier sent to the police. An unofficial inquiry by Governor Harris revealed that Walkinshaw was himself guilty of assaulting the migrant laborers in addition to not providing them food on time. A subsequent Inquiry by Major Fagan, the Protector of Immigrants concluded that "it was difficult to determine how or by whom the disturbance,"—in which Walkinshaw had reportedly "nearly been killed by the Calcutta coolies"—was started. The Indians testified that one of their number was struck by the proprietor first, and only then was he confronted by the rest of the indenteds. The

Sirdar, Henry Singh, failed to corroborate an important aspect of Walkinshaw's allegation—that Walkinshaw had fainted—and Fagan who had served in India believed the Sirdar: he was a "high-blooded *Rajpoot* whose evidence in India would be believed," he said. Lying would have lowered his status.[386] In the course of the Inquiry several inadequacies in the administration of indenture came to light. The following extract from the inquiry darkens Walkinshaw's aura of irresponsibility:

"*Huggins*: Have you now with you Dr. Meikleham's Register or Book of the sick from the first period of your receipt of coolies showing their names and their medical treatment, if so produce it to the Court?

Walkinshaw: From the time of their arrival down to the 19th of July no such book was kept, I not being aware that such was required of me. I now produce the Book kept since then.

Huggins: By virtue of your oath when was the sick book, now produced[,] commenced?

Walkinshaw: The 19th of July [1846]."[387]

This would have been deeply embarrassing to proponents of indenture who argued that Indians had access to medical treatment in Trinidad unavailable to them in India. Here was a case of a fairly literate and literary planter who suggested he was not aware of his obligations per indenture agreements. Dr Meikelham was also a planter who, more than a year after Indians had begun arriving, appeared as badly informed about the need for regular medical visits and timely treatment. The doctor was partly responsible for the death of Kundappa, the laborer who had ghastly sores on the soles of his feet, but who was moved by donkey-cart to another estate with upon the doctor's advice.

The medical needs and records of employees is a rather basic aspect of the indenture arrangements and Walkinshaw did not, as we discover below, excuse Indians for not being familiar with the new regulations in Trinidad. The sin of omission on Walkinshaw's part would have been overlooked but for his late payment of wages and failure to provide warm clothing, or even food in a timely fashion, to the East Indians who worked on his estate.

During the course of 1846 the Agent-General or Protector of Immigrants in Trinidad, Major Fagan, attempted to live up to the literal functions of his position. This was uniquely the first and last time a Protector would so challenge a planter: Fagan was destined to resign. Even before the charge of assault was laid against the indenteds by Walkinshaw, Fagan had informed Lord Harris that he had found the management of the Clydesdale Cottage estate wanting. In a rather coincidental twist, Walkinshaw had written a letter dated 12 August 1846 to the Colonial Secretary, an influential official in Trinidad then, whom most tried to befriend. In his letter, Walkinshaw made the case for harsher punishment of indented workers, and suggested that Indians who left the estate without passes should "forfeit one month's wages," that when fewer than six tasks a week were performed, the laborer should lose his Sunday rations, and he also proposed wage cuts of between two and four weeks for offenses such as eating cane, being drunk and for "disorderly" behaviour. Walkinshaw's enthusiasm to reduce the pittance in wages indenteds received—and on his estate irregularly—verges on sadism, as he had sworn that he was not aware of medical, food and wage requirements pertaining to the indenture system. By another coincidence the letter was not sent to Arthur White, the Colonial Secretary, on 12 August; the alleged assault on Walkinshaw occurred on 13 August and a *post scriptum* included the news of that day.

Governor Harris informed the Secretary for Colonies that Major Fagan had reported well before 12 August about Indian workers' complaints regarding their "not be[ing] properly supplied and were therefore discontented." After the Governor had received a copy of the letter addressed to White, Major Fagan and a local Magistrate were sent to Walkinshaw's estate. They found "Mr Walkinshaw had already laid a charge of assault against four of the coolys." Lord Harris took the singular measure of depriving Walkinshaw of the entire force of Indian workers: "I have felt it my duty, however painful," Harris wrote Earl Grey, "to remove" the workers from Mr. Walkinshaw's charge. He also informed the Colonial Secretary that he had found "considerable slackness to say the least in many of the proprietors and managers of Estates complying with the regulations," notably those pertaining to clothing and other necessities. He concluded with what might have seemed like the final nail in a coffin, "Mr. Walkinshaw had been in the habit of hitting and kicking them [Indian workers] in a most unjustifiable manner."[388]

Walkinshaw's clever defence, apart from the effort to ally with the Government Secretary, was to blame the authorities for having been too lenient with the indenteds. He reserved a special vehemence toward Fagan, who received many not very subtle insults during the Inquiry itself. On the 21 August, in the course of appealing to have certain documents for his defence, Walkinshaw offered this apology: "My conscience tells me that [I] must change my nature ere I could *willingly* wound the feelings of any human being; far less *intentionally* offer disrespect to a Magistrate. Assuredly in the whole course of my life I never had my patience put to so severe a test . . . [and] I did at one period of the proceedings allude in as mild a manner as I could to what I conceived a very marked bias on the part of Major Fagan . . . against me."

In response to Walkinshaw's repeated lack of knowledge of the indenture regulations, Fagan had sent a copy of them to him on 11 August 1846. This may have alerted the planter to his own omissions and neglect of the regulations. Hence the strategic letter to Arthur White. In the course of that letter Walkinshaw mentioned the problems with the indented worker, "Bitchie, who is much addicted to rum-drinking," and who had assaulted two fellow laborers and a constable who was called "to preserve the peace." When Bitchie was subdued by two other constables requested by Walkinshaw from the adjoining estate, Bitchie was marched off to prison for five days. Walkinshaw did not think the punishment severe enough and the magistrate, Knox, had refused to take the matter to court because the matter fell under the jurisdiction of

Major Fagan. Walkinshaw cited too, the case of Girdarry, who not only absented himself for nine days but who was guilty of "exposing his private parts to the Creole females."

Although Girdarry too found himself in prison, Walkinshaw was not satiated, perhaps because Bitchie and Girdarry found prison food better and more regularly given than at Clydesdale. The "criminals" returned with positive accounts of prison conditions: "Police very good place [. . .] plenty of rice and no work." Laurence noted this peculiar problem in the early years of Indian immigration, that of preventing indenteds welcoming jail-time because conditions there were sometimes better than on certain plantations. Managers who considered themselves good "disciplinarians" bragged how they had mastered the art of alternating punishment among jail, the hospital, monetary fines and extra labor.[389]

With respect to non-payment of wages, Walkinshaw blamed Major Fagan for having "peremptorily ordered me to pay on the last day of each month," when he had previously paid workers fortnightly. The laborers had become sour over this change and had refused to work on 26th, 27th and 28th July: "I was at great pains to show them that I was acting by the [Protector's] order— but in vain and because I would not issue rice to them unless they worked they armed themselves with sticks and surrounded my House intimating their determination to kill and eat the *Sirdar* unless I would give them rice. I was at the time bedfast from dysentery—and fearing that they might go to extremities—I gave them a day's rations on their promise to resume work the next day. . . . "[390]

There was no resumption of estate labor the next morning. No sooner had the indenteds seen their tasks measured for them than they returned to the barracks. In the absence of any explanation as to why laborers who had in fact turned out in the field changed their minds, one might surmise that the migrants thought the tasks unusually large. A "leader" of the migrants was sent off to the police, but the others followed in protest.

We might note the selective memory and obedience to regulations on Walkinshaw's part; he ignored instructions regarding food and supplies from the magistrates because they accrued to the benefit of the workers, but the alleged suggestion of delaying wages was immediately adopted. In his lengthy note to Arthur White, Walkinshaw had alluded to problems at a neighboring estate: "Mr La Croix of Fallerton Estate was pelted with stones and mud lately by his gang . . . unless a very severe example is made, and that immediately," the immigrant laborers would be incapable of improvement. Already, Walkinshaw added, "They are incorrigible thieves."

The subsequent history of indenture in Trinidad confirmed that the Walkinshaws won over the Fagans and that the big losers were first, free labor, including that of Indians; secondly, fair-minded whites like Major Fagan; and thirdly, the entire post-emancipation society-in-formation. Especially, because slavery had not yielded full freedom. "The system of indenture was one thing where the Ordinance[s] . . . were concerned. The reality was a horse of a different colour," Eric Williams had observed. Williams found irony in the British having appointed a Protector of Slaves to protect the slaves from their masters and for Indian indenteds the equivalent officer was the "Protector of Immigrants [who] was in effect the protector against immigrants." The whips of slavery gave way to a "system of indenture [where] the principal incentive to labour was the jail. Indentured labour was, to paraphrase Carlyle, slavery plus a constable."[391]

We came to agree with evaluations such as Williams' with some reluctance because Walkinshaw, as we detail below, displayed those qualities in human beings one is literally amazed at encountering, despite an intellectual awareness that all kinds of personalities obtain among our species. Walkinshaw was eventually investigated over three separate cases of brutality. The Clydesdale Cottage incidents were the first, but summarized in the charges of the indented worker, "Jhandoo" against Walkinshaw. Jhandoo had been left sick and starving without any visits for five days, even from a doctor. In those five days, he also received no food. The charges in general indicated that the proprietor "was in the habit of doubling the size of the normal task, forcing labourers to work from 6 am to 5:30 pm, and denying them rations until the task was done, often a two-day affair." The second matter of investigation concerned the death of Kundappa due to "ulcerated feet [being] left unattended until it was too late." The third related to Beechook who had been ill for a week but on the first day back at work, Walkinshaw "beat and kicked" him for no reason other than that Beechook sat "down in the field to rest during work." To make matters worse, Walkinshaw had offered the victim twenty dollars *not* to report the incident to Fagan.[392] Yet Walkinshaw's was not the only controversy in this period, nor was he the only planter found wanting in terms of employers' duties to Indians.

The incidents during and after the case involving a Mr Justice Anderson, owner of Carolina Estate, hastened the end of Major Fagan's career. Anderson had assaulted one of the indenteds, Bhodu, and cut a wound on his head with a whip during a dispute over delayed wages. The planter refused to pay the arrears, despite Fagan's reminders, even as late as May 1848. Anderson counter-charged Fagan with seeking to force a wage raise for Indians to 40 cents a day.[393]

The fact that Walkinshaw was not the only example of a cruel planter in Trinidad may have persuaded Major Fagan to write to London and suggest a total reorganization of the labor system. Although Fagan was not opposed to the system itself, he called for systematizing it and plantation management in the West India colonies. His confidence that "the same principles of action that influenced my career in India govern me" was resented by colonial Trinidad especially because Fagan found the situation so horrendous there that it made "oriental barbarism, in its darkest day," look like "civilization in comparison with the moral destitution prevalent in the West India colonies." Fagan blamed the objectionable quality of managers on the plantations:

As a result of this system, men of straw, on becoming appointed attorneys, rapidly rise to affluence and apparent consequence, living at the same time in princely style, while the absent proprietor gradually sinks into comparative poverty . . . It is obvious that, to carry out such a system of plunder and corruption, the overseers must be selected from a low and demoralised class, to whom a license is thus unavoidably conceded, to practice frauds to any extent for which his situation may afford opportunity. In time this worthy aspires to, and actually acquires, the management of an estate.[394]

That Fagan did not call for an end to Indian indenture, that he and Harris had jointly authored the first pass laws which London could not allow, that he sympathized with absentee owners, were all ignored because he had dared to speak his mind. Or, that he had sufficiently demonstrated that if necessary, he would confront planter-owners like Walkinshaw and Anderson, and this filled them with indignation and dread. Also, in May 1848 a melee involving Fagan occurred at the governor's residence in Port of Spain. The magistrate had accompanied some 35 Indian indenteds to Lord Harris. The indenteds sought redress from Fagan because they had not been paid for seven months. The Indians, along with Fagan himself, were ejected by Thomas Johnston, the Acting Colonial Secretary.[395] The dominant class now spoke its mind. For "the sake of our adopted country, of our own self-respect, we protest against the truth [sic] of the villainous picture which he has drawn of the inhabitants of this colony," and the punishment of social ostracism was ochestrated against Major Fagan. He was promised that he would "meet only with the contempt and indignation" for his "libels."[396]

It is not clear whether Major Fagan resigned or refused to accept more of the indignities he had endured while performing his duties. Harris had suspended him following the melee in May. In any event, Fagan left Trinidad forever in August.

Ironically, some of Walkinshaw's more outrageous ideas on making indenture more stringent on Indians eventually became law in Trinidad; Major Fagan received the utmost scorn and cold shoulder from both planters and the governor. The latter flirted with justice for the Indians but when confronted by the political will of the planters, Harris distanced himself from Fagan and justice. Despite the accolades received by Fagan from Indians who came to trust him as their only hope for redress in Trinidad, and the coloured newspaper *Trinidad Spectator* praised his knowledge of Indian languages and customs and other attributes—it recalled his "sterling qualities as a man"—Fagan was not forgiven by colonial Trinidad.[397]

Within a few years of Fagan's departure, Indians were "coerced" into three-year contracts with fines of L2 10s each for the next two years unless they were indented for a full five years. Free return passages were withdrawn; after an "industrial service" of 10 years Indians could leave, but only if they contributed L7 15s for the return passage.[398]

By 1870 if not sooner, Walkinshaw's desire that Indian workers who left the plantations without tickets or passes ought to lose a month's wages was adopted in terms of 30 days imprisonment for males. An "emigrant" had to survive the long wait at Indian ports and the 100-day voyage on a sailing vessel, only to discover the odds of getting a master who was psychologically locked into a slavery mindset might be greater than one who defied his milieu and island racialism. And of course there were the police, pass laws, ordinances, courts and prisons. Those who were allowed to buy out their indentures did so with money borrowed at usurious rates of interest; such sacrifices spawned a proto-capitalist class. Those whose masters refused to release them from contracts at any price courageously stood the test of time, took advantage of the generosity of the evangelical missions, and gave their children a chance at the better lives for which these adults might have left their homeland. Gradually, there was an inter-generational adoption of a creole or Indo-Trinidadian value system, blending not only East and West but also melding the three great traditions of Hinduism, Islam and Christianity. By the 1880s, the elements of a middle class were in place among Indo-Trinidadians so as to hold its own, incrementally, against remaining resentment. Arora's study acknowledges the Governor Sir Arthur Gordon who began land-grant commutations for repatriation, and the Protector Dr. Henry Mitchell, were more sympathetic to the Indian plight in Trinidad and aided them in some ways.[399]

Both by their value to the British plantation and by their peculiar cultural background, Indians were the most consistently exploited segment among Trinidad's laborers in the nineteenth century. This is not to say that Portuguese and Europeans or African indenteds enjoyed an island paradise upon migrating to Trinidad; Chapter Two has already argued the contrary. In terms of absolute numbers, duration and intensity of their ordeal as free laborers, the Indo-Trinidadian case remains unparalleled for that island's history. After leading the fight for Emancipation, Britain gradually replaced African slavery with Indian servitude. Oddly, too, laws which the Colonial Office rejected as draconian in the initial years of indenture had become acceptable in later years. Additional research may reveal whether this was the result of changes in thinking and attitudes at the Colonial Office or of effective lobbying by planters and their allies.

CHAPTER FOUR

SOCIALIZING THE IMMIGRANTS;
SEGREGATING THE SCHOOLS

"Until the last ten or fifteen years the Indians of the island
have been characterized as the most illiterate ethnic group
and the group most resistant to education. It was estimated
[in] 1945 that at least 60 percent of the Indians were illiterate
in any language."[400]
Paragraphs 138 and 141 of the Keenan Report: "The new
education system was established in 1851, but up to the
present time no attempt whatever has been made to
comprehend the Coolies under its provisions . . . Indeed I
did not meet with a score of Coolie children in all the ward
schools of the island . . . One of the cleverest children I fell
in with was a Coolie boy in the borough school, Port of
Spain. Indeed, wherever I met with a Coolie child who had
been a reasonable time at school, I found him, in all the best
qualities of the mind, to be immeasurably superior to the
creole of African blood. In powers of discernment and
reflection, the Indian ranks high, the creole low."[401]

Education in nineteenth-century Trinidad appears, from an Indian
perspective, to have been yet another experience in segregation.
Schools kept migrants from India a separate and distinct group
much as the plantations had done with their lives spatially on
isolated estates. Whereas Indians needed passes for visits outside

the geographically imprisoning plantations, they needed to have been free and accepted for thousands of jobs in the towns before they could benefit from the urban bias of the education regime in the years up to 1870. It is illuminating that the only "school" for Indians during the first 25 years of their residence in Trinidad was the Tacarigua Orphanage. Founded in 1857, it was evidence of the many deaths among Indian adults, the inability of a community under indenture to care for its defenseless children, and that orphans were more fortunate in comparison to the thousands of other Indian children who labored with, if not as, adults on the plantations all day long.

We could summarize the development of education in colonial Trinidad as having occurred over five or more periods. In the first phase up to 1834, Trinidad lagged behind other colonies in providing education for non-Europeans, namely the slaves and the free coloureds. A second phase between 1835 and 1845 neatly coincided with the period before the arrival of the Indians, but when charity or endowed schools took the lead over governmental efforts at public education. In the third period 1845-1869, the Indian presence and numbers received island-wide concern but while there was a perceptible increase in schools for black and white Trinidadians, the education of Indian children was sorely neglected. In the fourth phase from 1870 to the end of our period, Indians made gains in education in separate Canadian Presbyterian mission schools, but these did not bring Indians the change in curriculum and job opportunities as did the ward schools for other Trinidadians. There is a fifth phase from 1890 onwards when government and denominational schools focussed on separate geographical areas for expansion in a tense but generally workable division of common efforts at education.

The colonial state in Trinidad did less for its masses both before and after Emancipation in 1834 than had neighboring colonies at a similar stage of development. The vacuum was filled by the churches and various denominational schools. Recent writers have suggested that until the oil boom after 1973, the post-colonial state under Eric Williams did as little for education as had the colonial state. The debate about the divisiveness and waste of resources under church schools which raged on for most of the nineteenth century, found new life when Williams charged that denominational education put the "national culture at risk."[402]

Although we end our account of educational development in 1888, problems with teacher training and shortage of school places evident in our study, endured into Williams' tenure as Premier. In striving for balance in our discussion, we situate Trinidad's efforts within its historical context. That context was one in which Britain had already discovered the value of public education and regular school attendance, and also made available the Negro Education Grant to the colonies (L30,000 sterling for the years 1835-45).[403] In spite of being a colony, Trinidad did have choices and opportunities for the early promotion of education. It received encouragement from London, as in the "elaborate scheme of agricultural education" of 1847 but which Trinidad felt "no obligation to implement." Planters in Barbados and Jamaica set up charity or "endowed" schools during their "slave plantation phase." Trinidad's planters did not. Other colonies improved their rates of literacy through acceptance of evangelical missions and their schools. Again, Trinidad did not. One writer commented that Trinidad, "went through its slave plantation phase without a golden age of sugar prosperity which might have released the philanthropic urges of successful planters and merchants."[404]

Although the wealthy classes of Trinidad could and did send some of their children—sons in preference to daughters—to European schools, there remained an educational need for their younger children and for the poor who could not send even their first-born to private schools. Many shortlived private schools did appear as did schools and private tutors for girls. Trinidad was not without some educated individuals but this distinction was generally the preserve of the elites, which included a handful of coloured families.

After the arrival of the Indians in 1845, Trinidad had a choice as to whether to deploy Law or Schools to regulate order, promote economic growth and socialize a diverse population. In Chapter Three, we saw that the laws and regulations, police and courts were deployed against Indian laborers who comprised one-third of the population by 1870. That these sometimes unjust actions did not apply to other non-European groups with similar intensity may point to the priorities of the labor-hungry plantation colony. Yet, all of Trinidad needed schools especially for socialization and long-term stability.

Did Trinidad rely on Law alone to educate and socialize Africans and Asians between the 1830s and 1888? One scholar has indicated that such a situation did obtain in Trinidad right up to 1900, a society whose *raison d'etre* was the production of staples for imperial Britain and that slaves and their successors were expected to be obedient laborers and not much more.[405] There was no school for Indians between 1845 and 1869. In 1869, a Canadian Presbyterian minister, the Reverend John Morton, began teaching three pupils at his doorstep.[406] This was duplicated by a few other Churches up to 1870. One is urged to ask, therefore, whether post-emancipation governments did not appreciate schools as vehicles for socialization and economic development?[407]

It is tempting to agree that a myopia typified officialdom's efforts and outcomes in nineteenth-century Trinidad. Yet, fear of an education which could be liberating and therefore dangerous to the interests of the elites had all but dissipated with the Emancipation Act. Formal schooling made more sense when slavery and the whip had just lost their place in the freedmen's lives. But Trinidad did not seem to appreciate such thinking. One may be dealing here with a question about the nature and degree of balance between Trinidad's reliance upon law and education for socializing its populace after the demise of slavery. The context—a colonial one where English was yet to become the *lingua franca*—made the educational road problematic.

One may proceed by conceding that the presence of numerous schools is not an infallible index of a superior program of education and socialization; nor would the obverse always obtain. Especially where societies take a clearly different route from a defunct philosophy of education, the lack of infrastructure for schools become overriding factors in the rate of success. Such infrastructure would comprise geographical or county divisions, personnel training and supervision, budgets, spatial planning and related factors of easy access. The latter includes culture, language and the costs in releasing children's time and money from households. Some of the infrastructure necessary for educational development in Trinidad were in place in 1838 or about the time the Indians arrived in 1845. Yet other evidence presents Trinidad as a laggard in a comparison with colonies like Guyana; the sources concede that Trinidad had problems of geography and a more dispersed population and competing local whites—Protestant and Catholic, or British, French and Spanish. Education became a vehemently contested terrain among whites, thereby relegating non-whites to the background. With hindsight one can too easily read the mistakes and opportunities which were lost in Trinidad. British government and non-governmental funding, the end of slavery, and the presence of Churches were important availing conditions for rapid advancement of education. The attitudes of different sub-groups became the major obstacle to formulating an effective educational policy in Trinidad.

A comprehensive plan of education was recognized as necessary if not inevitable especially after Indians began approaching the proportion of a quarter of total population in the 1860s. Until the very end of that decade, however, the only government school provided the Indians was an orphanage where a few dozen children lived in a commune that aimed at self-sufficiency. Demography might have focussed attention on the educational imperative even if the indenture agreements did not specify a right to free education.[408] Western languages would have spread faster and festivals like Carnival and Hosay would have interpenetrated the society and become better understood, thereby reducing white fears about festivals turning into demonstrations against them.

Had Trinidad taken the education of free coloureds seriously
during Sir Ralph Woodford's tenure as governor (1814-28), a
foundation for mass education would have been in place sooner.
That foundation, we argue, might have been readily added to by
Governor Henry McLeod. Woodford disallowed coloureds from
opening independent public schools but in the 1820s consented
to the opening of *Cabildo* schools—the Cabildo being a town
council which endured beyond Spanish rule. Two such schools,
one for each gender, had begun offering an elementary education
"to whites and free coloureds of lesser means" in Port of Spain, but
Woodford's "strong theme" remained a stable "and ordered society
in which every race and class would know its place." After the
establishment of the Indians, the intra-white, the black-coloured,
and black-white faultlines of Trinidad society were replaced by a
coming together of Christian groups in one camp in opposition to
"a non-Christian oriental . . . mature, alien, resistant culture . . .
different from all [the] other peoples in the colony."[409] Yet there
was no effort to westernize Indians.

Even with the ex-slaves, a recognition of the Colony's duty "to
mould them into good citizens," had urged Trinidad's governors
to seek a plan of education which would "consider their condition
and necessities."[410] But neither creoles alone nor the incoming
Indians and their acclimatization to the dominant norms were the
dominant concerns in the educational discussions which followed.
The other non-Indian groups included coloureds, ex-slaves and
white Catholics, some of whom were suspicious of British
educational objectives. A complicating factor was that literacy levels,
cultural values and popular fetes were divergent among the different
sections of the population, within and across racial lines.[411] The
Indians did not create Trinidad's complexities and divisions; they
simply added another layer. But in being a non-Christian layer,
the Indian presence reminded the rest of Trinidad of the culture
they had come to share.

From an Indian perspective, colonial Trinidad was agile, even
enthusiastic in preparing the jailhouse rather the schoolhouse

for East Indians. Such a startling statement was shared in 1869 by Patrick Keenan who was sent by Britain to report on education in Trinidad (see below). The jails and the confines of the plantation were the only avenues of socializing Indian laborers into what was expected of them and their children. Gone was slavery, but a society to replace its legacy of attitudes and institutions remained to be created. Production of export crops was still the priority in metropole and colony, and insufficient thought was given to the day when indented laborers would be free of the plantations, just as the slaves had broken their chains.

The Keenan Report on the State of Education in 1869 had noted that official Trinidad linked police actions and schools:

"The police arrangements are admirable . . . I have just suggested how the police regulations might be made ancillary to an effective inspection of the schools. I believe that an extension of the police organization, by aiding in the suppression of squatting, by favouring the settlement of remote places, by securing order, and inspiring public confidence in the Government, would materially aid in promoting the establishment, on a permanent basis, of a flourishing system of education."[412]

Public education and its socializing role gained respect slowly in Trinidad where the positive contribution of Governor Henry McLeod (1840-1846) was crucial. Despite obvious advantages for Trinidad, affordable mass education as a great leveller—anticipated by McLeod—was not the most pressing concern for the Secretary of State for Colonies. Formal education was thus a laggard in Trinidad.

An explanation for the island's entanglement in delays, detours and distractions was intimately connected with its dominant elites being sharply divided between Protestant and Catholic, or British and French-Spanish camps. British Trinidad had tried to blend Protestant and Catholic traditions in the erstwhile Spanish colony, but the demand for equality on either side became difficult to satisfy. The failure to develop a broad view of education resulted in existing schools making policies of anglicization a substitute for education. The incoming indented Indians spoke almost no English, yet nothing was done to systematically teach English to them and their children. In fact, Indians were as likely to learn a patois of Spanish or French as they were to receive training in British ways. Some of the first Indians could not communicate with Trinidadians: "The *sirdars* on the Cedar Hill and Carolina estates who speak Creole French with fluency, acted as . . . interpreters."[413]

C.J. Latrobe who had prepared an earlier education Report, "Negro Education, British Guiana and Trinidad" (1839) praised neighboring Guiana and explained Trinidad's failures. Guina planters had already voted L34,000 for the "dissemination of religious instruction" in 1838. Trinidad's planters would respond slowly and visibly when the Canandian Presbyterians began setting up mission schools after 1870. Latrobe explained that Trinidad "has labored under greater disadvantages" than other West Indian colonies, "from the prevalence of the French and Spanish languages," and of the Catholic religion, and from the way in which its "motley population is found scattered in distinct and often isolated groups. . . . "[414] The 1797 Capitulation Agreement included the guarantee to Spain that the rights of its former Catholic and coloured subjects would be respected.

Trinidad also failed to bring the various social and racial groups in any one public place for any length of time, except to produce sugar and other staples. Leisure pursuits were generally non-existent and as late as 1884, there was no theater. Sports and exercise, especially for girls and even during school hours, were unusual.[415] Oddly, the disparate subcultures mixed only at the horse races.[416] Among whites, the seasonal fairs were about the only break from the monotony of cocoa and sugar[417] but for a minority among this minority who joined the fetes of Carnival and Hosay. The Public Library in 1858 had 80 subscribing members.[418] It had been opened in 1851 when ward schools opened on the basis of the efforts made by McLeod and his successor, Lord Harris.

A study of educational development in Trinidad begs the question about socialization. Indeed, nineteenth-century educational debates in the island devolved into narrow debates about the rights of various Christian denominations. A missionary recounts, "Closely allied to matters ecclesiastical was the educational question. The history of education in Trinidad reveals a prolonged struggle."[419]

The post-emancipation policies of Trinidad's colonial government suggest that socialization was translated into anglicization directed first at French creoles and other Catholics, then at Africans and Asians.[420] We believe that the want of more leaders like McLeod, Harris and Sir Arthur Gordon led to official failures in education and socialization. The latter processes are interconnected much more than Trinidad seemed to concede at least up to 1870. This failure explains why the Colony had to allow outsiders, the Canadian Presbyterians, to do the job which it had hardly taken up as late as 1870, according to Inspector Patrick J. Keenan. We examine the Canadian Presbyterians and their work among the Indians, below.

By the 1850s all the major population personae were on the Trinidad stage; those who were rising in numbers were balanced by the tremendous political clout of French, Spanish and British planters and personalities. To some whites, the island may have seemed unmanageable because the institutions of socialization— church, school, leisure activities and festivals—were not uniformly accepted by the various actors on the island stage.

4.1 NOTABLE EFFORTS AND CONTROVERSIES IN EDUCATION

In the controversy over anglicization as with most conflicts in public life Indians were compelled onto a middle ground if not the background largely because they had been brought over to exert their bodies, not their minds. The Hindus and Muslims were incidental to the education debates, despite their numbers. When discussion about society or education did extend to the futures of non-Europeans, the complexities of Trinidad became confounded with preconceived racial notions and biases.[421] The many valid reasons why Indian parents would not or could not send their children to school were reduced to stereotypical explanations. Mutual antipathy between Indian and African was assumed, which continue to revive images of "weak coolies" and the "negro quashee."[422] As late as 1888, Rev. Moore of the Church Missionary Society thought that segregated schools existed in India which necessitated separate Indian schools in Trinidad.[423] Such erroneous thinking conflated "caste" and race.

Where British law and integrated schools[424] would have been the natural means of socializing a colonial potpourri of peoples, the assumed African-Indian differences may have led educators and churchmen to maintain the divide. On the other hand, French and Spanish creoles resisted perceived anglicization and violations of the letter and spirit of the Anglo-Spanish Agreement of 1797. In seeking to avoid discord and too rapid a transformation of Spanish institutions and laws, Trinidad retained certain Iberian traditions long after the British takeover of Trinidad. The Cabildo of the capital, for instance, was replaced with a Town Council only in 1840.[425] Those Portuguese immigrants who were Catholic were provided with a minister at government expense.[426] A few Spanish laws continued in Trinidad well into this century.[427] These concessions were not timely or adequate enough to get Catholics to accept British ideas on education.

Individual governors did seek to allay Catholic concerns; in fact, "successive English Governors bore the title of 'Patron of the Catholic Church'" through 1844. An Ordinance 'For the better regulation of the duties of the United Church of England and Ireland in the colony, and for ensuring the more effectual performance of the same' (1846), finally gave advantages to the Church of England in that the mother country's ecclesiastical laws became supreme. This state of religious inequality was resolved by

Arthur Gordon in 1870 with the repeal of that ordinance.[428] This set the proper tone for an island-wide plan of education. Until 1870, then, a single-minded attention to, and plan for, mass education had not been possible.

A minority of slave children had been educated along with a minority of whites and coloureds before Emancipation and the arrival of the Indians, but "the education of the negro" was continued "under every disadvantage." Colonial legislatures, proprietors and administrators "were openly adverse" to public education. Rather than a purely racist phenomenon, concluded C.J. Latrobe in 1839, "the restricted principle upon which the parochial and so-called free schools were conducted," reflected the uncaring attitude of the age. Donald Wood accepted that interpretation.[429] Yet Britain itself was promoting schools.

At this time in the West Indies, the "few private teachers" were sometimes regarded aas being "of the lowest standard in point of qualification."[430] It would be at the turn of the century before teachers were adequately trained in the island.[431] Coloureds constituted the vast majority of teachers at least up until Keenan's investigation which found only three whites among a total of 34 teachers. Keenan said he did "not venture to advance any objection" to this, but thought it "extremely desirable" that several "European female teachers" be hired. One is left to draw one's own conclusions from Keenan's opinion that this was of "the weightiest moral importance."[432] A later paragraph in the 1870 Report revealed that white parents were reluctant to send their girls to school partly because, "To some of the masters, exception is taken on the grounds of alleged immorality and . . . In one case the Catholic priest issued a positive interdict against the attendance of girls."[433] Such opinions might have impacted negatively on school attendance.

Following Emancipation, *de facto* segregation was promoted among Trinidadians,[434] with amicable "race-relations" coming to mean good relations between Catholic and Protestant whites only. Occasionally whites were foresighted regarding the non-European population. L.A.A. de Verteuil believed that the "adoption of a general and liberal system of primary instruction" had become essential, "not only to eradicate the ignorance so deeply rooted in the soil of slavery," but also to acquaint the populace with English.[435] Little was achieved up to the 1850s, again because education was embroiled in questions of nationality and patriotism. Mixing education with thorny issues of faith and nationalism was blamed on a pro-British "attorney-general."[436]

The first major educational venture in Trinidad amounted to the adoption of the "Mico School System" as developed in Britain. The Mico Charity was the earliest educational force on the island, and significant for the region as a whole. In calling for a "gradual" spread of English and a critical assessment of the Mico schools, Henry McLeod distinguished himself as a preeminently fair governor. For one thing he discontinued government aid to the Mico Charity in 1840, when L500 had been given the previous year. He explained: "On proceeding to deliberate on this subject, therefore, I feel it my duty to . . . see whether [educational aims] cannot be attained, as Lord Glenelg hoped, through the aid of the Mico schools. If the Trustees of the Mico Charity would, at least in regard to Trinidad, so far consent to modify their Regulations as not to insist on the use of the Bible as a school book, I have no doubt that I should find little difficulty in carrying Lord Glenelg's intentions into effect."[437]

The use of the Protestant Bible as a textbook within the Mico school system became an issue; the Catholics "entertain[ed] strong objections" to it. McLeod was doubtful that the Charity would abandon the policy, concluding "there is little hope" of cooperation.[438] Two years earlier, the Latrobe investigation had saved its few positive words on Trinidad for the Mico schools. This was possibly because Latrobe had equated education with christianization and anglicization. In contrast, McLeod saw how a secular approach might strive for fairness. Latrobe thought the Mico Charity offered the "promise to overcome differences hitherto existing in the way of bringing an efficient and sound" education to those with "differing forms of faith, and especially of the large

Roman Catholic population." He evinced optimism—"a strong probability of success"—for the Mico schools.[439]

Latrobe's optimism had been presumed on white Catholics accepting the Mico schools as neutral. In reality, Lady Mico was its benefactor, and the ruse of using the Protestant Bible in the education of Catholic pupils backfired. Catholics protested to McLeod and began looking for alternatives, while some Catholic parents continued to send children to Mico schools.

Within a year of the Mico Charity inaugurating its work in Trinidad, two Catholic seminaries—for each of the genders—were established in Port of Spain under the patronage of Bishop Dr. Macdonnell. St. George's College enrolled boys "from all parts of the island," where the French and Spanish languages were included. In promoting their own languages without excluding English, Catholics took the moral high ground. By 1858 this dayschool had 57 pupils who each paid "4 dollars per month." The second seminary called 'The Convent' was founded by the Ladies of St. Joseph "a religious sisterhood originating in France." They did not receive government aid yet provided free education to "300 poor girls," in reading, writing, scripture, history, "the four elementary rules of arithmetic, needlework, and the church catechism," plus a "higher education" for another 120 girls.[440]

The Mico schools proceeded to found 24 "Mico system schools" in Trinidad by 1838. Mr. Bilby was the Charity's Agent and the superintendent in charge of the schools. Bilby himself lived in Port of Spain where four Mico schools were in operation. There were five Mico schools each in Naparima and Diego Martin, three in Manzanilla and seven in Carenage. All were run as "public schools," with 1,562 pupils. Girls constituted 34 percent of pupils attending the Mico schools.[441]

It engendered hope that a group of private schools enrolled pupils "of different religions," in Port of Spain. D. Evans instructed 17 boys; W. Jenkins taught another 32; Mrs Brambley ran a private school for 17 girls; W. Clunes, T. Hinde, Mr. Turin and P. Guise conducted private schools for boys, numbering 37, 35, 11, and 29 respectively. Enrolment totalled 178.[442]

When the Mico schools declined in the mid-1840s[443], it did so for at least two reasons. First, the system was a casualty of British economizing measures.[444] Secondly, in response to criticism of its veiled attempt to propagandize Catholic pupils, McLeod had not recommended any government grants to the Charity since 1840. The governor had met with Mr. Trew, Secretary of the Mico Charity in London, to plead removal of the Bible as a textbook in the case of Trinidad. Rather than accept compromise, the Charity began to focus its energy on areas such as Jamaica and the Bahamas. At the height of their work in Trinidad, the Mico Charity had 1,971 pupils on their registers but only 1,554 average attendances.[445] With its failure to modify policies in accordance with the local situation, Africans or Asians failed to benefit from the Mico schools and its bold legacy.

McLeod's sensitivity and sincerity in the interests of all Trinidadians was appreciated in 1858 already: Initially, "no distinction was drawn betwixt British and foreigners, and, I dare say, no essential difference of feeling existed. There has been lately, however, a tendency to abandon that broad and just cause for the pursuit of a narrow . . . line of policy [which] has for its principal supporter and organ, our present attorney-general . . . [His allies] contend that the habits and feelings of the inhabitants *must* be *purely* British . . . They account it almost a crime, on the part of *foreigners*, to be unable to speak a language with which they are unacquainted. . . ."[446]

Both the Catholic Bishop and Governor Hill, McLeod's predecessor, were so casual about the interests of their denominations that they were criticized by their own. The Catholics were piqued that their bishop was not voluble about the bias in Mico schools; and Rev. Mulhauser of the Church Missionary Society commented, "though a Protestant, [Hill] bends his old knees publicly in the streets of the town in adoration to the consecrated wafer.'"[447]

Just as inter-denominational schools were rare, so too were schools with both boys and girls. Protestant schools numbered seven in the capital, two of them coeducational, and a roll of 609 pupils. Girls constituted 42 percent or 259 of all pupils. Two public schools in Savanna Grande were also co-educational, where 31 of 72 pupils and 11 of another 21 were girls. P.E. Westmoreland taught 92 boys in San Fernando, but the "mode of instruction" was: "Bible without Note or Comment[ary]; partly the National" system. Boys were also enrolled at Cocorite (25), St. Josephs (25), Tacarigua (90), Chaguanas (34), Couva (190), Savonetta (197). Total enrolment thus came to 1,651.[448]

Protestants had 267 more children in school than Catholics. There were 1,651 children in Protestant schools of whom 21 percent were girls, and there were 1,029 Catholic children in parochial schools, 48 percent of them girls. Almost as many Catholic girls were in schools as were boys, but only a fifth of pupils at Protestant schools were girls. While this is somewhat ameliorated by Protestants accounting for 62 percent of all children at school, when Protestant and Catholic girls attending schools are juxtaposed, 27 percent more Catholic girls attended schools. That a Catholic priest had cautioned against sending girls to schools with coloured male teachers had apparently not translated into a lower female attendance at Catholic schools.[449]

McLeod's approach after 1840 was open-minded and fair toward Trinidad's multicultural population; success, however, depended upon local political and financial leadership.

4.2 MCLEOD: TRINIDAD'S FIRST

EDUCATION GOVERNOR

Many if not most of the British governors of Trinidad wanted to promote the English language as well as Protestant culture in Trinidad. Of them McLeod was the first to work on a detailed

plan of education which might promote British ways without
antagonizing the influential Catholic segment of the island. Lord
Harris was fortunate to succeed McLeod in 1846, thereby adding
final improvements and his name to a plan that had been five years
in formation. Before departing Trinidad, McLeod had written a
despatch informing the Colonial Office in London about the details
of a plan he and the Legislature had devised.

The Original Correspondence files are unequivocal in showing
that from 1 May 1840 until his departure in 1846, McLeod wrote
persistent despatches on education. He was not deterred by an
unresponsive Lord John Russell in 1840 or changes at the Colonial
Office even when it entailed repetitious notes to Lord Stanley.

On 1 May 1840, McLeod had written Lord John Russell upon
"a question . . . on which I am most anxious to have your Lordship's
early opinion and commands, I mean that of education."[450] What
had brought home the issue for McLeod was the competitive
demands for financial aid then being requested by various churches:
"On my arrival here a letter was placed in my hands from the
Bishop of Barbados in which His Lordship expresses his intention
of calling for the assistance of government in the support of seven
additional schools—and a very few days elapsed before another
application was submitted to me from the Roman Catholic
Bishop . . . for the support of four additional schools which have
been opened under the auspices of his clergy. I learn that there is a
like application from the Wesleyan Ministers now on the
Council a Table, and I know that other sects will prefer similar
claims."[451]

McLeod pondered the implications and consequences of his
response. While he appreciated the interest in setting up schools,
he was not sure if this "originate[d] more in a spirit of rivalry or
jealousy than [being] regulated by any sound principle." This kind
of competition led to rival schools being opened in the same
neighborhoods without relevance to needs, numbers or economy.
On the other hand, government was being called upon to "fritter"
away funds, without a supervisory role or any other input. McLeod

then referred to the Latrobe Report and reiterated: "[T]here never was a country where some general system of education was more required than in Trinidad."[452]

The Colonial Office was informed that quite apart from the diversity attributed to recent immigrations, the island had a Catholic majority, while "the bulk of property l[ay] with Englishmen and Protestants." The widely dispersed population of diverse "creeds," left McLeod "only the alternative of devising some general scheme by which the rudiments of education" might be extended to all and "the gradual and general introduction of the English language ensured." McLeod felt as strongly about spreading the English language as other governors, but it is apparent that he wanted to proceed without offending the Catholic majority. This characteristic wisdom, sensitivity and concern for all Trinidadians is made McLeod a visionary and a democrat. When he protested the low wage rates that Burnley's group had decided upon for Indians, he was taking risks in the interests of fairness to safeguard a "simple-minded people." He had proposed that once a certain minimum wage was violated, the Indian laborers "should on that account [if they] wished . . . return" home at government expense.[453]

While McLeod's intervention on behalf of the Indians was ignored, he was equally sympathetic to the potential desire for landowning among blacks: The constant influx, however, of the large bodies of coloured people who are arriving here from the neighboring . . . islands and from America, make it incumbent on the Government to have some care for the future, and to provide for that state of things . . . when many of these Immigrants will emerge from the dependent condition of Laborers, with the means and desire to become Agriculturalists on their own account."[454]

This constitutes an important nuance to Brian Blout's point that Trinidad planters "manipulate[d] the laws" in order to "prevent small independent farmers gaining access to land."[455] A foresighted governor or two could thwart such designs.

McLeod did not think that many non-Europeans would become sugar planters, in part because large acreages were needed for this enterprise. Cocoa, on the other hand, was ideally suited to the small entrepreneur. If London were agreeable to selling Crown lands to the laboring classes, "I should have no hesitation in proposing to Your Lordship that certain districts and lines of Crown property should be marked out for sub-division into moderate lots", and for sale to individuals "on fair terms." McLeod again was adept at keeping the big picture in mind, as with the coincidental but vital anglicization role black North American immigrants could play. "[T]hey are a most valuable acquisition to this Colony," he wrote, "not only as tending to the more rapid spread of English customs and language," but also from their positive work ethic, their "correct moral conduct" and their religiousness. For all these reasons, they would "shew a valuable example which is much wanted" in Trinidad.[456]

Meanwhile the plan for education lay fallow. When he had had no response to his May 1840 inquiries, McLeod wrote again to the Colonial Office. In this despatch, he reiterated Trinidad's situation was unusual for a British colony. Apart from the Catholic-Protest divide, the large creole influx "renders the demand of an extension of the means of education of greater consequence every day."[457] These differences—"of language and religion"—made it "imperative" that a government-run system of education be adopted as soon as practicable. This would ensure fair and equal access to all and promote the English language.

Almost apologetic about his persistence, McLeod noted that two-thirds of Trinidad still spoke either Spanish or French "exclusively," whereas he considered it "absolutely necessary that people . . . claiming the benefit of British subjects," should speak English, if only to read the laws which governed them. The argument are prophetic in that poorly advertized restrictions on the Hosay festival, led to a tragedy in 1884. McLeod added: "I would therefore, respectfully claim Your . . . reference to my despatch before quoted, with the view to my receiving instructions on my mode of proceeding. I am the more induced to ask this, as the present system under which we are acting is to provide half of the salary of

the teachers of schools,—and I yesterday received a letter from the
Arch Deacon of Barbadoes [sic], in which he states his intention of
placing five additional schools on the list, and for which half of the
teachers salaries will be claimed. This may very probably call for a
similar demand on the part of the Roman Catholic Bishop."[458]

The Colonial Secretary had been tardy prior to vacating the
Secretaryship; his successor, Lord Stanley, finally addressed the
educational question in Trinidad on 8 January 1842.[459] Stanley
acknowledged that the question, "embarrassing enough in any of
the colonies is surrounded in Trinidad by peculiar difficulties."
With respect to English, Stanley thought the government ought
to "diffuse" it by every means in their "power" and that it was not
"unreasonable" to insist English "be made a *sine qua non* in every
school applying for aid." Stanley agreed with McLeod that the
colonial government not become party, through aid, to duplicating
denominational schools in areas where only one school sufficed. As
to withholding aid from schools not conducted along the lines of
"a single scheme," he was less sanguine, based on experience of
opposition in Ireland to the secular model. While that experience
gave Stanley doubts about the effectiveness of a similar route to
schooling in Trinidad, he hoped that a fairly representative Board
of Education might be a useful method of proceeding. By
"representative," Stanley meant the broad appeaal to all Christian
denominations. "I am of the opinion that if a Board could be
constituted," so that various denominations were fairly represented,
and if the clergy were mutually cooperative and cordial, "such a
system might be productive of great good in Trinidad." The
opposition of a single denomination might become "a serious
obstacle" to the introduction of the plan. In this eventuality, Stanley
suggested the adoption of the British practice of awarding annual
grants from the general revenues on the basis of attendance, results,
and so forth.

Stanley's experiences in Ireland did not make him averse to
McLeod experimenting with the Irish model in Trinidad: "In
conformity however with your wish expressed in your Despatch to

my predecessor of the 1 May 1840, I have given directions for supplying you with the principal rules and regulations under which the Irish system is at present carried on . . . [If] the result [is] such as I am afraid must be anticipated, it will be necessary to take steps for restricting within reasonable limits the liability of the Government to be called upon to aid in the establishment of schools of an exclusive character.[460]

By the mid 1840s, McLeod had concluded that Stanley was correct in doubting the efficacy of the secular model of education for Trinidad.[461] A Despatch printed in the *Parliamentary Papers* admits that the intended system "was met by great objections on the part of the English Church, as they seemed to think it had tended to deprive them of all control," read: advantage as given by the 1846 Ordinance. The established Church did not want to forego advantages accruing to it by being part of the ruling group and had opposed non-denominational education for this reason. Up to that time, McLeod's Government had continued to pay teachers' salaries, "irrespective of their religious tenets," and had accrued to the advantage of the Church of England. Its schools had "increased considerably in proportion to others." This windfall was being threatened by the withdrawal "of the Parliamentary grants, and some funds which were at the disposal of the bishop of the diocese." The colonial revenues could not absorb all these expenses. A vital plank in McLeod's platform of education could now be put forth: "After serious and mature consideration," he opted for "a system of secular education under proper supervision," and he enclosed the resolutions passed at a full meeting of the Legislative Council."[462]

The above document includes two vital enclosures which reveal that the essence as well as many finer points in the Harris plan of 1851 were in fact McLeod's.[463] Recommendations made by the Governor and the Legislative Council appear in Enclosure 1. First, "That it be humbly recommended to the Queen that, for the purpose of promoting secular education in the Island," a Board of Education for Trinidad be "appoint[ed]". Second, that an annual grant be voted for education—"as the Legislative Council may see fit to vote"—but not to exceed the sum of L2,000 sterling in the current year (1846). That any school supported by the Board of Education "be purely secular." To avoid the charge of a disregard for religion, a proviso added that no person be admitted to such schools "without a certificate under the hand of some religious teacher in this colony," that those under the age of 14 years received religious education from such teachers, and in the cases of those above 14, they were regular "at some place of religious worship." Another recommendation was that "whenever the inhabitants of any quarter" raised half the estimated expense of setting up a school by land acquisition, buildings and teachers' quarters, the Board could inspect such arrangements and if found satisfactory, grant "the other moiety of such expense," and to guarantee the teacher's salary. Finally, ownership of all land and school property was to be "vested in Her Majesty, Her heirs and successors." This document was signed on 17 April 1846, by "Johnstone," clerk of the Council.[464] Harris adopted these proposals but included ideas on funding by reorganizing Trinidad into wards.

As far as a neutral, non-preferential system of education went, McLeod and the Council had made an excellent beginning. The proposals for which Harris is famous, were explained to Lord Grey shortly after his arrival in Trinidad. Harris's proposals remained in abeyance from 1846 to 1851—the length of McLeod's tenure—and Harris was fortunate to have had three additional years in the island before becoming Governor of Madras in 1854.[465] The years 1846-1851 were utilized in reorganizing the island into wards and larger district units so as to inculcate local government. The wards were made responsible for the costs of upkeep of schools out of rates paid by landowners. Ordinance #8 of 1849 reorganized the island into "divisions, counties, districts, and wards." The system of quarters under Commandants in Spanish times had been eroding, and their functions had been taken by stipendiary magistrates after 1797, while the police force was now directly controlled from Port of Spain. Another Ordinance #14 of 1854 helped regulate the "appointment of wardens, the raising of local rates," and the rules for creating ward unions.[466] This meticulous spatial reorganization was to supplement Harris' educational plans.

The governor summarized that there were four ways to go on the educational question. First, "By supporting the schools of the principal, or of all the religious bodies willing to receive assistance," large and small. This would have to go, he thought, because it had been tried already, and without much success. Secondly, Trinidad might adopt a "uniform system of secular and religious education," wherein a "generalized" instruction on religion, meeting with the approval of "all sects," would obtain. Harris disapproved of this route, "more especially as there are both Musselmen and Hindoos in this Island." The third option appealed to Harris: "The system of purely secular instruction," as haad been proposed in McLeod's plan. There was a fourth option, though somewhat complicated: "secular instruction established and directed by Government, but combining with it religious instruction. . . ." Ministers of the denomination which happened to be "most numerous in the locality" would manage the program, but "no forced attendance" would be required in religious classes. Impeccable "inspection and management" would have been vital to the success of such a plan of education.[467]

Harris was, like McLeod, reluctantly persuaded to opt for secular education. As the missionary Grant had applauded, Harris' plan was comprehensive and wise, except that it neglected religion. "I decided," Harris said, upon this plan "with considerable anxiety and in no spirit of pride but rather that of deep humiliation." Differences of religion were insurmountable, he explained, "and though I acknowledge . . . the immense importance of this subject in developing the powers of man, I thought it better," in Trinidad, to leave that task to other agents.[468] Harris had carefully considered McLeod's proviso on the third of the four options, but foresaw several "new" obstacles: "With respect to the certificates [in lieu of religious education] I must state my disapproval. I consider that it would be either useless or objectionable; useless, if according to a construction I have heard put upon the terms of it, that a parent or a friend may be considered a religious teacher; objectionable because of the ministers of religion are alone to give certificates, the very children whom we desire most to educate, would be excluded, viz. the progeny of the abandoned, the wanderer and the profligate. We have also Musselmen in this island, and Coolies [Hindus?], many of whom may be presumed, or certainly are, without religious teachers."[469]

Harris was correct that non-Christian Indians did not have their religious teachers provided them; immigrant *brahmins* or *mullahs* did arrive regularly but they were sent to labor on plantations. Until later in the century, all Indians were "coolies" and none had been formally allowed to practice his or her "caste" occupation. There is no evidence that Indian "priests" were recruited by Trinidad to minister to the religious needs of the Indians. Rather, there were occasional requests that brahmins not be recruited since they, with warrior "caste" groups, were ringleaders on troublesome estates. The Portuguese, on the other hand, had been provided Catholic ministers after coming to Trinidad. Harris, like McLeod, thought about this matter fairly: "Are we first of all to force them [Indians] to go to a teacher of a religion which they do not profess, rather than first instruct them and open their minds?" The ideals of education, Harris indicated, were applicable to the Indian mind. Once education were offered to Indians, "they may of themselves choose the right from the wrong."[470]

Not to be outdone by McLeod in idealism, Harris also thought about the possibilities of compulsory education. That this idea was not seriously considered until a commission of 1895, and not adopted even then, is beside the point. Harris wrote to London, "I should therefore be much more inclined, not only to throw the schools open to all, but even to oblige the attendance of all." While acknowledging this objective would be well-nigh impossible to implement "amidst the scattered population of this island," at the very least, it would ensure a minimum of "regular attendance. . . .

"[471] The implementation and successes of the McLeod-Harris plan of education was initially quite limited.

When Harris' Education Plan had come before the Legislature on 2 April 1851, the entire management and control of the schools, the hiring and firing of teachers, the determination of the curriculum and choice of textbooks had been vested in a Board of Education. The Board comprised leading residents and officials. Model schools and a normal school for teacher-training, were opened in Port of Spain in 1851.[472] At the time the plan's introduction in 1851, Trinidad was "even more heterogenous" than it had been in 1847. Of 69,609 inhabitants in 1851, 40,627 were locals or natives, 10,812 had been "born in the different British colonies; 8,097 had been born in Africa; 4,915 had been born in other foreign countries"; 4,169 were Indian laborers; 729 were natives of Britain; and 260 were of miscellaneous origins.[473] Keenan accentuated this diversity by factoring in religious distinctions as represented below for populace in 1851: Roman Catholics = 43,605; Protestants = 20,440; Church of England = 16,246; Wesleyans = 2,508; Presbyterians = 1,017; Independents = 123; Baptists = 448; Other Christians = 98; Gentoos[474] = 2,649; Mahometans = 1,016; Heathens[475] = 880; Unaccounted For = 1,019.

These numbers show what we know already, that Catholics were the single largest religious group in Trinidad's population of 69, 609. Catholics were twice as numerous as Protestants and more than twice the size of all denominations combined. The 1,019 persons whose religion was "unaccounted" for may have been Hindu; especially because the 1,016 "Mohometans" represented 40 percent of the Hindu total of 2,649. In fact, about two or three in ten emigrants from India were Muslim, but four in ten is too high a proportion. As we shall see below, Indian Christians were a tiny minority and until the end of the 1860s, *not* converts to Canadian Presbyterianism. Other denominations did attract Hindu and Muslim converts, notably the Catholic and Anglican Churches. Muslims and Hindus together made up 3,665 Indians but Keenan himself listed 4,169 inhabitants as having been born in India. In order to socialize such a diverse population, the educational system needed to work doubly hard and especially well, not least of all because of the late start.

4.3 EDUCATIONAL PROGRESS

THROUGH 1870

By the later nineteenth century, the McLeod-Harris plan of education had failed to produce any spectacular results. One reason was the apparent neglect of Christian education. Harris had himself expected some resistance to the principle of secular education: "I believe the clergy of the Church of England universally," without necessarily thumbing their noses at government, "have a great dislike to it." In 1851 the Catholics had given tentative approval, the Wesleyans had "declared their entire disapprobation," of the plan but other "dissenters" were supportive.[476] By 1870, almost every denomination had, for one reason or another, rejected this secular approach to education. Campbell says that the wardens were the wrong people to entrust with ward schools: "These men were planters or planter-oriented and were not eager promoters of schools." They received good salaries in the prosperous 1850s, and the neglect of education cannot be explained in terms of a lack of financial means.[477]

When Keenan arrived in Trinidad in 1869, he was generally disappointed both with the slow growth and poor quality of ward schools. Harris had estimated that one in 231/3 children in Trinidad had been attending school in 1846; the population totalled 70,000 and the pupils were at public and private schools were 2,518 and 482 respectively).[478] Keenan visited 76 schools, "in which I examined 3,103 pupils," an increase of 103.[479] As we shall see, fewer pupils attended than were enrolled.

The male:female pupil ratio was 3:2 or 40 percent female, but possibly because the capital was not as "safe" for girls as were the out-of-town schools, the three borough schools had a low proportion of 12.9 percent female pupils. If we compare 33 girls in these schools with the approximately 20 Indians that Keenan observed, Indian school attendance at ward schools was not atypically low, as there were a few church schools on the estates teaching elements of numeracy and literacy. Reasons other than lack of interest in education could explain why so few girls attended borough schools. Indian pupils contributed fractionally to male pupil numbers, but independently they compare favorably with, what in our own time is the other minority, females. Keenan saw 1,214 girls present during his visits to schools in Trinidad, while the corresponding number for boys was 1,889.[480]

While there were obviously more pupils in schools of one sort or another, in his visits to non-Indian schools Keenan found attendance at 3,000. That was also what Harris had estimated as being total enrolment in 1846. Keenan explained that owing to omissions in the registers of "schools not aided by the state, I soon found that the returns exhibiting the quality of the attendance at such schools were unreliable."[481] As to the situation at State schools, the following summary is a guide:

Model, Borough and Ward schools had 1,780 prsent out of 3,692 pupils on the registers; "Other schools" showed 1,323 pupils in class out of 2,744 on their registers.

Of a total of 6,436 names on school rolls in 1869, Keenan had seen 3,103 pupils, reflecting, an attendance of less than 50 percent. The best summary of progress is that while enrollment had more than doubled between 1851 (3,000) and 1869 (6,436), total school attendance improved only slightly during these 18 years. It was more perturbing for Keenan that "only 1,600" of those already at school made even a 100 attendances for the year. The "desideratum" therefore was not for more pupil numbers as such, but "for a better quality of attendance" among those already enrolled.[482] Indian pupils were clearly not atypical in time and place, nor for school enrolment and attendance.

Despite the colony's perceptions, in terms of poor black and white school attendance up to 1870, Indo-Trinidadian children fared well in the comparison. Keenan had found no government Indian schools nor government-aided schools, but a few churches and an orphanage had begun educating Indian children by 1869.

A school in Newtown was conducted by the Reverend S.L.B. Richards; another at El Socorro was run by the Archdeacon of Trinidad. Keenan did not examine this last school because on the day of his visit, "the teacher was unfortunately suffering from fever. . . ." At the former, he met with "Miss Eliza Brown, age 38; Protestant," and the teacher. She appeared "immensely devoted" to her duties but Keenan was disappointed "she knows nothing of the language" of the Indian children, a "great drawback". There were 19 boys and 15 girls on the register, but only 12 (six boys and six girls) were present for the examination. During the "examination they showed themselves to be bright and intelligent, but they had got no farther than a little spelling." At the Presbyterian school Morton himself and his assistant "named Dixon" did the teaching. There were 12 children present varying in ages from 6 to 13 years. Only a "few" of them had been baptized, "but, whether Christian or not, they were all taught the Bible and Catechism." At the Tacarigua Orphanage Keenan examined the 42 Indian orphans (25 boys, 17 girls) who were "brought up as Protestants." Catholics may have resented this edge the Protestants assumed with potential Indian converts. Keenan added that, "[T]he Governor, when I brought the matter" to his attention, replied that if the Catholics "established a corresponding class of orphanage," it too would receive the small maintenance fee for each orphan at L10 a year.[483]

It will be obvious that while Catholics showed their objections to pro-British or secular education, Indians had little choice about schools. To their credit, they were willing to send their children to several Christian schools if that helped a new generation of Indians. As to whether the Tacarigua Orphanage ought to be considered a school is unclear even today. Writing in 1968, Wood regarded the institution as a school, which contributed to education of Indo-Trinidadians. Founded in 1857, the Orphanage was, in fact, an agricultural or industrial school, with the orphans contributing a large share of the upkeep. Wood saw this institution, early in the Indo-Trinidadian experience, as "the only means to disseminate European ways in an almost unapproachable society." At the time, however, Keenan had not viewed the Orphanage as "evidence of the public desire to educate" the Indians. It was, as orphanages continue to be, "a sort of poor-law necessity," although school activity might take up part of the day.[484] Until the Canadian Presbyterians "arrived to work solely among the Indians," the Orphanage had offered "the only real place" for Indian education.[485] UnorphaneEast Indian children had a longer wait before schooling in quantity or quality was available to them.[486]

Keenan's educational inquiry was positive about the performance of those Indian children in attendance at the four establishments he visited, though much remained to be done in making schools accessible to, and training teachers for, their community. In a few urban schools such as the Borough school, Keenan found Indian parents were beginning to send their children, although East Indians numbered no more than a score. Keenan found the Indian boys adept in math, but opined "the creole is utterly unable to deal logically with numbers." The comparison went on to say that the Indian child displayed a tenacious and reliable memory; "the memory of the creole is uncertain and weak . . . the Coolie's definitions or statements are off-handed and clear; the creole's are hesitating and obscure."[487]

Keenan's Report is a valuable document for reasons other than educational reflections alone. In the temerity of its comparisons, namely those between the races, and in chauvinistic perspectives, this document helps us understand the milieu in which arguments for education, or indenture itself, were occurring. Those comments not intended to insult, appear useful in other contexts, and anything but denigrating.

Paragraph 142 of Keenan's Report is as damaging to Indian girls as were the contrasts drawn between Indian pupils generally and "the creoles of African blood." The female pupils from the Indian population were "in flexibility and aptness [of] mind . . . immeasurably inferior to that of the male." Rev. Richards, also a teacher, apparently confirmed Keenan's suspicions when he "remarked to me that he had observed the same striking disparity between the minds of the boys and those of the girls. The reverend gentleman added, that whilst the Coolie boy, after quitting school, almost invariably turns out well, the Coolie girl, unhappily, does the reverse. I may here mention that I observed no such disparity of mind between the male and the female creoles."[488]

Certainly, the more controversial aspects of Keenan's Report relate to his comparison of "Coolie" and Creole. It is regrettable that published work on this subject does not show Keenan in his milieu: imperial Britain. Occasionally, Keenan's moralistic judgements are inflicted on the whites too. In Paragraph 56 of his Report, Keenan noted that the ages of pupils ranged "from mere infancy to 16, 17, and even 18 years . . . The variety is very curious." But Keenan was far from amused; he found it "objectionable" that "in the same school and under the [same] master," girls and boys on the verge of adulthood were to be found together. "Those fully-grown girls were rarely in the upper classes," and their "minds, habits, and characters being . . . quite unformed," the matter was "serious and dangerous."

If Keenan appeared to be even-handed in his criticism of the female Indian and white pupils, one cannot say the same about his comments on parents. It is striking that in this report on education, almost as much is said about Indian parents as about the pupils; by contrast very little is said about white, coloured and black parents. When reporting on Morton's Church school, for instance, where he had examined 12 Indian pupils, Keenan found their "manners" and general demeanor "very good." Lapsing into ethnocentrism, he added: "Nearly all the boys wore a becoming quantity of clothes, which is very uncommon amongst [C]oolies, whether children or adults."[489] The report had a redeeming side. During his tour, apart from problems of access to schools[490] and the inability of everyone but the Governor to locate the schools on a map for him, Keenan noted the virtual collapse of the principles of secular education. It was "as rigidly laid down that the school-rooms [and masters] were not to be employed for any purpose connected with [religious] instruction . . . Deviations from the system have recently occurred in this respect. The Cedros school is a place of public worship for the Protestants. The Erin School is also a place of public worship for the Protestants, and the teacher is the recognised stipendiary Protestant catechist of the district. The Point-a-Pierre School has likewise been used [by] Protestants on Sundays."[491]

The Protestants did appear more audacious in violating the secular principle, but there was a case reported by Keenan where a school at Arima was allowed "in favor of the Roman Catholic clergyman," for use on Sundays. However justified each of the decisions might have been on the ground, Keenan intimated, "in practice, because of their partial" or selective nature, it was "detrimental" to the system. The change ought to "have been publicly promulgated."

Keenan's stronger criticisms were reserved for teacher-training and school and classroom organization. The idea of building living quarters on the school premises may have been an incentive to teachers but by 1869 it was found that teachers would lie in their hammocks all day long while children were left to themselves. Where teachers lived next to the classroom with families, there was the additional disruption from infants and household chores. "At Chaguanas the crying of a baby in the teacher's apartment very seriously impeded my examination of the pupils," lamented Keenan. The ward schools had other problems.

Several reasons, including incompetence, led to the rental of schools, where purchase of properties might have been the intention of the educational plan. Out of 30 schools in 1869, the wards owned 13. All but two of the 17 hired buildings, and half of those owned by the Board of Education were unsuitable. "I certainly was not prepared for the condition of the school-houses; for the complete indifference exhibited, in the majority of cases, to symmetry, to stability, to appropriateness of design, to neatness, to comfort, and even to health and decency. There are 17 of the ward school-houses . . . which would bring discredit upon any country that recognises civilisation as a principle of government. Life is positively in danger in such a school as Oropouche, where the wood under your feet are rotten, where decay has seized the walls, where the atmosphere is pestilential."[492]

In this context, the use of cowsheds for the school premises of Indian children does not appear particularly distressing. Except that as late as 1882 when the Rev. Grant's teaching became an interest for the visiting Sir Neville Lubbock, chairman of the Colonial Company, that school was again a stable. "On finding that the school in question was conducted in a cow-stable, which was rented for a small sum while the animal was in pasture," Sir Neville promised to request the Board for a doubling of the annual grant from the Company to L120.[493]

Keenan's visits to non-Indian schools indicated that even when buildings became better and sturdier, obstacles to good teaching and learning remained. Classroom organization was found wanting in so many respects that he felt it would "be simply a tedious enumeration" to detail the defects which he witnessed, "a mere recital of the want of everything that gives character and tone to a well-worked school in Great Britain or Ireland." Teachers showed absolutely no preparation, furnishing the Inspector neither with journals nor with lessons and lesson-plans; there were no class time-tables, nor was homework given to the pupils. Yet, teacher salaries were high, the mean being around L200 per annum, with the "master of the model school [receiving] 300 pounds a year." The general assessment of Keenan is pithily expressed in his own words, "Teachers were inert; the public were indifferent; the Board of Education was unmoved."[494]

Following Keenan's recommendations for government aid to denominational schools to accelerate progress—but which called for continued segregation between Indians and other non-Europeans in education—Trinidad moved slowly towards a more effective dispensation. The first implementation of reforms occurred in 1870 in abandoning the Queens Collegiate School for a secondary school tied into the British higher education system. Keenan had recommended the closure of the Collegiate and teacher-training schools. The training of class monitors for teaching careers had been proposed.[495] The more important reform was the funding of all schools, including denominational establishments. It was Arthur Gordon who finally decided that state-aided denominational schools[496] could co-exist with the McLeod-Harris secular schools. This equality or balance between the two school systems gave the advantage, beginning in 1890, to denominational schools in terms of the decision to open government schools only where churches had left a vacuum. This lies outside our period of study, but that 1890 decision explains the anti-denominational stand of some educators and leaders in independent Trinidad.

Keenan's recommendations pertaining to free and compulsory education would see the light of day only in the twentieth century. Moreover, Keenan may have erred in recommending separate schools for Indians. Especially after the 1869 program of having Indians substitute their claims for repatriation with land grants of equivalent value, policy-makers ought to have recognized the need for multicultural education, integration and nation-building. Any of these objectives would have rescued the Indian community from obscurity and geographical isolation.

Keenan's most damaging criticism of Trinidad's failures towards the Indians, was contained in the paragraph: "No effort was made to induce him [the Indian], through the awakening intelligence and dawning prospects of his children, to associate the fortune and future of his family with the colony. It is therefore that— collaterally, and I believe legitimately,—I connect the magnitude of the periodical exodus of the Asiatics with the educational system, which fails to provide for their children acceptable schools."

Again, here was evidence that Indians would go to great lengths to show interest in their children's futures. The availability of good schools might have led more of them to commute their repatriation to India for settlement in Trinidad itself. However, problems of poverty persisted for many Indians, especially in the depression years of the third quarter of the century when European beet-sugar competition was weakening King Sugar in the Caribbean. Poverty impacted on continued low school attendance of Indians in town schools, something which began to change with an increase in village or plantation schools.

4.4 ISOLATED INDIANS, THE CANADIANS AND KEENAN

That aspect of the Education Report of 1869-70 which recommended separate schools be set up for children of Indian migrants, as far as was practicable, was welcomed in many quarters. For one thing, this fit neatly into the design of the Canadian Presbyterians. As John Morton would have expressed it, there seemed to be a divinely inspired coincidence about. "We believe in Denominational Schools," he said, "considering the state of the colony and population, although if we were in Canada, we might not take that view."[497]

While they labored diligently, Canadian missionaries found it convenient to keep Indians apart from other groups, in part to better learn Indian mores, their language/s and the potential for conversion. A training pamphlet published under the auspices of the United Church of Canada, said "[O]ur Eastern friends in the West Indies are unique in our missions. They have been transplanted as were the Hebrews in Palestine," but to an environment totally different from their former land, "with gods

more strange and daily influences more perilous to their spirits."[498]
The Indians' "uniqueness" meant, quite illogically, that they needed
separate churches and schools. Indeed, it is remarkable that a
separate Indian mission was slowly created out of the remnants of
several different Church projects in Trinidad, when they represented
opportunities for integrating Indians with the wider Christian
community in Trinidad.

When Rev. Morton had arrived in Trinidad for health reasons
in 1864, he could not help wondering about the many Hindus
and Muslims to-ing and fro-ing from the Caribbean. He wanted
to evangelize them but could not persuade the Church in Scotland
or Nova Scotia to make the initial investment. It was here that the
previous work and difficulties of the United Presbyterian Church
of the United States gave Morton his golden opportunity. The
poor health of its missionaries had led to their withdrawal, and if
Morton promised to continue the United States mission to the
blacks at Iere Village, the Canadians might have that church
property in Trinidad. On 3 January 1868, the Morton family landed
on the island for their life's work.[499] The missed opportunity in
this story is that the Canadian promise of "a weekly service in
English be given to the black and colored [sic] people who had
been gathered in," was gradually abandoned.[500]

During the time that Morton conducted church services for
the non-Indian congregation at Iere Church, he thought "it was
not easy to persuade the Indians to attend the same services as the
Africans." Instead of trying harder or being more imaginative,
Morton took the church to Indian homes and without spectacular
gains.[501] Morton would make "little excursions in the neighboring
villages to preach in the open," enter into discussions or join the
Indians in their simple repast which flattered them no end.[502]
When Morton got the idea of teaching the children at his home,
he had one more reason to call upon the adult Indians. Shirley
Gordon writes that Indian parents "were unwilling to send their
children to the schools attended by Negro children," and the work
of the Canadian Church therefore suited their needs.[503] The

religious and educational preferences of the Indians were overstated. That Indians may not have been socially progressive paralleled the racialism of the government of the day. Anachronistic views are seen for what they are when we recall that Indians needed passes to leave the plantations, but non-Indians could travel or school anywhere they wished. Non-Indians might have attended Presbyterian schools, but they did not; Indians were more unfree than other Trinidadians.

Sarah Morton recorded her husband's work in *John Morton of Trinidad* from his diary and letters, in which he made the case for "a purely Indian" church. A diary entry reads:

> "October 3, 1868.
> With respect to the village I thought it better not to attempt gathering the Indians into Church, where they would feel less at ease and where the discourse being more formal I might fail to gain their interest through want of acquaintance with the language. I therefore meet them in companies in their own houses, or sometimes by the road side."[504]

The Reverend Grant also noted the role of Providence in his duties, without recognizing the opportunities for integration which were lost. At the commencement of the mission outreach in San Fernando in 1871 he recalled, "[W]e had no buildings," and no funds either, "but a way was again opened up." One group's loss was another's opportunity. "The Scotch manse, through the retirement of the Rev. George Lambert, had recently become vacant, and in it we found comfortable quarters, but this arrangement for our first year involved to a large extent the pulpit supply and pastoral oversight of the English-speaking congregation. It had its serious disadvantages, for it imposed a dual burden that was almost too great, and seriously interfered with preparation in the study of the Hindi language for our own particular work."[505]

It is this sense of the missionaries' "particular work" with the Indians which appears to have unwittingly delayed their integration

into the larger society. Where planters who extracted Indian labor
did so without a knowledge of Hindi,—and where an understanding
of English was demanded of Indians even in adhering to complex
Hosay regulations, Canadians promoted Indian cultural persistence
and resistance.[506] And without tangible evidence that it aided
evangelization.

The work of the Canadian East Indian mission has not been
seen from a non-religious perspective. The Church most closely
associated with the Indo-Trinidadian population began work in
the island in 1868 and drew many laborers to sermons only because
they did not have a satisfactory repertoire of leisure.[507] Similarly,
with other churches and the relationship between Presbyterian
missionaries and planters, politicians and purse-holders, the
warmth of the welcome was also due to social and leisure needs
and, for the planters, the use of missionaries as a sort of policing
power over estate managers and laborers. But it would be wrong to
see the work of the Presbyterians entirely in this light. This chapter
combined both perspectives to tease out reasons for the
contradictions in Indian Presbyterianism.[508] This approach has
relevance for other minorities elsewhere.

A study of the Presbyterian Mission in Trinidad is fascinating
for at least three reasons. First, it allows one to assess the links
between nationalism, religion and imperialism on a concrete level.
Canada had won distinction as a nation only a year before Morton
pioneered the Mission in Trinidad. The desire to save heathen souls
from damnation also involved Canadians taking their place in the
sun among other evangelical, even imperial, nations. Second,
Canadian Presbyterianism proved uniquely helpful in Trinidad
where Catholics remained wary of Crown colony government. For
Britain, Presbyterians offered a window through which Trinidad
might be penetrated and anglicized without directly implicating
the Church of England. Even if Canadian culture was a variant
rather than a duplication of British culture, for the Anglo-
Trinidadian establishment it were better that Indians became brown
Canadians than brown Frenchmen.[509] Thirdly, the Canadians

supported British rule and indenture without being as closely tied to Britain in the minds both of East Indians and Catholics in Trinidad. In this context the educational work of the Canadians was crucial, even as Morton supported the continuation of Indian servitude.

Canadian missionaries clearly "shared the values system [sic] of the British Empire's ruling classes," and promoted those values as much as they could. "They wanted their charges to be loyal subjects of Queen Victoria and loyal subordinates of the planters."[510] At the turn of this century when the Trinidad Presbyterian Church celebrated one of its anniversaries, Sarah Morton still spoke about her audience, the majority of whom were Indo-Trinidadians, as "the strange people."[511] Mrs. Morton said that she had wanted the converts to be better British subjects.

The foregoing might portray the Canadian Presbyterian Mission in a new, less purely religious light, but without gainsaying their contributions to Trinidad's neglected Indians. The Canadians were the catalysts for transforming the British Indian "coolie" and creating the East Indian. They fulfilled some needs as well as created new ones which promoted social mobility and creolization. And as the experience of the United States missions had shown, the new disease environment took a heavy toll on missionaries, leading to their decision in 1867 to leave Iere village near San Fernando. That many courageous Canadians stayed on to work among the Indians despite deaths and resignations of members, redounded to the benefit of Trinidad.

In the short term planter-supported Presbyterian schools failed to testify to the suspicion that Indians would flock to Indians-only schools. If they did attend schools belatedly opened on or near estates, average daily attendances versus enrolment remained lackadaisical. By 1892, there were 2,951 pupils on 52 Presbyterian school registers.[512] On attendances, de Verteuil recalled that in 1896, "when the Presbyterian school system was well established and the official roll of pupils was 3,383, the average daily attendance was . . . 2,057 or 62 percent. Some of the pupils stayed away to help their parents in the cane fields. Others did not insist that they attend it."[513]

The absence of schools and poverty had impacted on irregular attendances among Indian children, but regular attendance among Indian and non-Indian pupils were similar over time. Well over a decade after Keenan's investigation, only 12 Canadian schools and five government-aided Indian schools were in operation.[514] That was the first year when L. Guppy, Inspector of Education since 1868, decided to include Indian statistics to the Education Report. Our view that human progress is seldom linear, with periods of gains occasionally reversed by losses, applies to Trinidad's labor system as much as to educational development.

In the ten years since Keenan's visit, all Trinidadians but Indians made their most spectacular gains. Between 1868 and 1878, the schools had more than doubled while average attendance increased by 317 percent. There was a drop thereafter and progress was remarkable neither in total school enrolment nor in average attendances among non-Indian pupils. Of the 58 government schools operating in 1883, two were closed at the end of June.[515] Other schools were denominational or partly state-funded, but excluded the 19 Indians-only schools.

From 35 schools in 1868—with 2,836 pupils on the roll and 1,333 average attendances—Trinidad had 86 schools in all by 1878 (6,290 enrollees and 4,238 average attendances). Three years later, in 1881, there were 100 schools with 8,060 pupils enrolled in Trinidad and average attendance at 68 percent (5,541). The following year there were five more schools open in the island with 7,895 pupils on the roll and attendance increasing yet again to 73 percent. By June of 1883 Trinidad had a total of 109 schools, with 6,567 pupils making the average attendance out of 9,951 on the registers; however, regular attendance had fallen to about 66 percent.[516]

TABLE 4

Indian Schools under Canadian Presbyterians, 1884-85

Location of School	Boys	Girls	Total	Daily Average
Tunapuna	47	11	58	42
Tacarigua	36	6	42	40
Orange Grove	18	19	37	24
Arouca	29	10	39	27
San Fernando	85	34	119	77
Canaan	43	16	59	37
Ceadr Grove	25	0	25	20
Picton	54	17	71	46
Wellington	22	7	29	24
La Fortune'	44	13	57	39
Point-a-Pierre	34	13	47	32
Harmony Hall	52	17	69	45
Tarouba	20	0	20	14
Usine, St. Madeline	55	37	92	68
Petit Mourne	14	4	18	12
Bonaventure	26	16	42	29
Belle Vue	24	12	36	36
Rusillac	28	8	36	28
Fyzabad	22	10	32	24
Barakpur	24	4	28	26
Hermitage	25	12	37	27
Coycoye'	30	9	39	27
Princestown	72	48	120	78
Mt. Stewart	48	2	60	28
Jordan Hill	27	10	37	22
St. Julien	22	6	28	16
Palmyra	25	9	34	25
Riversdale	29	6	35	19
Lengua	22	10	32	18
Brothers	22	9	31	18
Cedar Hill	28	10	38	22
Ben Lomond/Ben Intento	26	0	26	17
Exchange	48	12	26	17
Brechin Castle	52	39	91	57
Esperanza	28	12	40	29
Milton	26	14	40	26
Calcutta Village	15	15	30	25
Waterloo	20	12	32	25
Providence	20	15	35	20
St. Joseph	42	7	49	38
Caroni	31	9	40	29
TOTAL	1,3-60	530	1,890	1,286
new school (#42)	?	?	+72	+21

Source : The Presbyterian Yearbook (1884-8).

While the 1883 report failed to mention Indian pupil numbers and attendances, the 19 Indian schools reflected a fivefold increase between 1869 and 1883, thereby reflecting a growing need for schools and the Indian appreciation of education. By 1885 Mission and state-aided schools for Indians had jumped to 42 per Table 4, therefore matching in two years the doubling which had occurred in non-Indian schools over a ten year period from 1868 to 1878. If there were a hundred Indian schoolgoers in 1869 they numbered 1,900 seven years later, with attendance at 73 percent. The progress depicted in less remarkable statistics on Indian education should not blind us to the progress and more rapid advances achieved by that community in the 1880s. In view of the abject start in the education of Indian children, it is understandable that some gains were made seven years after the island-wide gains of 1878. And these achievements occurred in a very hostile social climate, as intimated in daily newspapers.

That in spite of the efforts of governors McLeod and Harris, Indians were maintained as a separate, distinct, unintegrated segment of Trinidad society is revealed in newspapers such as the *Palladium* in 1880. In a leading article "Civilisation and the Coolies" thinking persons wondered whether "civilisation" might be conceded to India and its people. The *Palladium* decided that civilization "denote[d] Education, Knowledge, Refinement." It acknowledged that Indians were "refined enough to be polite people in the ordinary sense," but their knowledge was confined to "pecuniary and material interests." The latter made them imbibe "artifice, dissimulation, and often falsehood. . . . "[517] Just as the Rev. Grant had found their religions the most objectionable part of Indian life, the editor decided that Christian conversion determined real civilization: "But they have not the knowledge of GOD which excels all other description of knowledge, and to which it is highly desirable that they should attain, otherwise they must remain morally degraded . . . How then is the Civilisation, we all commend and admire, to be promoted in regard to our Asiatic labourers? The answer is, *first*, schools should be established *specifically* for the instruction of this race." [original emphases][518] The newspaper lauded the Canadian Presbyterian efforts and cajoled other churches to follow their example.

In the year 1880, therefore, the most literate circles in Trinidad were reading a message that continued to call for the geographical and social separation of Trinidadians of Indian and non-Indian roots. In all probability, some Indian parents would have welcomed separate schools for their children, but when dominant elites thought so, it certainly affected the rate and consequences of integration.

As mentioned already, the warmth of the Canadians' reception by Trinidadian society was not all unselfish. Not a few planters offered donations which were little different than bribes to the Presbyterian church for monitoring both estate management and Indian laborers. Grant admitted, "[M]any of the proprietors were non-resident . . . and through their representatives in the island kept the Mission under close observation and continued their support as long as financial conditions made it possible for them to do so."[519] What Grant does not disclose is that on occasion, donations would be discontinued when certain missionaries failed to please. For instance, Thomas Christie was the first to receive a salary offered by planters at the Couva station. Christie found himself in "open conflict" with the donors. The Church explained this in terms of Christie's personality and he eventually resigned on the grounds of "health." In 1876 Christie disclosed that the planter's representatives in Trinidad had been "interfer[ing] 'in such a way that it threatened even the existence of the schools.' There were heated exchanges including letters to the planters' head office in Scotland." Two years later Christie's resignation had occurred, with John Wright being the replacement missionary. That the usual personality problem was overstated is indicated by Wright's conflicts with another large planter-donor, Cummings. Wright complained to the mission council that he did not consider it his duty 'to stand between the proprietors and their officers to watch conduct and report.' Wright stuck to his position, Cummings

withdrew his L774 in donations, and a second missionary had to
return home.[520]

The only truly negative criticism that can be made of the
Canadian Presbyterians—once the point is conceded that he who
pays the piper calls the tune—is that they employed a double
standard as in their attitudes towards their converted Indian flock.
The Church did not allow equality of salaries between Canadians
and Indians, and not a single ordained Indian minister for the
entire period from 1868 to 1888. If we look beyond our period of
study for a hint of related developments, we learn that the first
Indo-Trinidadian ordination occurred in 1892. However, a protest
in 1900—the Egbert Madoo Memorial—showed glaring double
standards in the Church especially in John Morton's attempt to
have his son, Harvey, tke over from him.[521]

Madoo, who had been a "member, communicant, regular
contributor" to the Church for "over ten years," wrote: "That your
memorialist submits most respectfully that unless justice, fairplay
and equal treatment are shown to all alike irrespective of nationality
in connection with the Church it is impossible for the work to
make satisfactory progress in the right direction, and your
memorialist with all deference and respect protests against the
appointment, not the person, of Rev. Harvey Morton as successor
to Dr. Morton. Preference should have been given to Rev. Paul
Bukhan who has been serving the mission under Dr. Morton
faithfully and very satisfactorily for over 25 years, and who
doubtlessly understands the language, customs, habits and manners
of the East Indians thoroughly . . . Even Rev. Lal Beharie and
[Clarence] Soodeen who acted for Dr. Morton for six months some
years ago have greater claims than Rev. Harvey Morton."

The petition also went into details of how the Church had
accepted government grants only for Canadian salaries but refused
them for Indian personnel, effectively limiting remuneration for
Indians at "[no] more than L100." Such developments may
persuade some of us to consider the opinion of writers who suggest
that one of several motivations for the Canadians Mission to the

Indians was a post eighteenth-century religious imperialism.   In an essay on missionary methods in the East Indian Mission retained at the United Church Archives in Toronto, Brinsley Samaroo concluded that Presbyterians must be seen in the context of imperialism and the post-eighteenth century revolutions. Following the colonial American and 1789 French Revolutions, "people returned to their time-honoured solace" of religion in a period of weakening bonds, traditions and values. In Europe and America, individuals and organizations, "fired by this religious fervour strove to spread the Christian word," at home and abroad.[522] Ann Martell's study of the Presbyterians placed Canadian missionary work in the larger context of European expansionism. She wrote, "The latter half of the nineteenth century found Canada passing through a very nationalistic, sometimes referred to as imperialistic, stage. Canada had only just emerged as a nation in her own right . . . The missionaries were very much men of their age, and when they entered Trinidad they became, in effect, supporters of the island's ruling class. They supported the rigid race and class divisions which defined Trinidad society, upheld the indenture system, aided the colonial office in . . . anglicization and in return received the ruling class' support for their work."

Martell also demonstrated that male chauvinism was very much alive within the Church. Women were made "subservient" or forced to recognize the seniority of people like Morton. "In most decisions on mission policy Morton was able to sway council to his way of thinking.[523] " Therefore, when it came to his successor, the Indians could hardly influence Rev. Morton.

On the educational front, the records in *The Presbyterian Yearbook 1884-85* revealed progress in the number of schools and Indian enrolment per Table 4.5. Religious statistics were not as encouraging, and even today, there is no overwhelming preference for any one Church among Indo-Trinidadians. The Yearbook reveals that 152 Indians had been baptized during 1884-85; 27 couples had had "Christian marriage[s]" and 42 schools had been in operation. At the schools, average daily attendance had been 1,307, with 1,962 Indian pupils on the registers.[524]

While it is true that not as many girls went to schools as did boys in the Indian community, that girls at all attended must be seen as progress. Only three of 42 schools did not enrol girls, and the Calcutta Village school was remarkable for equal numbers of boys and girls. A second school, Orange Grove, had a majority of Indian girls, 19 as against 18 boys.

By the endpoint of this study in 1888, laboring Trinidadians were more conversant with what was required of them to reduce their own difficulties as residents of Trinidad. Perhaps the massacre at their Hosay festival on 30 October 1884—the subject of the next chapter—also played a role in this process among the Indians. However, a great part of the credit for assisting Indians adjust to the strangeness of Trinidad society must go to the churches, pre-eminently the Canadian Presbyterian Mission and their many supporters in Europe and the Americas. More generally, the British Parliament ought to be acknowledged for their recognition that education was vital in eradicating the effects of bondage and unfreedom. Indeed, after 1835 Parliament had voted yearly grants for the education of ex-slaves and creoles. This chapter examined the shortcomings of that religion-based and charity schools which had received British funds until 1845 when financial constraints and other policy factors intervened. The problems of Trinidad, of immigrant newcomers from all parts of the globe and the Protestant-Catholic contest among the whites, also explain the convoluted progress of education in Trinidad. Amidst all, and most refreshingly, there was a recognition from white and non-white, from rich and poor, that education was, as it were, the wave of the future. By the 1880s, parents, Churches and officials had made a spectacular effort to improve upon the past and produce an educated younger generation in Trinidad.

This chapter has examined the entire context in which non-white, especially Indian, education in Trinidad was neglected until late in the nineteenth century. It is fair to conclude that it was neither malice nor deliberate policy which segregated Indian men, women and children, and delayed the integration process in Trinidad. Indeed, schools did not prohibit Indians and non-Indians from attending the same institutions; but the demands of the estates, especially the need for passes and for travel to the urban centers where such schools abounded, militated against Indian enrolment or mixing with fellow Trinidadians at school. Within seven years of blacks and whites having more than doubled their schools and enrolment, there was a quadrupling of Indian schools by 1885. Trinidad had lacked an abundance of creative leaders and education-oriented governors and so that many opportunities for integration at school and in the society were lost, thwarted or simply overlooked.

The first secondary school for Indians was not founded until 1900 when the Reverend Grant's sons had completed their primary education.[525] Grant was nevertheless incorrect when he said: "[T]here was no appreciation of education on the part of either parents or children."[526] The fact of interest is reflected in rapidly expanding enrolment and average attendances-unspectacular among the elites and other more urban groups—when Indians did not have to attend urban schools and overcome the pass system of the estates. Poverty and the need to supplement the meager estate wages was more of a factor among Indians than for other groups. Despite the depression in the 1880s, parents did give up children's earnings and sent them to schools more regularly; by 1888 some 3,700 Indians had attended Presbyterian schools alone.[527]

P.J. Keenan, the London-appointed investigator into Trinidad's educational impasse, had recorded that the only parents who had come to see their children inspected in 1869 were Indians.[528] That emigrants from village India, ensconced on rural backwaters after arrival in Trinidad, struggled to learn the norms of western culture while receiving little direct state help. That struggle is an index of their self-motivation. Without the Churches, however, Indian education and progress might have been delayed beyond the mid-1880s and with that, the development of an Indo-Trinidadian middle class. Hindu and Muslim Indian appreciation of education is reflected in their overcoming an initial aversion to Church-centered education, and sending their children to good schools of any denomination.

While there certainly were some Hindus and Muslims who did not allow their children to be exposed to catechisms and Christian evangelism—in the face of ongoing neglect by the government—the primary failure had been that of Britain. But even this failure has been placed within the larger context in which secular versus religious education had to be resolved among Trinidad's whites before mass schooling could begin.

Following the detailed description and analysis of the educational needs and potential of Indian children in the Keenan Report of 1869-70[529], the authorities may well be accused of abdicating the education of settler Indians after 1869. The land-for-passages policy, begun by Arthur Gordon, sought to improve the financial position of the colony by avoiding the tremendous costs of chartering return ships to India.[530] Many of those Indians who developed a stake in Trinidad by foregoing return passages opted to take the education offered by the Churches, and where available, from ward schools. Indians saw education as a key to mobility and their efforts were reflected in the singular jump from a hundred or so pupils in 1869 to an enrolment of 1,962 children some fifteen years later, with daily attendances improving to 73 percent at a time when Indian wages were falling. By 1888 the Reverend Grant could testify that 3,700 Indians had passed through Canadian Presbyterian schools.

Indians were at first bewildered in their adopted land, but adjusted with the help of their traditions and willingness to learn from the host society. In 1888 Reverend Grant told the Franchise Committee, "I have just noticed in my report this year that I had 3,700" Indians who had then "passed through my school," and these graduates now took "an intelligent interest in politics. . . . "[531] Lord Harris, hailed as the bestower of the Ward Schools in Trinidad, had noted the different but valid cultural values of Hindus and Muslims among Trinidad's population groups. He regretted Trinidad's undue reliance on legal mechanisms for "solving" problems pertaining to the laboring populations. The implication is that, given an opportunity, Indians would adjust to new world culture. Colonial legislation "never" attempted to solve "any higher problem" except what "quantity and what sort of law is necessary to keep a population" in obedience and "ensure the production of the greatest quantity of sugar."[532]

One writer went further in suggesting that the courts and prisons substituted for schools in Trinidad.[533] We have sought to avoid an extreme conclusion even though Law clearly failed to be the most effective means of socializing Trinidad's Yoruba, Rada, Hindu, Muslim and other Afro-Asian cultural players.[534] That government and other British well-wishers aided the Churches in their educational endeavors among non-white Trinidadians, may point to the complimentarity between Law and Education in Trinidad and for effective programs of socialization elsewhere.

The totality of Canadian mission work aided Indians in seeking to participate at higher levels of the society, for which elements of Christian culture and education were indispensable. Indian children, if they acquired some education, could become clerks in white stores or interpreters for the government.[535] Uneven attendance, especially of girls must be juxtaposed with the general state of public education in the nineteenth century and an admission that less than perfect attendance was a cross-race, general phenomenon.[536] In many cases context is everything: where it can be shown that Indians were *not* half as different or outlandish as other Trinidadians, notable myths may be laid to rest.[537]

Ultimately, for the colony to have brought creole and non-creole, Hindu, African and Jew, coloured and Chinese, black and white, Christian and Muslim, of all income and class groups under a common roof of education, would have been anachronistic or revolutionary. Not least of all because during the nineteenth century, numerical importance did not usually translate into political significance. Free education was long in coming, and

Britons experienced difficulties with Indians and non-Indians while trying to shape colonial Trinidad in their image.

In this milieu, European colonial functionaries seldom looked beyond the next harvest, the price of sugar, or wage increases and reductions. Consequently, nation-building or national consolidation, racial cooperation and multi-cultural perspectives on education were inconceivable.[538] Long after Emancipation in Trinidad, a freed people were not being guided into forming a coherent society. Once indented laborers were brought in, there were bound to be regular additions of free African and Asian children who would help integrating within a western, multi-cultural society. There were several peoples in Trinidad but a coherent society remained to be fully conceived.

CHAPTER FIVE

FESTIVALS AND PLANTATIONS:
THE RESORT TO LAW

"At 3:30 p.m. [on 15 September 1986] dancers raised the
objects to their shoulders and circled to the chant of Hosay,
Hosay, Hosay, Hosay! The ancient shout echoed from the
battle of Karbala, through the historical currents of Trinidad
and into the future . . . Despite ten days of fasting and a
long journey with a heavy load, the dancers found the
strength to return. The sacrifice mirrors the price Old World
peoples paid when they were brought to the Americas."[539]
"[T]he plantation was an absolutely unprecedented social,
economic and political institution, and by no means simply
an innovation in the organization of agriculture."[540]

In the initial issue of *Plantation Society in the Americas*, Carl Degler's
prospectus cogently outlined the untapped potential of the
"plantation" construct.[541] One of his many valid points is that the
"focus upon the plantation, irrespective of whether the labor that
worked it was legally free or not," helps us explore whether slavery
was truly unique or whether it is part of a continuum along with
other coercive labor regimes. Incorporating the ideas of Degler,
Engerman and others, this chapter demonstrates how Trinidad's
plantations shaped and affected mass celebrations and thus reveals
much about culture, the economy and the politics of leisure in
Trinidad for the period 1834-88.

In the period of our study there was limited social mobility in
a colonial island which treated non-Europeans as sources of menial
labor and not much else.[542] Nevertheless, this chapter allows the
lower classes to speak for themselves to the extent permitted by
the historical record. We analyze what these groups themselves
did especially during their leisure hours. Previous chapters have
analyzed Trinidad's economic problems, its schools, its courts and
prisons, all of which were impacted by the world of labor. In order
to get a glimpse of the real laboring men and women, African and
East Indian, we must look beyond the realm of work to the world
of play. In the world of leisure were found the authentic Africans
and Indians, in that little time they could call their own, in that
little space where their own values and metaphysics became
shoulders to lean upon, in limited spaces supposedly free of the
planters' power and stereotypes.

Before colonial Trinidad redefined its citizenry and urged them
away from previous systems of thought and belief, the state violently
attacked Africans and Indians at Carnival and Hosay festivls in the
period 1881-4. This was colonial law in action, an index of a heavy-
handed socialization process. The festivals were seen as repositories
of African and Indian autonomy and held both fear and fascination
for the elites. That was one view; the masses, however, were simply
salvaging their humanity.

The dehumanizing processes which turned first Africans, then
others, into slaves and units of labor for the plantations had initially
failed to destroy memories of earlier, autonomous lives. While it is
debatable whether the pre-plantation lives of Afro-and Indo-
Trinidadians were better materially, their cultural existence in Africa
and in India had been fuller and richer. It was only to be expected
that these laborers would recreate their lives in plantation Trinidad
through religion, leisure and street festivals. In doing this, Indians
in particular challenged their geographical or spatial restriction to
sugar estates and the christianization goals of the colonial elites,
school segregation having facilitated such goals.[543]

In terms of the analysis of the plantation in the opening quotations, any source of autonomy or *power* for the laboring groups had to be controlled or eradicated. The basic question of this chapter can be framed thus: Did the elites try to destroy street festivals they did not comprehend, or did they hope to avert labor and other alliances among Afro-and Indo-Trinidadians by weakening and separating their only arena of joyous, free and autonomous interaction? The data is at best ambiguous; however, some of these thoughts and motives are evident in the record, and in testimonies and depositions which were given at official Inquiries which followed the violence at festivals in Trinidad during the 1880s. In those instances where officialdom saw popular festivals only as powerful and dangerous vehicles, their response to them was coldly political. Real negotiation among the races was closed. The cultural and psychological needs of Africans nd Indians were ignored by the dominant elites in these situations or negotiations.

When Trinidad's elites observed their otherwise docile subordinates at their mass festivals, the latter were transformed into sometimes magnificient beings. These laborers were not any longer mere units of labor. At these moments in the annual cycle Africans and Indians reverted to something of their former glory or meaning. The planters and other elites could not understand their workers in this street arena. A struggle ensued.

The plantocracy spoke of the street festivals as powerful "things" and were often filled with dread. By the 1880s, the elites seemed determined to destroy Carnival and Hosay through state violence. That Carnival and Hosay survive in Trinidad today testify to the resilience of meaningful ritual in the lives of all human beings. This also suggests that the world of the plantation and its brand of divide-and-conquer ethnic politics did not succeed at every level. Indian-African relations suffered greatly under colonialism but there were positive outcomes from the nineteenth century as well, which is another reason why we ought to revisit the tragedies of the 1880s.

The elites openly expressed fears about the merging of Carnival and Hosay into a common celebration which seemed a possibility in the 1880s. With the benefit of hindsight, then, one might read the cultural struggles of the 1880s as a subtle process of negotiation. These were "negotiations" about the direction of the embryonic Republic of Trinidad and Tobago. Overt and covert goals were sought by all sides involved.

Paradoxically, it was the Catholic white immigrants who had brought Carnival to Trinidad in the years before Emancipation but had abandoned it soon after the slaves were freed; whites also helped resurrect Carnival into a national symbol since Trinidad's independence from Britain in 1962. In the immediate post-emancipation period, however, a slow but sure rift had cleft the street life of whites and non-Europeans, and these divisions came to a head in the 1880s. This was also the decade in which the Creole agenda for more democracy reached a head, a decade of poor economic times and increasing beet sugar competition as well.

It was, the elites felt, a most inappropriate time for Carnival and Hosay to rise as symbols of contest among competing values: between a plantocracy conscious of its small numbers and Christian civilization and the masses not yet awakened to their destiny as westerners and Trinidadians. Local elites were attempting to create a viable western-oriented society, one preferably English and Protestant, but the masses were instinctively opposed to some of these values.[544] Where the one sought a society with stable political and labor relations according to British norms, the other wanted more equal access to education and the freedom to control their own lives and leisure. With hindsight we can say that a peculiarly one-sided negotiation ensued between elites and masses.

All Trinidadians, wittingly or otherwise, were involved in fashioning a post-slavery society in which they would achieve a measure of comfort and progress. The negotiating parties became the ex-slaves or black poor; the Indians, both indented and indenture-free; the elites comprising the whites and some educated blacks, coloureds and and possibly few Indians or Indian-Christians; and the mass of coloureds extending from the middle class to the poor.

In this scenario, the ex-slaves generally lacked negotiating strength other than their numbers. The non-Christian Indians were even less influential proponents of their view of a just and progressive Trinidad. While coloureds were beginning to abandon that ambiguous status so long endured within a three-tiered slave society, individual coloureds could be swayed in favor either of whites or blacks. Some coloureds had useful resources, material and educational, which improved their negotiating clout. The white elite and their close allies, including missionaries and some Colonial Office personnel, had the greatest clout in these informal negotiations which helped shape present-day Trinidad. We know already that the powerful "negotiators" eventually responded to mass festivals with brutal force. The oversight of the colonial mother country was reduced to a policy of damage-control. Yet, violence had not been inevitable.

Although whites enjoyed the influence which colonialism and the plantation system conferred upon them, their small numbers made some of them nervous or inclined toward coercion in the aftermath of slavery. This tendency revealed itself whether the issues concerned labor, political reform—mounted by poor whites and coloureds—or determining the uses of religion,[545] leisure time and street festivals. Blacks and Indians could also choose violence in strikes or riots but they could not call upon the extreme levels of police coercion available to the elites.

The coercion of the plantations complemented the coercion of the legal system to compel Indians and Africans to deny those cultural practices which offended or intimidated the elites. Some aspects of each major fete were seen as offensive. In 1881 and 1883 Carnival was subdued with the island's police force; in 1884 two Carnival celebrants were killed; later that year, more than a hundred Indians were shot by police and soldiers who tried to prevent Hosay celebrants coming onto the streets, as had been the usual practice. J.E. Andre, a white Trinidadian, protested this "massacre" to the Anti-Slavery Society in London.[546]

These century-old tragedies still infuse a sense of vitality and community history for Carnival and Hosay celebrants even though both festivals have been changed in important ways since political independence. For instance, Earl Lovelace reminisced about the earlier Carnival in *The Dragon Can't Dance*: "But this Carnival, putting on his costume now at dawn, Aldrick had a feeling of being the last one, the last symbol of rebellion and threat to confront Port of Spain. Fisheye was under orders not to misbehave, Philo had given up on his own calypsos of rebellion to sing now the Axe Man. Once upon a time the entire Carnival was expressions of rebellion."[547]

Hosay was not co-opted in any way similar to Carnival. The colonial elites may have sought to destroy Hosay where they had modified Carnival to make it acceptable for the elites. Hosay survived the 1880s and has kept alive a tradition of resistance among Indo-Trinidadians. When Guyana hosted the 150th anniversary of Emancipation, Tommy Payne made the connection with the free village movement of Trinidad. "In fact, while recently in Trinidad attending a similar meeting to this one, I discovered they see as the start of positive Indian resistance the Jose [Hosay or Hose] riots of 1884, which came in the wake of riots by villages, for Villages also existed in Trinidad, and this was in the years 1881 and 1883."[548]

Payne is right to alert us that defenders of Carnival had come from what had been post-emancipation, free villages in Belmont, East Dry River and Levantille, and that these Carnival disturbances preceded the Hosay/Muhurram "riots" of 1884.[549] We will now explore those interconnections and the impact of the institution of the plantation on such cultural actors as Indians and Africans. Only a context in which the plantation is kept in mind will allow one to understand why the elites saw mass fetes as threats necessitating a violent response.

5.1 ORIGINS AND MEANING
IN TRINIDAD'S FESTIVALS

Just as slaves in many contexts brought remnants or living cultural vehicles from Africa and restructured them in the Caribbean, Indians had great success in reviving their annual *Muhurram* festival so popular in northern India. While this observance has its roots in Shi'a Islam, it had been celebrated by Hindus in India as it came to be the case in Trinidad. In the Caribbean, however, the festival had become creolized and is generally referred to as *Hosay*, also Hosein, Hose' or Jose.[550] The most popular post-emancipation festivities among ex-slaves and those linked to them were several observances subsequently submerged in a two-day pre-Lenten Carnival. Unlike today, elite whites neither participated fully in festivals nor did they take kindly to the "boisterousness" of the masses in the years after Emancipation. Some elites went so far as to label Carnival uncivilized, unchristian and vulgar.

Carnival has commonly been traced back to pagan customs, and especially to the Roman Saturnalia and Bacchanalia. In this common trajectory, modern Carnival has much to do with role reversal, "status reversal," and paupers being kings for a day. Samuel Kinser has another perspective: "The modern meaning of Carnival," he says, arose from the experiences of early modern Europe, namely the fifteenth and sixteenth centuries. "It is a consequence of Catholic and later also Protestant attacks on the celebration" of a holiday which, until 1450, had been "generally acceptable." In his etymological analysis of *carne vale*—root words in Carnival—Kinser does not relate them to the pre-Lenten fast, or avoidance of meat, but to the equally valid translation, "to lift up, to relieve from flesh." In this sense, there is room too for feelings of being elevated, of rising above the mundane and the oppressive in daily life. This is particularly true for Hosay. Carnival includes status reversal, but it is also much more. "Da Matta [and others see] Carnival in the usual manner as reversing the surface of everyday life in playful fantasy. Carnival, however, plays not only with the surface but [also] with what the surface hides."[551]

Nineteenth-century Trinidad festivals appear to have played the role of surrogate trade unions, political parties, welfare-related systems, and all manner of psychological functions. In this sense, Kinser's approach to *Carnival* is closest to the past realities of the island. Not coincidentally, the Norman Inquiry into the 1884 Hosay massacre said that the Indians enjoyed an "exaggerated" idea of their power.[552] Commissioner Norman did not specify whether this power related to politics, the plantations, labor-relations, or only to their personal lives.

The pre-emancipation Carnival had been the preserve of the dominant elites, who played masquerades and gave gala balls and fancy dress parties. Black slaves were excluded except when they were part of dramatic performances or played music for the whites. The coloureds were allowed to use masks but not in conjunction with white revellers, nor on the streets. This situation changed with emancipation, when the domain of public space was theoretically opened to all. One early eyewitness to black participation in the street Carnival was Charles Day, who wrote in 1848: "The maskers parade the street in gangs of from ten to twenty . . . The primitives were negroes, as nearly naked as might be, debauched with a black varnish. One of this gang had a long chain and padlock attached to his leg, which . . . the others pulled."[553]

Either the slaves were celebrating the end of their bondage in a satiric revel, or playing out in masquerade those recent memories which could provide dramatic material for Carnival. Now that freedom had triumphed over slavery, it was possible to find humor in the labors of the slaves. V.V. Ivanov observed that at "certain moments in the seasonal cycle,"—which will be different for each society—particular groups "exercise ritual authority over their superiors."[554] Day's snapshot of Carnival reveals contradictions which can best be reconciled in Kinser's perspective. There is nothing funny or humorous in depictions of slavery: only a freed slave might laugh at his past bondage. Others who might attempt the same, as in the scene witnessed by Day, might be construed as apologists for slavery. Then the reversal of roles and status consisted not in the dramatic material itself—the images of slavery—but in the dramatis personae. Day adds to this interpretation by observing, "[W]henever a black mask appeared it was sure to be a white man." This was possible in the post-slavery era; white revellers had enjoyed other masques before the 1830s.

Following Umberto Eco, a white person's imitating a slave might be comic material; when freed black persons imitated the white person's representations of slavery, we have satire.[555] Errol Hill observed that before Emancipation, "the planters themselves used to represent a similar scene," disguised as "negue jadin," driven on by whips. Torches had been used in such representations but after 1838 white Trinidadians expressed concerns about the torches causing fires.[556] Much had changed.

Quite apart from the scenes from the 1848 masquerade, one finds evidence in support of allegations that Carnival was becoming Africanized and "vulgarized."[557] D.J. Crowley described a rather "objectionable" masquerade called *Pissenlit*, literally "stinker." He compared this Africanized masque with the French upper class *Dame Lorine* mas' played in the yards of whites, including aristocratic French Trinidadians. *Pissenlit* probably went too far: it was almost always played by men in women's gowns or "menstruation cloths liberally stained with 'blood' . . . it was suppressed in the early years of this century."[558]

Few of the opponents of the post-slavery Carnival saw beyond the surface vulgarity. One Catholic priest echoed the worst adjectives of the island's newspapers when he decried the changes in the post-1838 festival. The Abbe Masse recalled witnessing Carnival in the 1870s and 1880s, but words such as "savage" and "mad" reflected his overall attitude. His opinions apart, he placed blame only where it was deserved. On 25 February 1882, the priest blamed Europeans for bringing the worst lessons to the colonies. "It is the Europeans who brought the masquerade into America with all the vices of a corrupt civilization." The "negroes" had paid more heed to these "missionaries of the devil" than to the message of the Bible which "the Catholic priests have come to bring them." He warned: "Instead of subduing the savage, these workers of satan flatter them. A time will come when they will turn against them and devour them."[559]

In terms of other responses to the post-emancipation Carnival, newspapers described it as anything from "a wretched buffoonery," "an annual abomination," to a "diabolical festival."[560] The specter of the Devil was raised again: On 20 February 1882, Masse saw the overture to Carnival, or the "Canboulay" (*cannes brulees*) procession. "At midnight I was woken up by the sound of several horns and numerous cries coming from all parts of La Brea [southwestern Trinidad]. It was the beginning of carnival. On Sunday everything is quiet and the least carnival-like manifestation would be swiftly punished."

Masse then described the significance of the Canboulay, which almost always ended in great disorder and accidental or drunken violence: "It is impossible to get an idea of the disorder which takes place. . . ." He described the scene from slavery days when fires were started by disgruntled slaves, in revenge upon some overseers for insults and injuries sustained by them. "It is a fact of this kind which they [ex-slaves] want to recall . . . It is those who have the horns with which . . . the alarm [is sounded and responded to]. From all sides negroes appear, some armed with sticks, others carrying on their heads what they are known to have most precious. All run in the direction of a centre where there are other negroes who have lighted torches and who stimulate a field of canes on fire. Then the sticks, the rags, anything that falls under their hands serves to put out the fire."[561] It was at this juncture that "disorder" was said to dominate the Canboulay, which allowed Abbe Masse to blame women and alcohol equally with the men. In putting out the symbolic fire, Masse noted that many participants "receive some good blows," on account of "the abuse of rum which the negroes and negro women do not fail to have." Accidents occurred at Canboulay which "begins as a farce but nearly always ends in a tragic fashion," for reasons already offered by Masse. "The kind of frenzy which takes possession of them, the abominable dances to which they give themselves up, the cries of the beast of prey which they give, the hideous masks which they have on their faces, the clash of their sticks, the noises of knives which several carry in their belts, sometimes the cries of distress of the gravely wounded unfortunates, all that in the light of torches carried by more than half of these negroes, produces a spectacle frightening and truly diabolic."[562]

At the same time Masse recorded the staid celebration of middle and upper class persons of color. On the very night of Canboulay in 1882, an "aristocratic negro of La Brea gave himself the benefit of a disguised ball." There is a sense of decorum and middle class standards having been observed at this venue.

The most prominent transformations in Carnival, then, were visible in the massification of the street processions and in the introduction of Canboulay.[563] The manner in which Canboulay became the Sunday overture to the next two days of Carnival is befuddled with controversy. The controversy arises because Canboulay appears to have been associated, initially, with the 1 August commemoration of Emancipation. Remember that Carnival precedes Lent and occurs in the first quarter each year. The observations made by Day also appear in Commissioner Hamilton's inquiry into the 1881 "riots," namely, "'The history and meaning of this torchlight dance or procession (the Cannes Brulees) is briefly this. In the days of slavery, whenever fire broke out upon an estate, the slaves on the surrounding properties were immediately mustered . . . the gangs were followed by the drivers cracking their whips, and urging them with cries and blows to their work. After emancipation the negros [sic] began to represent this scene as a kind of commemoration of the change in their condition, and the procession of the 'Cannes Brulees' used to take place on the night of the 1st August [August Day], the date of their emancipation, and was kept up much for the same reason as the John Canoe [Jonkonnu] dance in Jamaica. After a time the day was changed, and for many years past the Carnival days have been inaugurated by the 'Cannes Brulees'."[564]

For those who have helped to end slavery, namely the Church, there was disappointment that August Day was being overlooked by ex-slaves. Indeed, a useful perspective on Trinidadian festivals is gleaned from a comparative look at the Jamaican Jonkonnu. In the 1850s, "the John Canoe [fete] passed from public celebration of August 1st to the 'underground.'" This was a response to official hostility toward a value-less festival which could not be tailored to elite uses. The absence of possibilities of "us[ing] the day . . . for didacticism," led to the loss of white interest in, and gradual rejection of, Jonkonnu. A similar attitude confronted Carnival, yet unlike Jonkonnu, it did not go underground. Probably because Trinidad's elites enjoyed the fete and targeted only parts of it for destruction.

A decade after Emancipation, efforts had been made to control Carnival. Obstacles were raised against old and new aspects of the fete now that the non-white masses had become dominant and "disorderly" in the celebrations. Such obstacles comprised restrictions on Canboulay, ostensibly to assuage the fear of accidental fires; about whether blacks were to be allowed to masquerade on the streets; and in new rules for obtaining permits before Carnival observances.

Hosay, too, had grown in popularity among the masses as it did in unpopularity with some of the elites who saw it as an unpredictable force. Notable for joint Hindu-Muslim observances in India's northern states,[565] it soon attracted noticeable Afro-Trinidadian interest. Although Hosay arrived in Trinidad after 1845 with Indian indenture, it had grown rapidly among all Indians and the wider community. Active participation of blacks became conspicuous in the 1860s, which included fasting to build castle-like structures (*tadjahs*) and playing *tassa* drums.[566]

In time the most visible and attractive features of the Trinidad Hosay or Muhurram became frenetic tassa drumming, street dancing, feasts and parading of the model mausoleums for Hasan and Hussein. The concept of creolization helps in understanding this fete and its fate in the Caribbean. Muhurram came to be called the "East Indian Carnival," the emphasis falling on the element of fete, on its *carnival* aspect. The word *Muhurram* itself was creolized into "Hosay," probably traceable to the frequent calling out during the festivities, of the names of Hasan and Hussein, one or both names being improperly enunciated as *Hosay*. Yet, this was a way in which the martyred grandsons of Islam's Prophet Muhammad became relevant in plantation Trinidad.

Many non-Indians in Trinidad did/do not realize that Hosay is a ten-day festival, occurring during "Muhurram" the first month of the Islamic calendar, and that nine days of fasting, prayer, ritual weeping precede the final fete. In the nine days of fasting and solemnity, the elaborate model tombs or *tadjahs* are built. Most Trinidadians saw the fete but nothing of the austerity and deep spirituality inherent in Hosay. Scholars have drawn parallels between the sacrifices at Karbala and on the plantations; even contributions towards the decorative material for the tadjahs constituted a monetary sacrifice.[567] The drama and sacrifice recall the battle of Karbala in 680, when Hasan and Hussein were bloodily removed from succession to the fifth Arab *caliphate*.[568] Those who supported the blood line of Islam's Prophet came to be known as Shi'a or Shi'ites. The majority of powerful Arab leaders did not take kindly to the claims of the Prophet grandsons; Sunni numbers helped that sect triumph, the survivors of the Prophet Mahomad's bloodline now called "Shi'ites meaning sectaries." The generous and holy lives of the brothers guaranteed both a place in numerous hearts.[569]

Most of Trinidad's inhabitants saw Hosay mainly through the final day, *Ashura'* when the fete element predominates.[570] Many bonds were in fact being developed on the plantations which were omnipresent in Trinidadian life. The distribution of Indians and

Africans on the different estates created multiracial competitive
units and a division of labor extending to tadjah-building. The
Phillipine estate apparently had earned precedence in taking the
embellished tombs onto the roads.[571] The most eelaborate tadjah
would then lead the entire procession to the sea or river where the
tombs were surrendered. All along the way playful fencing with
hakka sticks, *tassa* drumming, and general merriment brought
women and children behind the tadjah of their respective
plantations. This parade drew white and coloured spectators to
their balconies. During the 1881 Hosay, we read that when bad
weather and hard times dampened the spirits of the sight-seeing
public . . . notwithstanding which, the galleries of the windows of
all the houses of High Street were crowded with the bright and
eager countenances of the fair sex, whose expectation was put to
severe trial from the unusually late appearance of the [tadjah]
procession.[572]

The place of the mixed-race or coloured population in mass
festivities was ambiguous. While many may have adopted Carnival
within the purview of French and Spanish culture, the arrival of
Britain had thrown an unfavorable light on the Catholic-influenced
festivities. Gradually, a significant number of British-oriented
coloureds came to share the hostility of their Protestant rulers
toward mass festivals.

Prior to Emancipation, coloured participation in Carnival had
been a privilege raather than a right. Yet, their situation was a
notch above the rest of non-European Trinidad. "The free persons
of Colour were subjected to very stringent Regulations and
although not forbidden to mask, were yet compelled to keep to
themselves and never presumed to join in the amusements of the
privileged [white] class . . . After [1833] things were materially
altered, the ancient lines of demarcation between the classes were
obliterated and as a natural consequence the carnival degenerated
into a noisy and disorderly amusement of the lower classes."[573]

The post-emancipation dispensation which had rendered all
Trinidad's people free to mask and join street festivities came too

late for those coloureds who had thrown in their lot with the anglicizing policies of Britain. As Barbara Powrie observed, some three distinct elements comprised the coloured middle class: Anglophile and/or Protestant coloureds; Francophile and Catholic coloureds; and free black immigrants. Only the second group continued to participate in their pre-Emancipation Carnival.[574]

A sizeable proportion of coloureds who had retained values imbibed from Spanish and French creoles had been seen at the Carnival of the 1830s. In 1833 *The Port of Spain Gazette* reported that when the Assistant Chief of Police sought to "check the shameful violation of the Sabbath," and arrested two coloureds, "his house was assaulted by a large concourse of rabble," who broke the windows and attacked Mr. Peake himself.[575] The British in Trinidad frequently used the "violation of the Sabbath" as an excuse to show their disapproval of Carnival. One "Scotchman" complained to the press about this "desecration" in 1838 and of "the disgusting and indecent scenes that were enacted in the streets." He concluded that British values made it imperative that the "wretched masquerade [which] belongs to older [Spanish?] days, ought to be abolished in our own."[576]

British disapprobation was less effective in driving all the whites from participation in Carnival. In 1881, and in the face of what Hamilton had concluded, his Report opined: "the conduct of the people generally appears to have been comparatively harmless, their performances being mainly of a low and stupid style of buffoonery. . . ." The Commissioner did explain that since the 1860s "certain bands of ruffians" had inserted themselves into the fete proceedings. The occasional disturbances owed their origins to "persons paying off old grudges under the cover of Carnival." No responsibility for the "riots" was attributed to police actions or to other factors, even though "The frequenters of the Carnival are not . . . restricted to the ruffians and prostitutes who take the chief parts in those scenes." Among the onlookers were also many "harmless people" as well as "a vast crowd of excited and excitable spectators, whom drink or irritation may at any moment involve in a general melee."[577]

Whether or not whites were included with the "large number of harmless people," the Commissioner had concluded fairly that Carnival was not dominated by "ruffians and prostitutes." In the first year of Emancipation, however, the streets were practically devoid of celebrants from the elites or upper classes.[578] As this was the first Carnival for the ex-slaves, it was understandable that some whites observed a cautious distance. The "disorderly amusement" of ex-slaves and "degenerate" and irreligious treatment of the Sabbath did not characterize Carnival at this time. Some elite revellers therefore returned to the street Carnival. Throughout the period 1834-1888, some of the elites always participated at the masquerades. Generally, however, whites opted for fancy dress balls.

With regards to the coloureds, their attitudes are again ambiguous. Those who were socially mobile in an upward direction stayed away from Carnival even if French creole in culture. For those coloureds "frustrated" by their condition, the fete became an important "safety valve." Carnival, for these status-static or downward mobile coloureds, presented an opportunity to voice their grievances and challenge authority. For them, Carnival was "one chance in the whole year when socially embarrassing facts of inheritance c[ould] be used to advantage, freely and openly."[579]

5.2 AMBIVALENCE TOWARD THE CARNIVAL AND HOSAY FESTIVALS

By the 1850s, all Trinidadians who classed as elites or the "polite circles," including some among blacks and coloureds, were expressing major reservations about the continued carnival license of the masses. There was a divide-and-rule strategy employed by the authorities, vis a vis the right to mask by coloured and black participants. Since the 1830s, the right to wear masks in the street festivities had been circumscribed by police discretion. In 1846, "on account of the general unrest in the city," the governor totally forbade masking in the 1846 Carnival. Three days later an announcement said that the prohibition did not apply to house-to-house masking. As only coloureds and whites observed Carnival in this manner, the real message was that only the masking of these two groups would be tolerated. Actions and regulations such as these had the effect of driving a wedge between coloureds and blacks.

A few years later, Ordinance No.6 of 1849 gave the police discretion in allowing or disallowing masking at Carnival. Without police authorization, masking would be "illegal." The Ordinance also restricted Carnival to two days in order to weaken Canboulay and "protect" the Sabbath from desecration.[580] The masses managed to retain Canboulay with the argument that it always commenced at midnight and therefore was a Monday event.

During the governorship of Keate in the 1850s, one of the most direct attempts was made to suppress the entire observance. Investigator Hamilton's Report of 1881 had recalled that in 1858, "an attempt was made to put down the Carnival by force." The masses "resented" this and prepared for a more "extended" Carnival in 1859. Keate sent the police to shut down the fete and a "serious disturbance" followed. The police then needed reinforcements, but none was forthcoming. A "body of unarmed troops" were called to assist the police, but they too "were attacked by the people and compelled to retire." Thereafter, the society seemed resigned to Carnival, at least until 1868.[581]

The alleged concern about accidental fires has been noted. Additionally, there was general white disappointment that ex-slaves were not commemorating Freedom Day since the 1840s. The first of these concerns began to be resolved in conjunction with a focussed repression of Canboulay. The second would be achieved through an orchestrated separation of Carnival and Hosay, in making Hosay and Indian culture less attractive to non-Indians.

An Ordinance of 1868 strenghthened the earlier regulation of 1849 requiring masqueraders to obtain prior police permission. Also, "the carrying of lighted torches became an offence if done to the obstruction or annoyance or danger" to any resident or passer-by in the street.[582] This was the core weapon with which Canboulay was to be attacked in the 1880s. The second of the above concerns allowed the realization of an odd alliance between erstwhile enemies—planters and many a missionary.

It is very likely that after 1834-38, Canboulay commemorated 1 August, Emancipation *and* freedom from forced labor, as per fire-extinguishing demands of the planters. The spectators and planters who witnessed 1 August commemorations also confronted unpleasant memories of the demise of their world.[583] Such unpleasant planter memories were wedded to righteous indignation of missionaries and their constituents when, by the 1840s, the masses moved Canboulay to February as the midnight overture to Carnival. While the precise details about how August Day was transformed into the overture called Canboulay are difficult to delineate, Day's 1848 account suggest that by that date August Day-cum-Canboulay had merged. Yet, for those who frowned upon Carnival, the apparent disregard for Emancipation Day was the insult added to injury. The black and coloured middle class and their missionary friends resented the neglect of August Day for joint black-Indian celebrations of Hosay, or alleged defilement as in the lewd frivolities of Carnival.

Until the jubilee decade of Emancipation, this was precisely the group, the status-conscious non-whites and missionaries, who observed the end of slavery with speeches and dinners.[584] There is a question about the timing of the decision to move from an opposition based on newspaper criticism to the recourse of state and police violence.[585] Both Governor Keate's use of police power against Carnival in 1858-59 and the case of the Hosay violence in 1884, occurred during economically difficult years. The anti-Carnival "riots" too occurred during the lean 1880s. The increasing role of the shiftless and unemployed from the slums of Port of

Spain, and of the *jamette* class (*diametre*) gave a sense of urgency to the elites who now presented their anti-Carnival mood as a concern for law and order.[586]

Hamilton reported that unemployment, prostitution and slum conditions had been turning out Carnival adherents in Port of Spain throughout the 1850s. By the 1860s, these "jamets of the urban slums, organised into bands," were more visible during Carnival.[587] The downtrodden of society found comraderie and neighborhood organization in the bands: "The jamets of the towns were organised into bands for the purpose of dancing and fighting. These were territorial and semi-secret organisations: each sector of each region might have its gang. Such gangs may have derived from West African secret societies, and their existence in Trinidad was noted as early as 1808 . . . Each gang had its Roi, Reine, Dauphin, Grand Judge, soldiers and alguazils. The 'avowed object' of these slave bands was to hold African dances. Membership in these bands was a test of manhood; initiation sometimes involved the shedding of blood in street rituals . . . Crossing the boundaries of any band's territory was a signal for ritualised conflict, which was usually arranged for Carnival days."[588]

This was known to the participants, but almost nothing of this perspective was possible for Carnival's enemies. Black and coloured elites too, whether they sought rapid anglicization or simply the rapid westernization of the masses, failed to appreciate this as well. As the black newspaper *New Era* put it, the masses, those "immoral" people, based "their right of existence on their power to outrage all that society hold most sacred, and all that religion impose[d]."[589] Anyone who valued personal success or social mobility would reject Carnival.

The media attack on a mass fete which lacked didactic opportunities was accompanied by the hope that Carnival, by 1871, was dying a natural death. This demise did not occur, and in 1877 the *Port of Spain Gazette* cautioned, "the thing which with the majority of the lower classes here goes under the name of masquerading acquires a new strength and fresh vitality every year it is tolerated." There was a note of frustration and urgency in this subtle threat. It may have been here that the battle lines were drawn. Carnival riots occurred two years later, in 1879 and more seriously, in 1881.

Several factors made the Trinidadian authorities nervous in the 1870s and 1880s. Such anxiety culminated in the Muhurram Massacre of 1884. One was the economic depression to which beet sugar competition from Germany and France contributed; then there were increasingly forceful labor action from indented Indians; and thirdly, there was the approaching jubilee of Emancipation Day in 1888. Politically astute blacks and coloureds like William Herbert, J.J. Thomas and Edgar Maresse-Smith began preparing for a massive fiftieth anniversary of slavery's demise.[590] All this made the elites so wary of "instability" that they failed to separate the context of art, leisure and ritual from revolt and terror.

On the streets, the content of Carnival was always as much artistic and religious as it was political. A recent study of several Caribbean artistic celebrations led authors Nunley and Bettelheim to declare that depending on "specific moments" one or the other of the three elements—political, religious or artistic—might prevail in Trinidad's festivals.[591] The political and labor-union style roles of both mass festivals in Trinidad became evident in economically lean years. But there were other Carnivals in which Indians participated as ordinary maskers, as ordinary Trinidadians. Indians were famous for their *burroquite* (donkey) representations accompanied by songs during the 1870s, but their favorite was Coolie Devils or *jab jabs*.[592]

Another political element in Carnival came to stay when the "jamets," regarded as the flotsam and jetsam of the sugar colony, anticipated Carnival as the event which was the highlight of each year. Carnival bands which existed year round competed in the street festivities for all that gave meaning and personal respect to its members. These downtrodden people from the slums found that in Carnival they might be kings instead of paupers for the day, and also an occasion on which to lampoon the dominant society and vent their frustrations. Carnival had come to symbolize the "rejection of the norms of the superstructure" by those who aspired to respectability but had been excluded because of "colour, traditional mores, lack of education and poverty."[593]

The activities of the bands made Carnival, in the eyes of the elites, vulgar and abominable. But the elite withdrawal from the street Carnival had left "a post-emancipation social order in the making," to the masses and their band culture. Indeed, the first bands had emerged in the Belmont district of Port of Spain, "a village of mud and thatched cabins that cradled an African culture."[594] The Radas of West Africa had been settled in the vicinity. Not until the 1870s did opponents of Carnival arrive at the conclusions that Carnival was not dying because of elite withdrawal, and, that the withdrawal had meant a surrender to the culture of the masses. Consequently, a decision to reassert control over Carnival was taken, a decision in which Captain Arthur Baker and his police played a crucial role.

The Superintendent of Police, Baker, took his first action against mass festivals in 1880, when he had suddenly appeared at Canboulay. Baker and his men arrived just as the celebrants readied for the midnight procession. The police surrounded the revellers and compelled them to give up their torches, staves and drums. The element of total surprise worked to the advantage of the police and resistance was minimized. Without torches, staves and drums there could be no Canboulay procession. The masses, nonetheless, returned to Canboulay in 1881 sufficiently prepared to resist further police action. In 1882 Baker and his men found no surrender like that of 1881. A major riot ensued. Some participants were injured, but 38 of the 150 policemen too were injured. Canboulay had bought a short lease of life.

The Carnival riots became widespread news, and the masses were gratified that many black and coloured social elites protested the role of the police. They saw the police action as wanton interference. Governor Sir Sanford Freeling did not have pleasant alternatives. His decision to reinstate the celebration when the masses "promise[d] not to make any disturbance or break the law," angered Baker's men.[595] This was a pyrrhic victory for the masses. The anger of the police and that of the public at the "riots" led to the Hamilton Commission, which not only upheld Carnival restrictions, but extended constraints on Hosay.

The defenders of Canboulay made one last stand in 1883, leading to what is known as the second Carnival riot. Police power and legislation combined to neutralize the masses and their lively Carnival overture. The last Canboulay was that of 1883. The attention of the elites now turned upon Hosay.

While there is a temptation to see a machiavellian design to suppress Carnival bit by bit, and then move on to obstruct large scale Hosay observances in Trinidad, it is equally probable that the mere desire to send Trinidad along a Protestant Christian direction led to a repressive policy. The fateful decisions may have been the result of ad hoc measures, and not necessarily premeditated by evil genius. The question of anglicization of Trinidad was evident in newspapers, particularly in connection with the negative impact of heathen Indians. Was there an urgency for the elites to maintain the direction of post-slavery Trinidad by carefully controlling "unchristian" festivals?

Bridget Brereton argued that well into the last quarter of the nineteenth century, "carnival was an arena in which class antagonisms were worked out."[596] With respect to the Indo-Trinidadian Hosay, K. Haraksingh saw in it "undisguised demonstrations of opposition to the established order."[597] Both of these interpretations have some truth, but seen entirely from such perspectives, Carnival and Hosay lose their inherent artistic, cultural and festive merits. The authorities, however, operated within the plantation orbit where the value of non-Europeans depended upon docility and work, not art.

After 1870, the intensifying competition from European beet sugar made Trinidadian planters feel hemmed in, and they responded with coercive measures against blacks and Indians, whether it was in response to labor actions or festival rights. It is in this context of the giant looming shadows of the plantations, and the efforts to anglicize and christianize Indians and Africans completely, which made state violence upon Carnival and Hosay revellers feasible or attractive. There continued the perennial planter petitions for "reliable" indented laborers, even as Indian confidence and labor strikes grew in number and intensity during the 1870s and 1880s. What irked and possibly frightened planters was the closer relations between laboring blacks and Indians, especially in their cooperation in building tadjahs and mutually celebrating each other's festivals. Could persons who played together, someday fight together?

As early as 1859 the *Port of Spain Gazette* had called for controls on Hosay. "It must always be a grievous sight to see in a christian [sic] country," the newspaper opined regarding Hosay festivities, "the *false* and *foolish* worship, paraded openly and unchecked." The editorial looked to that "joyous" day when there would be "heart worship of the only true God."[598]

This pro-planter medium was matched in its disapproval by the newspaper of the coloureds, *The Trinidad Sentinel*. In 1857 that newspaper regretted that August Day, "once so remarkable" in denoting "the greatest epoch in West Indian history" had been allowed to pass without "a single mark of the tribute of recognition and respect due to its memory." To exacerbate this sad state of affairs, "the day was very unpropitious for the exhibition of the paper-decorated" Indian tadjahs despite inclement weather which might "have caused a postponement of the Coolie celebration."[599] This newspaper of upwardly mobile coloureds sensed that their interconnections with the blacks, who were now joining the "Coolie Festival,"[600] would bring the opprobrium of fellow Christians upon them all. Besides, blacks would reduce their opportunities for social mobility if they imitated non-christian Indians. During the Hosay fete in question, it was not possible "to mark any difference in the multitude of Indian and creole labourers whose creed, or whose love of novelty," the newspaper surmised, accounted for black creoles joining in the "tumultuous" Hosay festival.

The opponents of Hosay missed its role in the generally drab, unlightened life of a transplanted people. Keith Hjortshoj writes that Muhurram/Hosay emphasizes those "basic human bonds, human virtues, and human needs," which were violated in the murders of Hasan and Hussein. In India he was told that "'Anyone can be a Shi'i at heart . . . Muslim, Hindu, or Christian.'"[601]

The elites and social engineers in Trinidad succeeded in driving a wedge between Hindu and Muslim, and in maintaining the divide between Indo-and Afro-Trinidadian. Hosay critics had the influence to wean non-Indians away from the Coolie Carnival. Law was again called upon to nip in the bud any potential fusion between Indian and creole festivals. A few months ahead of the October 1884 Hosay, legislation was passed, in July, to now restrict Hosay to Muslims alone. No permits for parades were granted the Hindus, and blacks were forbidden to participate.[602]

Legislation supported by fear, prejudice, or both, conspired to prevent Trinidad becoming a cultural and social melting-pot, and Hosay from assimilated into wider Trinidadian life. While the restricted room for social mobility and frustrations among coloured and black creoles led them to prize and gallantly defend Carnival, the planters' insistence on combating declining sugar prices by increasing the daily tasks of indented workers, may have politicized the 1884 in particular.

Creoles who joined the Indians in Hosay posed a particularly anxious problem for the elites. The Norman Inquiry into the Muhurrum Massacre of 1884 revealed the creoles' expectant waiting for the Indian processions to reach the towns, notably San Fernando in the south, where they would join in the march to the sea. Commissioner Norman also recorded one white testimony about creoles having urged the Indians on when the riot act was about to be read. The deponent said, "I heard the expression from the crowd at different times in Creole accent,'I hope there's a row, a damned row.'" A constable testified that "a creole man, George Andrew" was sentenced to six months imprisonment with hard labor for "inciting" the Indians against the police.[603]

This active creole participation in Hosay was viewed as a dangerous sign; but it is not clear what such participation actually signalled. Given the many ways in which Indians had been isolated from other Trinidadians, a common leisure pursuit was arresting. The elites may have anticipated a labor, or worse, a proto-political alliance among those who "played" together. More likely, creoles had joined the Indian fete for a combination of curiosity, fun and neighborliness. Research has already demonstrated that on Trinidad's plantations, solidarity was more often than not based on the estate work group, in spite of race. In 1859, when competition and assault became blurred during Hosay observances, "Creoles and Chinese went to the help of their workmates; loyalties to the estate transcended those of race in the fighting." It is equally important to examine those elements which make festivals universally attractive, as noted by Historian Donald Wood. "Both Carnival and [H]osein were processions, and the animation of a march has a more exciting effect on a crowd than a function that takes place in one spot. And perhaps most important of all, each had a strong competitive element in it. In Carnival it was, and still is, the rival bands that compete in the ingenuity of their themes and in the magnificence of their costumes. In [H]osein it is the rival taziyas that compete for admiration, and to be first in the procession or first at the edge of the water. The rivalry of [H]osein was between estates and it was the working group and not religion or the same home district which determined the allegiance of those who took part."[604]

This understanding of the masses and their festivals lay ahead, in the twentieth century, and not with the colonial elites of the 1880s. When planters saw "coolie-creole" cooperation and celebrations, and with the indenteds' increasing role in shaping their workday and remuneration, they became unsure about the fullness of their control in Trinidad. By then, too, Indians comprised more than one-third of the island's people. Falling sugar prices accompanied by poor planter-indented relations had strained relations "between the British and their subjects."[605]

In 1877, indented laborers had raised the issue of how their
"lost" days were being calculated; days on which they were ill or in
jail had been "factored" into giving planters an "extension period"
at the end of the Indians' servitude. Indians objected to planters
"alone presen[ting] the total number of lost days, making it
impossible for the[m] to give lawful excuse for absence." The fact
that indented and free Indians "could be arrested for so trivial an
offence as merely crossing a highway," did not endear the regime
to any sector of the new workers.[606] As we have seen in Chapter
Three, every Indian in a public place could be regarded as requiring
a pass.

One can again contextualize the brutal actions against Carnival
and Hosay, without condoning them, by examining other demands
which planters confronted in the 1880s. Apart from ex-slave and
Indian grievances, colonial Trinidad was being buffeted by a
resuscitated on-again, off-again campaign for greater representation.
Harking to the point made by T. Payne, the Hosay disturbances of
1884 are linked to the Carnival disturbances of the earlier 1880s.
If one takes the argument further as Anthony de Verteuil does, the
period from 1881 to 1888 were the years of revolt, and the title of
his book. The disadvantaged and displaced whites had, in fact,
mounted a "revolt" of their own. This was not a violent revolt, only
constitutional agitation for political reform. Perhaps, de Vertueil's
work ends in 1888 because in that year the Royal Franchise
Commission investigated the feasibility of granting voting rights
to the populace.

That the Franchise Commission considered the future of Indians
in Trinidad was a positive sign, in terms both of educational/
material progress made by Indians and in the sense of justice and
the dream of democracy. Indian numbers dictated that only gross
racialism would continue to exclude them from discussion. Kenneth
Grant testified on 9 April:

> "Chairman : Could you give the Commission any rough
> idea of what proportion of the coolies speak English;

when I say coolies, of course, you know I mean Indian immigrants, but it is a shorter word; what proportion of them do you think speak English?

Grant : It would be rather difficult to answer that directly, sir. Many of them understand English, but they are accustomed to use the Hindustanee language [Hindi] in their own homes. But a great many understand it.

[Question]: Do many read it?

Grant : Oh, yes; I have just noticed in my report this year that I had 3,700 that have passed through my school, and I suppose most of those understand English fairly [well].

Chairman : . . . You think they can take an intelligent interest in politics then?

Grant : Many of them can.

Chairman : There is no reason for making any distinction between them and the others?

Grant : I don't think so."[607]

This issue of Indian numbers and their future *political* clout led some of the elites to argue that Indians were quite different, in fact lower on the social scale than the rest of the populace. Then again, for coloureds as much as for ex-slaves, the many political and social consequences of the Indian presence weighed heavily upon their own futures. The leaders among the creoles may have realized that political power was the key to winning victories over the former slaveowners as well as securing their own best interest. Coloureds had mounted their campaigns for equality and political reforms almost from the beginning of British rule; after 1838 black leaders collaborated in politics with lighter-skinned coloureds. Not surprisingly, therefore, coloured and black leaders and newspapers protested against Indian immigration (as a symbol of planter recalcitrance) and against blacks joining in the celebration of Indian culture in Trinidad. The chairman of the Franchise Commission conceded the principle that Indians deserved the vote with other

Trinidadians. Some Indians were "considerable owners" of property; but if immigration were to continue "at the rate at which it is going on . . . the Commission has to look very much further ahead," when some day, "the very people who imported those coolies" for estate labour and "upkeep . . . may suddenly find that they have to be governed" by these same people.[608]

Indo-Trinidadian population increase, even if not a surprise to those who continued to covet Indian labor, came at an inconvenient time. For those who opposed Indians coming into a full partnership within Trinidad, no time would have been convenient for democratic principles. If only these indented workers would disappear after their work were done on the estates. . . . Coloured creoles appeared to be the group most threatened by Indian numbers and influence; they were best placed to take over from the British overlords.

In the aftermath of the terrible price inflicted on Hosay celebrants, British authorities and local whites declared that Indian laborers had become intoxicated with their importance-a sense of their "power."[609] If simply recreating an observance they had enjoyed in India made indenteds powerful, it was a power of which they were largely ignorant. Trinidad's officials saw long-term implications in the spread of Hosay which political culture and their duties imposed upon them; they could see, too, the dangers of having repeated confrontations with a growing part of the population. Those who sought to justify the unjust and disproportionate response to Hosay in 1884, pointed to increasing labor disturbances on the estates as an Indian grab for power. When the Indians' success in fighting off Hosay restrictions since 1882 were added to the equation, Indians were seen fulfilling such prophecies.

In 1882, the attempt to enforce controls on Hosay had been relinquished in the face of rumors that Indians were stockpiling petrol and weapons to defend their festival.[610] Two years later the authorities in Trinidad were determined to stop Hosay with a virtual army of soldiers and marines, who had been carefully preparing for the 1884 event.

The authorities in Trinidad set out to prevent a continuance of Hosay as a grand, island-wide, multi-racial festival led by the Indians. In July 1884, with the governor in London, but with the connivance of the Protector of Immigrants, an ordinance was introduced to prevent Hindus and blacks from participating in Hosay festivities.[611] The idea was to reduce Hosay to a Muslim observance in the privacy of the estates, although traditionally, the tadjahs were deposited in a waterway. Indians were not, in 1884, seeking to do anything different from what they had done at previous Hosays in Trinidad. Like all rules governing indenture, they could be changed when it suited any one colony; in Trinidad we saw a dramatic and tragic consequence of such unexplained changes only because a very large group of Indians were involved. In almost every other case, rule changes affected Indians as individuals, or they were expected to go to courts and prisons as individuals (the Walkinshaw Estate situation was an exception to this in 1846), and the effects were severe, but out of view.

Opponents of Hosay who were acting in Christian conscience failed to understand the vital role the festival played in the monotonous, dreary lives of the indented and indenture-free Indians alike. Hosay made the year's suffering and exile tolerable for isolated Indians. (Some, though perhaps not all, Indians made a comparison between their fate and that of the beleaguered Shi'ites[612]). Haraksingh reminds us that Hosay was also a healthy antidote to strained headman-laborer (or Indian-Indian) relations.[613] To the extent Hosay was therapeutic to various levels of the estate labor force, the plantocracy failed to see how they benefitted from Hosay.

The latest restrictions on Hosay were met with dismay and indignation by the Indians. A petition was drawn up under the leadership of Sookhoo, a headman of the Phillipine Estate. The petition was summarily dismissed: Sookhoo was told that Hindus had no reason to resent being excluded from what was a Muslim festival. This idea that Muhurram was purely Islamic was not true in undivided India in the nineteenth century; Tinker, in treating the entire question of Indian interaction with plantocracies, said: "It was an absolute principle" of the indenture system that "no Indian labourer become a recognized leader . . . Their only recognized role was that of petitioners: and humble petitioners too."[614] Sookhoo was being told what Indians in India did when he had been born Indian; he may very well have felt deeply humiliated.

The brusque treatment of their petition angered many of Sookhoo's colleagues on the estates. A groundswell of feeling against the unjust restrictions asserted itself among some of these Indians. Sookhoo was reported to have declared, 'We will have no more petitions; we will fight it out with the strength of our hands.' It came exactly to that, despite Indians having *hakka* sticks, necessary for the staged fights.

While Sookhoo displayed some leadership in 1884, there is no evidence that he sought (or succeeded) in convincing Indians on other estates to his point of view. The established prestige which the Phillipine Estate had earned in previous Hosays was at stake for Sookhoo and his brethren, but the estate management's general hostility to the laborers precluded clear thinking. In nineteenth-century Trinidad, where the plantation had not as yet succeeded in destroying important non-western ways, its elites saw a potential threat posed by Indians very seriously. The old fear of the slavemasters about slave rebellions in the thick of night were exhumed; no one rationally examined how prepared Indians or blacks were to take over Trinidad in the 1880s. That the elites believed Indians posed a threat in 1884 unleashed the full barrage of police power upon Indian celebrants, killing 16 on the roads and wounding well over a hundred more.

Subscribers to the *Times* of London read a letter from a Trinidadian on 8 November: "About 14 or 15 were killed and about 87 wounded, some of them will probably die before long. The details of this atrocious massacre, as narrated to me by trustworthy eyewitnesses, are so ghastly that, although it took place a week ago, ever since my sleep has been very disturbed, and my blood has been at fever heat at the idea that such an unparalleled atrocity [has been] committed at the present day under the British flag."[615]

The nation was stunned; the Colonial Office scrambled to prevent British India learning about the gory details; Indo-Trinidadians themselves still live the trauma of that event, generation by generation, as Hosay quietly continues to spread its message of the dignity of the downtrodden.[616] That Hosay was diminished yet refused to die may be seen as a victory for the victims of indenture, and for those who died on the battlefield of the estates on 30 October 1884.

5.3 THE NORMAN INQUIRY INTO THE HOSAY MASSACRE (1884-85)

The number of Hosay celebrants who were killed on 30 October 1884 vary in different accounts. Some fatally wounded Indians ran into the cane pieces where they were found only later. Hence the number of fatalities noted on 30 October was less than the final count. Singh's study—the only recent study to be published on the Muhurram massacre—concludes that 16 Indians died on 30 October and 150 were wounded, but that "Some of the injured were still dying in January 1885."[617] Andre's letter was sent to the *Times* by the Anti-Slavery Society with the comment, "A parallel case would be calling out our troops to fire on 5th of November [Guy Fawkes Day] bonfire men."[618] The Earl of Derby looked for a commissioner to conduct "damage control."

Another observer in Trinidad had sent a letter critical of the local authorities two days before Andre's letter. This "English Observer" was appalled that the Indians fired upon at Hosay with the usual *hakka* "sticks were practically unarmed." His letter added that among the casualties "are said to be women and children."[619]

The enormity of the police brutality may be captured by the translator conveying from two of the Indian witnesses at the Inquiry: "[We] did not hear the Riot Act read," and besides, at no time was it told us, "we would be shot" for going onto the roads as in previous years.[620]

Both before and after the appointment of Norman to investigate the events leading up to the police firing upon Hosay, an important debate on indenture took place in the pages of the *Times*. A letter signed, "Trinidad, on Nov. 6." criticized the "false" benefits offered to Indians by the proponents of indenture. Additional remarks show, had s/he been asked, this observer may have been a useful witness: "The fact is that the rest of the population is afraid of the [Indians], and so take these stern measures to keep them down. But whether we are justified in compelling our fellow-creatures to serve us for five years, whether they want to or not, in order that we may make money, and then shooting them down because we are afraid of them, seems a doubtful question, and one that requires some investigation."[621]

The debate was then joined by "An Indian Civilian," whose letter to the *Times* appeared on 29 November. In a particularly critical letter the writer asked whether the celebrants' "opposition to an arbitrary police regulation," was not seized upon "to shoot them down wholesale." The entire issue of low wages and increased tasks was cited as a justifiable grievance on the part of the Indians. The whole system of indenture was being indicted. The West India Committee decided to join in the fray.

The West India Committee's Acting Chairman, Quinton Hogg, wrote a rebuttal to the *Times*. He said, "[T]here is no justification whatever for the attempt made to represent the *riot* as having arisen from any increase in the daily task or in any reduction in the daily wage. The dispute has been from the first simply one between the Government and the Coolies, and had the law been more firmly enforced in the first instance I believe the calamitous event in which it culminated would have been averted."[622]

The letters of protest on the one hand, and of the West India Committee on the other, agree on the "calamitous" nature of the events of 30 October 1884, but on very little else. The spokesman for the planters saw the Indian Hosay as nothing short of a political festival with political aims. Hogg sounded much like Walkinshaw of Clydesdale Estate, insisting that government's "indulging" the Indians had created the problems, which were supposedly preventable by squeezing more concessions from indented Indian laborers.

Where Andre found a massacre, Hogg saw a labor riot which had nothing to do with labor conditions. Hogg's letter is exceedingly clever for relieving planters of blame in what was being called a simple "dispute" between "Government" and Indian laborers. Would the Commissioner examine this vital question as to whether the "dispute" was between Indians and their employers, or between the "Government" and the indented?

The Colonial Office made Sir Henry W. Norman the sole commissioner into the "Muhurram Disturbances." Norman reached Trinidad on the last day of 1884 and began work on 1 January. By the end of a week, Norman's task was completed with apparent satisfaction. In his Report, he declared that he had "examined 34 persons," that he had found no reason to blame the authorities in Trinidad, and added, "H.W. Norman, General. Governor of Jamaica on Special Duty," on 7 January 1885.

The idea that a current governor should investigate a massacre of plantation laborers on a neighboring sugar colony could only have worked because the victims were defenseless non-christians. It is inconceivable that the highest imperial officer of one British colony would condemn the government of another equally dependant on cheap labor and sugar exports. Norman seemed to exemplify this injustice by ignoring the question of whether planters had in any way contributed to the state of tension in Trinidad in the 1880s. Indeed, even as Norman felt compelled to listen to the testimony of Andre, he did his best to portray Andre in a negative, unpatriotic light. The effective point made by Commissioner

Norman was that "There can be no doubt that the Coolies feel their power, or rather, I should say, have an exaggerated idea of that power, and that concession would now be looked on as weakness . . . if the present rules [against Hosay] were withdrawn. As an additional reason for not now altering the rules, I would ask attention to the statements which bear testimony to the improved demeanour of the Coolies since the 30th October, and to the very remarkable opinion expressed by a missionary who is devoting his life to the[ir] benefit."[623]

The logic of the forces involved in damage control could not have been expected to show consistency. Between Hogg's letter to the *Times* which saw the tragedy arising from a dispute between "Government" and indenteds, and the more substantive aspect/s of Norman's Report, came testimony from planters and missionaries that the "Coolies" were better laborers after 30 October. Even if the loss of life was regrettable and even if the massacre was not connected with labor issues, the tone of Norman's report indicated that the price was worth the "improved demeanour" among Indians. One moment nothing in the lives of the workers had to do with labor, the next moment festival restrictions are maintained so as to allow planters "improved [coolie] demeanour."

Norman also failed to ask why a force of 346 armed men, a warship and buckshot ammunition were prepared in advance and deployed against the island's population which was clearly unarmed.[624] Another glaring omission in the Norman Inquiry was to question the Governor, Sir Sanford Freeling, or to investigate whether his absence from the island was not taken advantage of by planter interests. One of only two references to the governor, relate to the Indian casualties:

> "All were the result of buckshot, which was issued to the police in lieu of bullets some time back [1882?] by order of Sir Sanford . . . The question of whether rifle bullets or buckshot should be used . . . is not one upon which any opinion I can give will be of value . . . As to the actual terms

of the regulations, I may observe that they were issued by
the late Sir F. Barlee, in pursuance of the decision arrived at
by Sir Sanford . . . in whose absence he [Barlee] was
administering the Government, that they were approved of
by your Lordship. . . ."[625]

The Hosay tragedy and Indian deaths were treated too casually by
the authorities in 1884; in determining what course Trinidad was
to take, Indians certainly had a weak negotiating hand. Sir F. Barlee,
acting governor for a period in 1884, and central to the tragedy in
Freeling's absence, probably died soon after the 1884 tragedy.

Whatever the verdict of history and historians, a largely
unprotected group of migrant Indians were shot and killed in
Trinidad, during an Indian cultural festival. The only opening to
make an excuse for this preventable massacre lies in the fact that
the Indian festival had become creolized. In that sense, we come
full circle to the unenviable position of the Indian in plantation
Trinidad: they could be effectively portrayed as the wrongdoers or
the recalcitrant people. This seems true, too, had they rejected
creolization completely. To indulge a paternalistic analogy, few
adults today publicly applaud other adults who succeed in quieting
troublesome youth through corporal punishment. In a way,
Trinidad congratulated itself for a massacre of colonized Indian
workers far away from home.

It might appear that Norman did not completely lack a sense
of fairness because, both he and Quinton Hogg had invoked an
Ordinance of 1882 restricting festivals—which was "disobeyed"
by the Indians. On further examination, this issue further also
questions the fairness of Commissioner Norman, because he failed
to show a connection between that ordinance and the customary
rules of (the creole) Hosay.

The Ordinance #9 of 1882, a "decision" of Governor Freeling's
was not identical with the *Regulations* of July 1884. Crucially (for
the Indians), Freeling did not have a direct say in framing the
latter in 1884, cleverly foisted onto Ordinance #9. This, in spite

of the 1882 Ordinance stipulating, "The Governor is hereby authorized to make from time to time regulations," for the observance of all "immigrant festivals", of "defining the routes of such processions."[626] Defining "routes" is clearly different from a ban: routes would have been redundant if a ban were in place. While in 1884 control over Hosay was interpreted as its outright prohibition in public, the governor had, in 1882, himself indicated that the Ordinance had been effective when, following a pledge against disorder from the celebrants, he gave his full blessings for Hosay 1882. He had been similarly gracious toward Carnival in 1881.

It was for this reason perhaps, that a meeting in May 1884 was held in Governor Freeling's absence. The press reported "a meeting of planters took place at the office of the Protector of Immigrants [sic], the object of which was to pass certain rules" against Hosay. It was also reported that the "rules are to be recommended for approval by the Governor." We do not know if the governor ever approved it. As the governor was excluded from the meeting, the reference to his approval may have been mere subterfuge. These officers of government were the ones with sole negotiating advantage.

The *San Fernando Gazette* assumed, arrogantly as it turns out, that Hindus had no role in Hosay: "The Hindoos only join in the fray on the same principle and for the same motives as the Port of Spain [Carnival] bands, to enjoy the excitement of the day, and, too often, to pay off old grudges. The only plan would be to forbid Hosein processions entirely on the public roads . . . Asiatics are easily cowed. They are cruel and treacherous, but a real display of force, at San Fernando and at town, will settle the matter at once and for ever after."[627]

It would be little exaggeration to say that such opinions translated into the idea that once having labored to make planters successful in Trinidad, Indians ought to die quietly and enrich the earth. *The Trinidad Recorder* had cautioned, "[I]n consequence of the implied promise by Sir Sanford Freeling, it would be unwise to interfere with [Hosay] entering the towns."[628] We know from

Norman's Report that Barlee, not Freeling, had given the final approval. The events in October 1884 unfolded almost precisely as the planter newspapers had hoped.

The iron-fisted policy toward Hosay, it was argued even by Commissioner Hamilton, was needed to balance restrictions on Carnival. Yet, if the merchant James Drennan's testimony is indicative, "The Creoles [who] have had their carnival stopped . . . tried to incite the [Indians] to keep up their festival."[629] Rather than justifying fears that " . . . anything like a war of races should be engendered if it were put into the heads of the creoles that any privilege", was allowed to Indians "but withheld from them,"[630] instead we see a creole concern that Hosay not also fall victim to the elites.

Although it is inaccurate to assert, as planters and British officials seemed to suggest, that nineteenth-century Trinidad festivals were purely political events, it might be useful to make general observations about the latent political force within festivals. (Remember, though, that artistic and cultural aspects of festivals were never completely submerged at any Carnival or Hosay celebration, even ones which were politicized by proximate events.) From antiquity festivals have captured and strengthened the culture and aspirations of ordinary peoples in the face of the burgeoning power of the State to define culture, morality and work ethics. Mikhail Bakhtin, in *Rabelais and his World*, wrote that "Carnival with all its images, indecencies, and curses affirms the people's immortal indestructible character. In the world of carnival the awareness of the people's immortality is combined with the realization that established authority and truth are relative."[631]

The idea that "authority and truth" are relative was clearly resonant among Afro-and Indo-Trinidadians in the 1880s. I.M. Cumpston said of Africans and East Indians, "They were not readily affected by fear of the law."[632] This calls into question the recourse of Law for purposes of socialization better left to schools and educators. On the other hand, reports of dominant groups about the character of people under their subjection or tutelage, are almost always contradictory. For instance, the missionary W. Gamble, in describing free blacks mouthed adjectives later to be used for Indian indenteds: "The liberated classes and their descendants cannot be said to have attained to any high standard of moral character . . . they are litigious, and somewhat lax in honesty." The Indians, in this early phase of their stay, however, were "a mild and industrious race . . . more steady and obedient."[633]

Norman's report spoke of the need for being consistently tough on the masses, so that they did not seek to protest for basic rights, be it wages or cultural or religious fetes: "There is little doubt that the Indian immigrants looked upon the processions as a sort of means of demonstrating their power. It is not as if the processions were confined to Mohamedans. If they were so confined they would be of manageable dimensions, but as Hindoos and Mohamedans alike joined in them they would become unmanageable, except under special restrictions."[634]

This investigator and researcher in historical data cannot say "there is little doubt" the plantocracy deliberately shot Indians in the dusty streets of Trinidad. The massacre certainly happened and it was certainly avoidable; one can never be as certain about the motivations both of the Indians and Trinidad's elites. The concern with steady labor, however, was paramount.

Much more was at stake in Trinidad during 1884, as the reference to relations of "power", and the words "unmanageable" and "restrictions" convey. Unfortunately, the report did not explain why the festival would be unmanageable when Hindoos *and* "Mohamedans" celebrated it. There is no recorded incident of Hindu-Muslim clashes at Hosay, even between two individuals. Nor did Norman explain why Hindus and Muslims had jointly celebrated Hosay in Trinidad (if not in India), despite their differences.

The Enquiry left the impression that deliberate Indian disobedience of critical regulations necessitated police action on 30 October 1884. Yet, the expectation that laws be obeyed presumes that the public either understands the laws, or might be expected to get access to, and read, laws and regulations. This was not the case with the restrictions on Hosay 1884; London "approv[ed] of the regulations which have been made under the Ordinance" on October 6, three weeks before the festival![635] None other than the Acting Colonial Secretary, W.R. Pyne, testified before Norman, "I cannot say whether the Government instructions were thoroughly understood" by the Indians. He added that "it is difficult to make them understand what is wanted, since a large proportion of them cannot read."[636] It might be assumed, however, that of those Indians literate in English, some among them would have read or heard about the restrictions. Others certainly had not. If we recall the words of Trinidad's governor McLeod, the failure of education had been stark precisely because as late as the 1840s two-thirds of Trinidad still spoke either Spanish or French "exclusively," and McLeod considered it "absolutely necessary that people . . . claiming the benefit of British subjects," should speak English, if only to read the laws which governed them.[637] When laws are contravened, therefore, it need not be true that the Indians' "self-confiden[ce] and insole[ce]" are the only possible explanations, as Mitchell, the Protector, had indicated. On the other hand, certainly a few Indians (like Sookhoo) had exhausted peaceful appeals to allow the Hosay to go on as usual. The testimonies given by Indian deponents at the Enquiry also that not all Indians were aware of the anti-Hosay rules. That ignorance of the law is no basis to plead innocence (invalid in legal battles?) does attract sympathy in civil society even today. Not so in plantation Trinidad.

Within the plantation system the laboring classes had to be kept in line. Hence, Ryan (and Beckford) remind us, one needs to acknowledge the continuing power of the plantocracy between 1838 and the turn of the century.[638] Trotman also argues that the sugar interest had direct access to the policymakers at the Colonial Office through their powerful lobby, the West India Committee. The absentee planters, from their vantage point in London, almost always influenced the choice and subsequent conduct of the governor of Trinidad. The Legislative Council (as an advisory body) was dominated by planter interests, members of which were nominated as both official and unofficial members throughout this period. Trotman shows how other colonial officers, like Sir Joseph Needham, were connected to planter interests. Needham, chief justice in 1884, owned a lucrative 433 acre cocoa estate near the capital, devoting only two days per week to his duties."[639]

As for barristers and officials who risked the plantocracy's anger, the fate awaiting them was either being hounded out of the island or the misery of social ostracism in a colonial backwater. With regard to the Protector of Immigrants, an officer supposedly mediating between the larger Trinidadian society and Indians (whose only possible protection in their new land lay in this office), he too was entirely dependent on white creoles for hospitality, often a planter himself. Moreover, when Major Fagan lost his battle on behalf of Indian indenteds at the Clydesdale Cottage estate in 1846, the Walkinshaws continued to win in Trinidad until after the Second World War.

In the years just before and during the Hosay massacre of 1884, Charles Mitchell, owner of Paradise Estate, was no Major Fagan and no "Protector" of Indians. A creole newspaper in an 1880 editorial had criticized Mitchell for delaying many from a release from indenture. "It is somewhat strangely suggestive," the paper said, that outstanding days, "which are reported to be improper, and to be an unfair advantage in favour of the proprietor of the estate . . ." should be redeemed on Mitchell's "estate" as "unpaid labour."[640]

The Protector benefitting from days allegedly lost on other planters' estates, indicates why the Protector might not have questioned the veracity of planter claims against Indians. The Norman Enquiry explicitly, albeit reluctantly, criticized Mitchell for "want of influence" among the Indians. It was the only time Norman criticized anyone other than Indians for the massacre; but he prevaricated: "I do not blame the Protector" but where "Indian immigrants form an increasing part of the population," the officer ought to have "Indian experience, and [be] well known for his power of influencing natives."[641] We have seen this omission with regards to Hindi-conversant officials in Trinidad already in Governor McLeod's stay on the island in the 1840s to P.J. Keenan in 1869, in connection with aides and teachers recruited for Indian children by the Presbyterians.

Having come to his post in 1883, Mitchell's prefatory remarks to Norman were defensive about his qualifications, after which he commented on the alleged massacre: "I can only speak [sic] Hindustani very little. Most [Indians] after they have been a year or two in Trinidad, understand English . . . Until I came here about a year and half ago I had not been in Trinidad for over eight years. I had plenty of opportunities of seeing the [Indians] before that. When I returned they had greatly changed: they were more insolent as well as independent, and I ascribe this to their knowledge of their power."

On the issue of just grievances Indian laborers might have, Mitchell hinted at the true situation in spite of himself. "Their complaint is that their task work is excessive," he said, and countered with, "This complaint is not real, as they always refuse to work by time instead of by task." Two sentences later, he concedes, "The tasks this year, are, I think a little heavier than they have been before, owing to the low price of sugar." Yet, Quinton Hogg, possibly in a comfortable London chair, stated that the events of 1884 had nothing to do with labor. Mitchell ought to have known better, being a local planter.

The last two paragraphs of Mitchell's testimony, on the measures he had taken about informing celebrants of Hosay restrictions, appear contradictory:

> "I did *not* instruct Mr. Pasea, the assistant inspector, to go
> round the estates, but I believe he visited several of the
> estates, and he told me he had seen the people and made
> them understand the Regulations would be carried out.
> Before the Regulations were issued I went round *some* of the

> estates with Mr. Pasea, *telling him to visit the others*, and
> informed the people that *some* instructions concerning the
> Hosea processions were going to be issued, which they would
> have to obey, and I inquired of them what they considered
> the religious part of the ceremony."

From his own testimony, the planter-protector did not already have the regulations in hand; he was carrying out a survey, official or otherwise. Mr. Pasea testified that he was "a planter . . . for 11 years" before coming to his post in 1881, spoke "Hindustani just enough to make the [Indians] understand about their work." Yet, with reference to the restrictions on Hosay, he "took every opportunity of telling *all* the people about them and whenever I visited an estate I spoke about the Regulations." Given his own poor communication skills with the laborers, it is no wonder the indenteds "never cared to discuss the subject."[642]

5.4 THE STAKES

In the context of colonialism, one important line of conflict in Africa and Asia had been the struggle of the natives to prevent the death of the Old Society. In the Caribbean, the contest consisted in non-European "immigrants" seeking to shape the order which was being created for them. They did so more in displaying cultural persistence and resurrecting old world observances, especially festivals, than in a clearly articulated debate, or even negotiations. From the available evidence, Indo-Trinidadian cultural survivals were believed to pose a "danger" to the elites. The failure of planters and the Protector to say something other than that Indians were, in the 1880s, "more independent," "more insolent" and obsessed with their "power," we are unable to fully assess the "danger" they posed. Paradoxically, these powerful Indians could not determine the size of their tasks or negotiate better wages for themselves. In those instances where officialdom saw popular festivals as powerful and dangerous vehicles, their response to them was coldly political. In terms of their duties, these officials had performed impeccably in shaping post-slavery Trinidad.

A valid question which begs an answer is why no action had been taken against Hosay until the 1880s, when the brunt of planters' cost-reduction measures during the depression fell upon the Indians. (Of course, planters saw a big fall in profits: whereas 54,496 tons of sugar had earned L886,172 in 1883, the higher production of 60,961 tons fetched only L642,255 in 1884[643]). Labor grievances led Indians toward more effective strikes. And finally, Indians constituted about a third of the population, Table 3.5 tabulating 48,829 Indians in a population of 153,128.

In 1882 there had been serious labor disturbances at the Cedar Hill plantation, owned by the powerful British-based Colonial Company. The *San Fernando Gazette*, referred to the "murderous designs of a senseless and infuriated mob armed with clubs, hoes and agricultural forks," which attacked both the Company's attorney and the manager; two policemen, sent on horseback were quite ineffectual, one of them dying from a cardiac arrest. It was only an armed detachment led by Captain Baker, which arrested the ringleaders and restored quiet. The *San Fernando Gazette* pointed to labor disturbances on other estates as evidence "that there is a fermentation of some kind not yet laid bare." It rambled ominously on about Indians, "-at all times weak and passive because of [their] isolation," become confident and "powerful" if not "made subservient to strict and unflinching discipline." The paper called for a strong police presence at the forthcoming (1882) Hosay. The point about Indians being "weak" in "isolation" reflects a continuity in thinking among missionaries and the elites.

That there was fear among the elites in 1882 or a preparation to punish the Indians was indicated by military precautions. San Fernando's police force was tripled with reinforcements from Port of Spain (reflecting that the capital was less prone to the Indian "danger"?) The public was asked to "keep themselves armed" and "ready to fire" on the Indians if there was disorder. Additionally, the government requested "three warships" from Barbados. Despite rumors that the Indians had stocked up "petrol and powder," neither they nor the government side resorted to violence in 1882.[644] Violence was not inevitable. The fact that the town of San Fernando, center of the sugar planting area, but not Port of Spain was reinforced point to Hosay's links with labor not political calculations.

Governor Freeling may have succeeded in protecting Carnival in 1881 and both Carnival and Hosay in 1882, but his subsequent absence from office gave the enemies of the Indian workers their opportunity.[645] During the Enquiry, Pasea testified that he had "introduced a deputation, concerning another matter," to Governor Freeling, and told him "I thought this was a good time to talk about the Hosea." Following this meeting, the Governor had "asked them if they thought it a privilege to go through San Fernando, and they answered, 'Yes.' He then said, 'Well, as long as you are quiet I will not interfere with your processions going through San Fernando . . .'" Pasea then testified that recent mild treatment had made the Indians "very impertinent" giving as an example the acquittal of those involved in unrest at Cedar Hill:

On 30 October I was in San Fernando but saw nothing of the *riots* [emphasis added]; I thought it best not to go to either of the parties of the police lest my presence might lead the [Indians] to believe they would not be fired on . . . The results of the riots has been very marked; it has produced a very beneficial effect. I see no spirit of resentment among the Indians but they are much quieter and better behaved in every way.[646]

This testimony indicated that Pasea that the Hosay would be fired upon; he stayed away for that very reason. He added, "I was not consulted on the issue of the Regulations" against Hosay and "I thought they would probably cause some trouble, particularly after Sir Sanford Freeling's promise" of non-interference if the Indians cooperated.[647]

There was a subtle but distinct difference in the treatment meted out to Carnival and Hosay festivals in colonial Trinidad. The elites sought to control Carnival and keep it from becoming too Africanized or dominated by lower class motifs. Rarely would members of government or the elites call for the abolition of the entire Carnival. The fete which originally took place over three days (and now, two), was amenable to modification; creoles could give up aspects of it to mollify the powerful. With Hosay being a one-afternoon street parade, the only way to reduce it was to outlaw it. Hosay had to be accepted or rejected outright. When Indians in 1884 took their model mausoleums onto the roads they generally kept to the negotiated understanding with Governor Freeling since 1882. Perhaps the police and upper classes did not respect this negotiated settlement because of the alien-ness of Hosay. We've seen that Baker's men were angered by Freeling's sympathetic approach to Carnival in 1882 (several policemen had resigned but were persuaded to withdraw these). Indians were not represented in public space, where help was usually found.

The Indians could not, as long as they remained human, ignore the reality of plantation harshness; they would have had to make a stand for cultural survival if not for human dignity. Hosay 1884 was their stand for cultural survival. Hosay 1884 may not have been the choice of a majority of Indians for a showdown but the questionable role of the Protector (in Freeling's absence) may indicate the government wanted *the* showdown in 1884. Had the elites focussed their repression and police action on one plantation, Cedar Hill in 1882 for example, that lesson would have had to be repeated elsewhere. This may point toward why (in view of the evidence for labor problems in the 1880s) the Indians were disciplined into becoming "quieter and better behaved in every way." That is how plantations operated.

The plantation preceded slavery and lingered on after Emancipation because it was the only institution which could rapidly order the new societies which Europeans inherited after Columbus. In Chapter Two, we saw plantation society opt for thousands of new workers rather than negotiate with ex-slave workers; in Chapter Three, we saw the plantation complex willing to use jails to criminalize Indians who sought some freedom from their imprisonment per long indentures; In Chapter Four, we saw a lack of will among planters and government to provide quality mass education, especially to Indian children; it was consistent (although not inevitable) that plantation society would use the law and British soldiers to suppress the East Indian Hosay, where they might have opted to rely on schools and education much more, and sooner.

In the late 1880s when Indians totalled 50,000 in a population of 153,000, only 2,000 of their children were at school (with an average attendance of about 1,300). Estimates suggested (Chapters Three and Four) that almost 13,000 children were, in fact, Indo-Trinidadians: they were born there. Yet, a society which did so little to educate these island-born children, readily shot down their parents over a festival coming off the plantations onto public roads.[648] Only to the extent there was a governor McLeod, a Mr. Andre, and a few kind missionaries, are we reluctant to agree with Trotman that Law, not education, was used to socialize Africans and Indians in plantation Trinidad.[649] Yet, it was interesting that the elites thought an Afro-Indian majority could take over the State had they aspired to. There is no evidence that they did.

Missionaries had complained no end about the complication of having to contend with Eastern religions.[650] That missionaries might have had a sophisticated approach to their agenda is also suggested by Singh, whose evidence (contrary to missionary ideas) shows that multi-racial Hosay celebrations had been going on for about 30 years instead of ten. Also, it was Reverend Grant who encouraged certain Muslims to draw up a petition against Hosay observances.[651] These Muslims were all Sunni, adversaries of the Shi'a, based on the theological issues at stake when Shi'a commemorate the martyrs who were indeed killed at the hands of Sunni Muslims. According to Hjortshoj Shia-Sunni violence during Muhurram celebrations in India became common only after the punitive actions of the British following the Indian colonial revolt (1856-58). The Shi'a rulers of Lucknow were deprived of much of the wealth and prestige for their perceived disloyalty; Sunnis were able to rise in material status, and after 1905, sought a separate identity when the idea of communal representation was proffered.[652] Most indented Indians arrived long before these differences could turn them against India or Pakistan and Hosay.

This discourse of negotiations within the colonial society of Trinidad has in some very obvious ways been part of a discourse about power. The masses did not verbalize this in any way like planters and government officials did: in Chapter Two we saw how Burnley and Governors Hill and Mein talked about the "power" which the freed population enjoyed in the labor arena. In this chapter, there was a great deal made of Indians having an "exaggerated idea of their power" vis a vis the Hosay festival. Trinidad had come full circle.

It was serendipitous for Indians in particular that shortly after the Muhurram massacre, an enlightened governor came to Trinidad. Governor Robinson (1885-91) opened up prime Crown lands for sale to the masses, including Indians.[653] This was a salutary development, and it may have assuaged some of the frustrations of indented and indenture-free Indians. The former could look forward to the day when they too could buy quality land for petty capitalist ventures. Where the commutation of return passages for less valuable land during the brief period between 1869 and 1880 may have increased Indian grievances, the sale of quality land seemed to make good the expectations for which many might have left India in the first place. Ironically, their successes in retail ventures and market gardening would be so remarkable that the harsh details of plantation indenture could be forgotten by themselves and others.

Ultimately, whatever actions the laboring classes took was bound to leave an impact upon the society-in-formation. Among the positive consequences of riots, labor unrest, even of being killed or shot at during street festivals, allowed the colony to offer some room for hard-working people to improve their material conditions and aspire to upward mobility, especially for their children. In that sense, labor negotiated the best deal possible in post-emancipation Trinidad. The negotiations may have been many-

sided and unequal. But Carnival and Hosay represented an arena
in which the disenfranchised majority insisted on shaping its life
out of the wreckage of slavery and indenture. They continue to do
so, irrespective of whether we call the process negotiation, a search
for human dignity or cultural persistence.

CONCLUSION

There were major mistakes made during the colonial period in Trinidad that have bedeviled race-relations in the modern Republic of Trinidad and Tobago. This study has tried to understand how some of these mistakes—major and forgivable—were made in the period up to about 1900. While Trinidad was a colonial caste society where whites were at the top and non-whites always at the bottom, there were no monolithic groups of the dominant and oppressed. Cleavages of race, nationality, religious affiliation and outlooks cut across each racial or ethnic category; some members of the laboring classes also experienced upward mobility. Accounts of colonial realities in London were oversimplified, wrong or too colorfully written. Sometimes, as we have seen, two visitors would represent the same colony in rather contradictory terms, as in the accounts below written barely 20 years apart:

> "If I ever turn planter, as I have often had thoughts of doing,
> I shall buy a cocoa plantation in Trinidad. The Cane is, no
> doubt, a noble plant . . . [but] sugar can never be cultivated
> without negro labour."[654]
> "[Indenture is] more cruel than what obtained in the times
> of slavery when the Negro, if unable to work from age or
> sickness, had a right to be maintained by his owner, and
> could not, like the coolie, be driven to perish on the
> roadside."[655]

The visitor to the West Indies in 1826 was sufficiently impressed with the region to desire to settle there, but he despaired of sugar being produced without African slavery. With the benefit of

hindsight and history, we have shown that the visitor's despair and
that of many post-emancipation planters evaporated with the
coming of large-scale Indian indenture. With British Indian labor,
many plantations could simply go on with business as usual. This
prodded a twentieth-century historian, Eric Williams, to charge:
"One can only wonder today how it was possible for any country
that had abolished slavery on the ground that it was inhuman to
justify Indian indenture with its 25 cents a day wage and its jails.[656]

Trinidad, we have discovered, had no post-Columbian
economic history outside of voluntary and involuntary labor
migrations, a trend which continued with the post-emancipation
reliance upon African, European and Indian indenture, the last
beginning in 1845 and secured by 1860 when Britain took direct
control of India. We have made the case for treating Indian
indenture as part of the ordeal of free labor in Trinidad, as well as
regarding Indo-Trinidadian history as a part of a global labor
history. We cannot insist on ethno-historical approaches only
because the nationality of labor had changed with post-
emancipation arrangements. One of these arrangements was the
triangular one which included Britain, India and plantation
colonies. However, India was not an equal player with Britain or
even with the plantation colony of Trinidad: the planters who
dominated the society if not the governemnt had an effective lobby
in London which could persuade, even sway, British politicians.
And they did both on matters concerning plantation labor.

While Trinidad had recruited Chinese laborers in 1806—eight
years before the first free blacks from the United States were settled
on the island—this arrangement was less efficient in yielding a
continuous supply of cheap labor because China retained a portion
of its independence and officially at least, declared migration an
act of treachery. Unofficially, the Chinese cooperated with western
agents or governments when it was convenient to do so. The few
hundred Chinese who entered Trinidad in 1806 demanded
repatriation en masse in 1807. Subsequent efforts showed the
contrast with India, especially the difficulty of conducting indented

migration from an semi-independent China.[657] As Walton Look Lai's study, *Indentured Labor, Caribbean Sugar: Chinese and Indian Migrants to the British West Indies, 1838-1918*[658] demonstrated, Indians were taken to Afro-Asian plantation colonies while the majority of Chinese migrants went to Hawaii and the USA, in the West. Also, Chinese were not usually taken out of China by an imperial, impersonal structure under foreign control, but by Chinese already established in the West and "for better or worse," the communal credit ticket system.

Trinidad has a Chinese minority today, and they also shared many of the harsh experiences of Indians on and off the plantations. The British Indians have had more of a presence and progeny in the Caribbean, and have been transformed into Indo-Trinidadians. A case is sometimes made that the Indo-Caribbean people are emerging from marginalization, but the tiny Chinese population is still a rather invisible part of the Republic of Trinidad and Tobago.[659]

But was Indian indenture in Trinidad worse than African slavery? The answer is not central to any of our arguments in the preceding chapters. Although Indian labor migrants were, at times, *treated worse* than were slaves of Trinidad as is evident in the views expressed in the works of Eric Williams and C.R. Ottley, the Indians themselves were clearly *not slaves*. And there was the rub: precisely because they were bound for a limited time, the plantation management generally exploited every sinew and muscle in the indentured man or woman before they were free of the plantations. While Indian migrants were certainly free, in terms of *de jure* status, their *de facto* status was closer to that of slaves than to that of free persons. When we began peeling away past the generalizations and euphemisms about the indentured trade, the core of the onion, we discovered, had little substance in terms of the Indians' *freedom* in Trinidad during 1845-88. For this reason, Indians needed passes to move about in Trinidad (but no one else in the island did); Indians could be imprisoned for allegations that they violated their contracts, while other Trinidadians faced, at the very worst, a civil case on the same score; and Indian children were ignored in official education policy for almost 25 years. As late as 1884, poorly advertized changes in local ordinances could become the basis upon which the colonial state would unleash its instruments of violence on Indians at their annual street festival, with sixteen immediate deaths on that October day.

The Hosay or Muhurram has been a useful vehicle, a window almost, into the colonial plantation as well as into the lives of a mainly English-illiterate population. Indian migrants had neither newspapers nor political organizations in the years before the massacre of 1884, but their frustrations as a foreign labor force in "an almost unapproachable society" surface in the events during and after the festival on that fateful October of 1884. In the years immediately following the massacre, Indians appear to have left the plantations as far behind them as it was possible to do. To some extent, the Canadian Presbyterian schools were attended to the advantage of more and more Indian children (with other state-aided schools belatedly playing their part), but the acquisition of land where Indians established themselves as small farmers and independent entrepreneurs was probably the most significant development for their economic futures. It was perhaps in recognition of their problems and their desire for independence that Governor Robinson (1885-91) began selling fertile Crown lands in 1885, a year after the October 30 massacre. It may be helpful to remember the "opening up of Crown land," was distinct and separate from the shortlived land-for-passages policy (1869-1880) of Arthur Gordon. Those early grants were of poor-quality land; "owing to the poorness of the land . . . difficulties of communications, and want of organization, these lands had . . . in many cases been abandoned, the immigrants preferring to buy land like other people in places chosen by themselves."[660] While opportunities for Indians improved after 1885—and indenture remained onerous for many newcomers—the difficulties of the Walkinshaw years are to be comprehended in the context of Trinidad being a new, potentially wealthy, sugar colony yet to exploit its agricultural potential.

Britain had arrived as Trinidad's colonial mother relatively late in the age when Sugar was King in the West Indies. In 1797 when Britain did effect a military takeover of Spanish Trinidad, the decision had more to do with European power politics than with sugar or cocoa or slavery. The Napoleonic Wars convinced Britain that Trinidad were better resurrected as a sugar colony than that it fulfil a role as base from which to wreak havoc on a rival (Spanish) American Empire. Once redirected on this route of sugar and slaves (tried by Spain since 1783), Britain discovered the disadvantages of its late start.

First, British Trinidad like Spanish Trinidad learned that the indigenous population was on the decline, and that the island lacked both capital and slaves in quantities which facilitated a plantation economy. The island actually had more slaves at Abolition in 1807-08 than in 1834 at Emancipation (respectively 21,895 and 17,539). Second, Britain discovered that it had become a place for experiments which British abolitionists hoped would stop the extension of slavery into newly acquired colonies. These factors accounted for Trinidad's divergence from the plantation history of older West Indian islands like Jamaica and Barbados. Trinidad slaves were more urban and more free than were the slaves in older British colonies, and Trinidad's settlement itself was accomplished by mixed-race (coloured) immigrants and black free persons.[661] Free blacks included disbanded soldiers from British regiments who had fought in the United States, neighboring creoles and other African-Americans welcomed by Governor Ralph Woodford during 1814-1828.

Abolition in 1807 was a boost for free blacks as much as for Trinidad's coloureds, but it also sealed the fate of coloureds as potential leaders, both in the short-term and in the long-run. Asian newcomers forced coloureds to opt either for an alliance with the ex-slaves or withdraw into obscurity. Abolition and Emancipation witnessed the drying up of a supply of ready and captive labor

force for the emergent plantation economy yet to experience its
"take-off" stage. Thus arose a cry of labor "shortage" in Trinidad
which has spanned an entire century, ending only in 1917 when
India abolished the indenture and transportation of its people to
the West Indies.

   The coloureds, whose numbers and high proportion of total
population had made Trinidad unique among West Indian colonies,
opposed East Indian immigration from the start, including through
the petitioning of government as in the Thomas Hinde petition
bearing 140 signatures. They complained that the plow, animal
and mechanical power were not being as extensively used as in the
United States; the work of J.U.G. Asiegbu and P.D. Curtin
corroborate these and other counter-assessments that Trinidad had
no real labor shortage. Asiegbu found that outmoded methods,
absenteeism among the new British planters and mismanagement
cut into planter profits after Emancipation, when they had to pay
cash wages.[662] Curtin denied any large role for the ending of
"protection" (West Indian sugar having long enjoyed a preferential
entry into the British market) or purely labor-related problems for
the post-emancipation complaints of planters. He cited lack of
technological innovation, the competition from beet sugar and
planters' inability to adjust to a free labor market for their failures
and lower profits.[663] Our examination of testimony given by
Trinidad planters to the 1842 Select Committee on the West India
Colonies (Chapter Two) led us to believe that planters (William
Burnley, Edward Walkinshaw, Justice Anderson) were avaricious
both of indented labor and of high profits.

   Planters did succeed in winning sympathy from British officials,
in part through their effective lobby (the West India Committee),
to sanction various labor schemes after 1834, from indenting
Africans and Portuguese to the longer servitude of Chinese and
British Indians. The coloureds who had constituted more than
8,000 of Trinidad's total population of 32,000 in 1812 and were
almost thrice the size of the white population, were aghast at the
planters' insatiable appetite for Asian laborers. The fact that on the

eve of Emancipation in the 1830s the population of 16,285 coloureds had become equivalent in numbers with slaves (17,539) may point to another reason for their concern over Indian indenture. A group which had its share of suffering and scorn, was, as it were, robbed of its place in the sun by the planters' turn to Asia. This perspective on the anti-Indian slant of coloureds in nineteenth-century Trinidad needs further exploration.

We are confirmed in our belief that the very segregationist nature of Indo-Trinidadian indenture reduced the opportunities for greater Indian-creole and Indian-Trinidadian interchanges, whether in schools, during recreation or at Muhurram each year. Apart from the sympathy some creoles showed in October 1884 that the Indian fete not be circumscribed by the colonial authorities, Indians and creoles had shared the same barracks on some plantations. The educated coloured elite may have remained aloof, but they were not anti-Indian, as is clear in the record of the controversy at the Walkinshaw estate.

The newspaper which, during the heady days of the experiment with Indian indenture reminded Trinidad about Major Fagan's "sterling qualities as a man," also knew that the indenteds had "confidence in appealing to him" because the migrants learned that "from him only can they be certain of obtaining redress for their wrongs."[664] In his short tenure of two years, Fagan had felt that in some respects, the Indian was treated worse than a slave. He brought to the attention of the authorities in London the forced removal of sick or disabled Indians, so that many died like animals on the roads. This treatment was meted out to indented Indian women as well; they would be encountered on the roads, virtually naked and penniless. Even when Indians suffered theft (in April 1848 black laborers from Nevis ransacked an indented Indian's room) and other difficulties, creoles were able to differentiate between the people and the system. On the robbery incident of April 1848, the *Trinidad Spectator* noted growing opposition "to the coolie" but also, that the creoles and others had simply wanted "to drive the coolie out of the labour market."[665]

In retrospect, the Thomas Hinde petition with its 140 signatories had viewed the planters' temperament accurately. Hinde had mounted a spirited opposition to indenture in 1844-48, and continued to criticize the system of labor intermittently in the decades thereafter. The temporary suspension in the trade in 1848 (through 1851) may have weakened this anti-indenture movement with a false sense of success. These voices are a proud record in the history of Trinidad because politically weak people nevertheless took on the colonial system of unfree labor. The work of Mahatma Gandhi, Gokhale, and Rev Andrews was but a continuation of this strand of public opinion against new forms of unfreedom.

Indians did not arrive in Trinidad in the way illegal immigrants arrive in present-day North America; if they were not always abducted, they were offered an invitation, to enter or remain in Trinidad. But for a tiny minority, Indian migrants were transported by the British on British or chartered vessels, with British personnel, to fulfil the wishes of mainly British plantation owners.[666] The planter elite and officials may have ignored the long-term consequences of their turn to India but by 1870, Indians were increasingly local instead of transient. By then, Governor Arthur Gordon had begun offering less fertile lands to indenture-free Indians to induce their settlement in Trinidad as opposed to repatriation to India. Those who insisted on repatriation stood to lose five or ten acres in Trinidad, contribute a third part of passages back home, and the arduous readjustment to "caste-conscious" India. Although a small minority of Indians accepted the commutation of passages policy up to 1880, one 1888 estimate declared that Trinidad saved a quarter million pounds with commutation schemes, an issue raised at the first meeting of the Franchise Commission:

> " . . . there is another very important matter which I may call
> the coolie vote [because many] have not completely settled,
> for there are [those] entitled to back passages—so many,

that sometimes the Protector of Immigrants frightens us at
the Legislative Council with the very large bill we should
have to pay . . . if all the coolies . . . were suddenly to claim
them."[667]

Of course, that right to return, like most of his or her other rights,
needed to be translated into practical reality, in this case their
insistence that a ship be chartered when migrants were ready to go
back to India. Britain's Indian subjects did not enter a labor situation which had distanced itself from plantation slavery. While
they rarely had a voice in interpreting the contract with planters,
and no voice in determining their wages, laws, the prison system,
educational curriculum or legalizing traditional marriages, they
have been blamed for the decline in ex-slave wages in Trinidad. We
have examined the Indian "Middle Passage" and seen how indented
Indians suffered the indignities of labor in a state of bondage.
William Green's assessment is therefore eminently fair:

"There was a great deal of deception and injustice in the
indenture system, some of it blatant but most of it subtle . . .
Like the [1833-38 slave] apprentices before them, indentured
workers had limited legal recourse against improper treatment.
Stipendiary magistrates . . . were alienated from the immigrants
by language, religion, and customs, and they remained dependent
upon the planters for hospitality and social intercourse."[668]

The experiences of Indians were both similar to and different
from the experience of former slaves and new indented Africans,
Portuguese, Chinese and other replacement workers on the erstwhile
slave plantations of Trinidad. In Chapter Three we found them to
be a group readily victimized by Trinidad's prisons. Whereas they
were about a third of total population, in the period up to 1888,
Indians usually made up half the prisoners simply because of labor
disagreements. While they were part of a continuity in Trinidad's
post-Columbian history, East Indians became a group apart because
of their non-Christian culture. This distinction is critical: Trinidad's
opting to seek Indian workers was not atypical. Indians became

atypical upon entering the Caribbean because of their cultural tenacity and dubious acceptance of western religions and values. This state of affairs came to a head in the 1880s when their worlds of work and play were turned upside down as the elites insisted on curtailing street festivals (especially Hosay) when laborers were unwilling to accept less and less wages for longer and longer indentures.

Chapters Four and Five demonstrated how labor difficulties along with the failure to socialize Indians in readily accessible schools allowed the Hindi language and the non-Christian Hosay to grow in popularity among Trinidadians. When increasing dissatisfaction with their low wages and restricted lives pushed Indians into more organized strikes and labor revolts, Trinidad violently suppressed Hosay. The elites may have treated Hosay as a privilege, which, with less docile labor, had to be withdrawn. This action ignored the sympathetic role and agreements between Governor Freeling and the Indians (1882) which, with the virtual connivance of the Protector of Immigrants, was nullified by regulations against the street Hosay in 1884. When the indented workers apparently disobeyed the new regulations publicized—poorly, to boot—three weeks before their fete, they experienced a notorious massacre which still reverberates among Trinidadians today. That tragedy was avoidable, had officials respected indented Indian lives. At the time, Indian lives were cheap, or considered less equal that the lives of other Trinidadians.

Colonial officials in Trinidad generally followed the wishes of the elites, especially the planter elites. They had little to gain—as Major Fagan found out in the years 1846-48—if they supported an alien people simply out of principle. It was said even of Trinidad's governors that, while each was expected to be impartial, his "whole social life in Trinidad" was spent in the company of white creoles, "and if he paid no deference to their wishes, life became hardly worth living."[669] The same situation obtained through the 1880s, even in the Legislative Council. For instance, of the eight nominated Council members in 1880, four were sugar planters, two were cocoa and sugar planters, and one each a merchant and barrister. The presence of professionals and entrepreneurs may have indicated a dilution of planter power, but this was not achieved until the twentieth century. If we again examine the middle class elements in the 1880 Council, the merchant was closely "linked with the sugar interest."

Other government officers, Sir Joseph Needham for instance, were routinely connected to the planters. Chief Justice in 1884, Needham also owned a lucrative 433 acre cocoa estate near Port of Spain, devoting "only two days per week to his official duties."[670]

If there was poetic justice in Indian immigration giving Trinidad its twentieth century majority group, Indians had to experience the pain, the pathos and the prisons of the plantations as well. For they had been brought to Trinidad at a time when slavery was outlawed but plantations themselves had yet to reach their zenith. Trinidad's best sugar harvest was in the year 1826, barely eight years before slavery was outlawed. The fateful duo, sugar and slaves, had become Indian indenture and Trinidad sugar in the years 1845 through 1888 and beyond. As has been pointed out, the Indians proved adept at making the best of a bad situation. After the depression of 1884—and the Hosay massacre—the majority of Indians left the plantations for rural towns and villages. By 1891, some 54.68 percent of Indians were outside the direct control of planters, 11.8 percent having moved to the Naparima Ward Union (the highest concentration) and the lowest but significant concentration of 5 percent of all Indians moved to Port of Spain.[671] Anne Martell leaves us an anecdote which demonstrates that the Hosay massacre had not smothered Indian dignity: Rev. Morton met an Indian brahmin working at field labor, "'who drew himself up before me with the dignity of a prince . . . And his eyes flashed with haughty dignity as he claimed me for a brother, though a carriage stood at hand for me and his hoe awaited him.'"[672]

East Indian indenture was clearly an imperial decision, sustained by imperial oversight and guarantees, which had brought Indians to Trinidad, Indians who otherwise might not have come to the Caribbean. Thrown into a new plantation culture, Indians struggled to make meaningful lives for themselves against all odds. By 1888, Indians had seen the worst of indenture—at least better medical services were provided, and the schools had begun the education of their children with some earnestness now—they had begun to spawn a middle class of their own, and had begun to creolize.[673] Some had already taken advantage of the few Church schools which had been available in 1868-1870 to become interpreters and clerks, others set up small businesses or benefitted from aligning with Trinidad's other staple, cocoa (which also helped former slaves climb up the social ladder). This is an inspiring story of hard work, sacrifice and self help. It is also a testament to the potential of the capitalist route and its increasing freedoms.

The years following Patrick Keenan's 1869-70 report on the state of education in Trinidad evinced some notable efforts towards improvement. School buildings in particular were strengthened, improved and fitted with latrines. While bearing in mind how some governors are lauded by authors for very personal reasons, Gordon's willingness to allow denominational schools to coexist with secular ones is credited for giving a spurt to school openings for a decade. Eversley recalled his "lineage" and personal qualities were needed at a time when, "Clique and party were rampant, and the insolence of office [was] unrelieved by those virtues which alone can adorn the investiture of official power. The crucial test [after having sanctioned denominational schools was] . . . his conversion of the squatting district of Montserrat into a legalised settlement of prosperous cacao planters, and his policy of throwing open the hitherto shut up lands of the Crown."[674]

Eversley blamed Gordon's predecessors for spawning "pernicious" effects of squatting because they shared an age-old fear about the rise of "a yeomanry class, or a class of small proprietors." However, there are several other sides to this question, including the government's huge responsibility for providing roads where small farmers planted in cocoa and other crops.[675] There was a desire to grant Crown lands equitably, especially among blacks and East Indians, for the sake of harmony and better government.[676]

Despite the colonial policies, segregated education and after 1884, separate street festivals, race-relations in Trinidad have been remarkably good when compared with the nineteenth-century anti-Portuguese riots in Guiana/Guyana and more recent and violent Indian-African conflicts.

What had rendered this group of immigrants so distinctive? Was it simply their religion, or their race, or both? It was race, religion, and numbers as well. At one level it was paradoxical that Indian indenture did not fail. A predominantly male community, with few of their religious and social functionaries present (or if in Trinidad, circumscribed in their traditional roles), the non-recognition of Indian religious marriages, and especially the neglect of their children's education—less than a sixth of 13,000 Trinidad-born Indian children were in school as late as the 1880s—augured ill for such a people in an alien environment. Yet, Indians persisted, suffered blows, prisons, and a violent attack on Hosay, to emerge intact, if not as a group, then as "East Indians." If modern ghettoes may be likened to the imprisoning plantations of yesteryear, the Indian achievement is a useful model.

Finally, it is imperative that Indian indenture be treated as an integral part of Trinidad's labor history. Amerindian and African slavery, seasonal peon labor, black, white and brown indenture are part of this reality. It is unacceptable that the Indo-Trinidadian experience be relegated to a separate episode of ethnic or immigration history. Ethnicity and immigration are consequences only of Trinidad's post-Columbian reliance on outsiders for labor and development. Trinidad had invited Indians to settle, and actively so since 1869, thereby saving Trinidad huge costs in chartering return ships to India. Colonial Trinidad was not willing to pay the full cost of indenture; the Indians made the best of their new conditions. This needs to be fully acknowledged, lessons learned, and useful models upheld. Trinidadians and other Indo-Caribbean immigrants to the USA have certainly seen a refreshing contrast as

their Hindu, syncretic beliefs and festivals are revived in places like
Toronto, Boston, New York even Epping, New Hampshire, where
there is little condemnation of East Indians and opposition is
through the courts. Perhaps time has finally pushed caste-based
politics and community relations in the background where they
may rest, until the next balloting for elected office. On the
optimistic side, ethnic politics may become obsolete in our lifetimes,
because most forms of segregation and apartheid are being
overtaken by deepening global democracy in the global village.

Table 5

Caste Breakdown Among Indian Immigrants (1879-80)

Caste Breakdown Among Indians Introduced in 1879-80

Muhammadan	---	648	Bhuiar	---	6
Chamar	---	274	Koibucto	---	
Brahman [brahmin]	---	175	Bhogohan	---	2
Kurmi	---	125	Bostom	---	1
Lodh	---	73	Pattahar	---	1
Teli	---	59	Tamoli	---	1
Dosad	---	54	Onaie	---	1
Kunbi	---	49	Ghahai	---	1
Bhurr	---	47	Jaswar	---	1
Kessan [farmer]	---	34	Kosoriban	---	1
Gowala [cowkeepers]	---	31	Manjee	---	1
Jat [warriors]	---	26	Kol/cooly	---	3
Buncah	---	24	Patowa	---	4
Kumar [potter]	---	19	Christian	---	4
Bhungi, Mehter, Halkote	---	19	Katick	---	19
Barai [carpenter]	---	16	Kalwar	---	13
Halwye [confectioner]	---	12	Musahur	---	10
Mali & Bari [gardener]	---	15	Dhurkhar	---	4
Sonar [goldsmith]	---	4	Bahalea	---	6
Ajoodhabasi	---	1	Ghatwar	---	1
Lohar/smith	---	18	Napith	---	3
Takoor, Chatri, Rajput	---	294	Tucha	---	2
Ahir and Satope	---	255	Arrock	---	2
Kahar	---	128	Bagdi	---	1
Kori	---	88	Beldar	---	1
Koiri	---	72	Goriah	---	1
Muraisand Murao	---	57	Banspore	---	1
Passi	---	52	Chundul	---	1
Kachi	---	49	Jogi	---	1
Nonia	---	45	Suri	---	1
Gararia	---	32	Benhoneg	---	1
Kandu	---	30	Boes	---	3
Naoand Hajam [barbers]	---	26	Kanu	---	3
Mullah [religious muslim]	---	22	Rungwa	---	4
Dhobi [launderer]	---	19	Gour	---	4
Kyesth/clerks	---	15	Dhanuk	---	15
Mochi [cobbler]	---	15	Bhuja	---	11
Gosaine & Athit [brahmin]	---	7	Bind	---	6
Kewat [boatmen]	---	15	Tatowa	---	7
Bhatt [Bengalibrahmin]	---	2	Mahurutta	---	5
Thanuand Tanta	---	1	Awasti	---	1
Bhurboojoo	---	1			

SOURCES:

The translation of "caste" names was aided by A. Gupta, L. Singh and R. Beladakere at Silver Spring, MD (22 September 1991). The "CASTE" list is "Census of the Indian Population" in Comins, Note on Emigration p.37.

APPENDIX A

SUMMARY OF REPORT OF SELECT

COMMITTEE INVESTIGATING THE STATE

OF THE WEST INDIA COLONIES IN 1842

1. That the great act of emancipating the slaves in the West Indian colonies has been productive as regards the character and condition of the negro population of the most favourable and gratifying results.
2. That the improvement in the character of the negro in every colony, into the state of which this Committee has had time to extend inquiry, is proved by abundant testimony of an increased and increasing desire for religious and general instruction: a growing inclination to take upon themselves the obligation of marriage, and to fulfil the duties of domestic life: improved morals: rapid advance in civilisation: and increased sense of the value of property and independent station.
3. That unhappily there has occurred simultaneously with the amendment in the condition of the negroes a very great dimunition in the staple production of the West Indies, to such an extent as to have caused serious, and in some cases ruinous, injury to the proprietors of estates in those colonies.
4. That while the distress has been felt to a much less extent in some of the smaller and more prosperopus islands, it has been so great in the larger colonies of Jamaica, British Guiana and Trinidad as to have caused many estates, hitherto prosperous

and productive, to be cultivated for the past two or three years at a loss, and others to be abandoned.

5. That the principle causes of the diminished production and consequent distress are the great difficulty that has been experienced by the planters in obtaining a steady and continuous labour and the high rate of remuneration which they give to the broken and indifferent work which they are able to procure.

6. That the diminished production is caused partly by the fact that some of the former slaves have betaken themselves to other ocupations more profitable than field labour; but the more general cause is that the labourers are enabled to live in comfort, and to acquire wealth without for the most part labouring on the estates of the planters for more than three or four days in the week, and from five to seven hours a day; so that they have not sufficient stimulus to perform an adequate amount of work.

7. That this state of things arises partly from the high wages which the insufficiency of the labour supply, and their competition with each other naturally compel the planter to pay; but is principally to be attributed to the easy terms upon which the use of land has been obtained by the negroes.

8. That many of the former slaves have been enabled to purchase land and the labourers are generally allowed to occupy provision grounds subject to no rent or to a very low one, and in these fertile countries land they thus hold as owners or occupiers not only gives them a supply of good food, but in many cases a considerable over plus in money, altogether independent of, and in addition to, the high money wages which they receive.

9. That the cheapness of the land has been the main cause of the difficulties that have been experienced; and that this cheapness is the natural result of the excess of fertile land, beyond the wants of the existing population.

10. That in considering the anxious question of what practical remedies are best calculated to check the increasing depreciation of West Indian property, it appears that much might be effected by judicious arrangements on the part of the planters themselves for their own general advantage, and by moderate and prudent changes in the system they have hitherto adopted.

11. That the one obvious and most desirable mode of endeavouring to compensate for the diminished supply of labour is to promote the immigration of a fresh labouring population to such an extent as to create competition for employment.

12. That for the better attainment of that object as well as to secure the full rights and comforts of the immigrants as freemen, it is desirable that such immigration should be conducted under the control, authority and inspection of responsible public officers.

Source: Parliamentary Papers Vol. XIII (July 1842) pp.273ff.

BIBLIOGRAPHICAL SOURCES

This study has benefitted from libraries and inspiration that spans Indiana University through Trinidad, Canada, the United Kingdom, and South Africa. Research and sources for this dissertation have come, therefore, from many places within the United States and, of necessity, overseas archives. Prominent among these are Indiana University's superb Inter-Library Loan Department, the archives and libraries in the United Kingdom, and the United Church Archives of Canada. Interviews were conducted during 1990 in Trinidad, and informally (with Richard Blackett 1986-90), who provided the germ for this thesis in his observation that there has been more similarity between African slavery and Indian indenture than is evident in the historiography.

Parliamentary Papers (the Irish University Press series) were used extensively and freely at the University of Maryland at College Park (MD., USA) and on Micro-card at the Johns Hopkins University, while the initial location was London.

1. PRIMARY SOURCES:

1.1. Documentary Sources

British Parliamentary Papers. Despatches (by governors), reports on immigration, and colonial statistics. India Office Records, London (and University of Maryland, College Park.)

British Sessional Papers. These are also part of the Parliamentary Papers, but because the Irish University Press Series has separated them by "topics", their volume numbers are not the same as other such papers. "Command Papers" are also found in this category. University of Maryland, College Park and Institute of Commonwealth Studies, London.

Hansard's Parliamentary Debates, Third series. Volume XLI, 1837-38. The Johns Hopkins University, Baltimore, MD.

Original Correspondence Files: These C.O. files in the Public Record Office (Kew Gardens), United Kingdom.

Papers Relating to Her Majesty's Colonial Possessions. Several large volumes of these papers have been collated and bound at the Institute of Commonwealth Studies, London.

Report of Messrs. Peck and Price, who were appointed at a meeting of the Free Colored People of Baltimore, held on the 25th November, 1839, Delegates to Visit British Guiana, and the *Island of Trinidad; for the purpose of ascertaining the Advantages to be Derived by Colored People Migrating to those Places.* Baltimore: Woods and Crane, 1840. Institute of Commonwealth Studies, London.

Royal [Franchise] Commission, To Consider and Report as to the Proposed Franchise and Division of the Colony into Electoral Districts. Trinidad, 1888. UWI Library, Trinidad.

State Papers Colonial. Public Record Office, Kew Gradens and Institute of Commonwealth Studies, London.

Trinidad Council Papers. Detailed papers on the Trinidadian scene and its reports for the period since 1874. Royal Commonwealth Library, London.

Trinidad General Registers. These documents contain each ship's list of Indian immigrants arriving in Trinidad, and data on caste, and age. Trinidad Archives, Port of Spain.

West India Planters' Memoranda. The record of correspondence between the planters lobby and the British authorities since emancipation. Included in these were invaluable papers such as *West India Committee to Colonial Office* (24 March 1877) Thomas D. Hill (chairman) to Lord Carnavon, subtitled *Chinese Emigration.* Institute of Commonwealth Studies, London.

West India Association Pamphlets. In this category were included a few rare books and general surveys of Trinidadian conditions. Institute of Commonwealth Studies, London.

1.2 Interviews

8 June 1990: (Friday): Anthony de Verteuil, at St. Mary's College in Port of Spain, on Madrasi emigration to Trinidad.

21 June 1990 (Thursday): Dr. Ken Boodhoo and Mr. and Mrs. Narine Singh at the latter's home in St. Augustine, Trinidad. Topics ranged from the history of Christian missions and Indian culture, to hymns and music.

28 June 1990 (Thursday): Interviewed Mrs. Rosabel Seecharan, a doctoral candidate being supervised by Dr. Brereton, at the St. Augustine campus of UWI, Trinidad, on her personal history.

29 June 1990 (Friday): Joseph Harry at his home in Tunupuna, Trinidad, on the subject of Hosay.

30 June 1990 (Saturday): Mookish Babooram and Sita Mahabir, at the former's home in Orange Valley, Trinidad, on the Indo-Trinidadian perceptions of history and society.

1.3 Newspapers

These following papers were consulted at the Colindale Newspaper Library (London), while the newspapers consulted for selected articles were purchased or personally acquired.

1. *New Era*
2. *Palladium*
3. *Port of Spain Gazette*
4. *San Fernando Gazette*
5. *Star of the West*
8. *Times (of London)*
7. *Trinidad News*

8. *Trinidad Recorder*
9. *Trinidad Review*
10. *Trinidad Sentinel*
11. *Trinidad Spectator*
12. *Trinidad Standard and West India Journal*
FOR SELECTED ARTICLES ONLY:
13. *Sandesh.* Article on Hosay, 28 October 1988.
14. *Sunday Guardian.* Address of J.R.P.Dumas at the Central Bank Auditorium in Port of Spain, 10 June 1990.
15. *Trinidad Express.* 23 January through 18 December 1990.
16. *Trinidad Guardian.* "What can Selwyn Ryan Find? (PP.9,11) 25 June 1990.

2.SECONDARY SOURCES:

Ahmed, Imtiaz. "The Shia-Sunni Dispute in Lucknow 1905-1980." Pp.335-50 in M. Israel and N. Wagle, eds. *Islamic Society and Culture Essays in Honour of Aziz Ahmad.* New Delhi: Manohar, 1983.

Anthony, M. *Profile Trinidad A Historical Survey from the Discovery to 1900.* London: Macmillan Caribbean, 1975.

Arora, G.S. *Indian Emigration* (New Delhi: Puja, 1991) .

Asiegbu, J.U.G. *Slavery and the Politics of Liberation 1787-1861 A Study of Liberated African Emigration and British Anti-Slavery Policy.* New York: Africana; Longmans, Green and Co., 1969.

Bakhtin, M. *Rabelais and his World.* Cambridge: Massachusetts Institute of Technology, 1968.

Besson, J. "Family Land as a Model for Martha Brae's New History: Culture Building in an Afro-Caribbean Village." Pp.100-32 in C.V. Carnegie, ed. *Afro-Caribbean Villages in Historical Perspective.* Kingston: African-Caribbean Institute, 1987.

Beckford, G. *Persistent Poverty: Underdevelopment in Plantation Economies of the Third World.* New York: Oxford University, 1972;1983.

Bhana, S. and Brain, J.B. *Setting Down Roots Indian Migrants in South Africa 1860-1911*. Johannesburg: Witwatersrand University Press, 1990.

Birbalsingh, F. ed. *Indenture and Exile* (Toronto: York University, 1989).

———————————ed. I*ndo Caribbean Resistance* (Toronto: TSAR, 1993). Blouet, B. "Land Policies in Trinidad 1838-1850." Journal of Caribbean History (9) 1977: 43-59.

Blum, J. "The Condition of the European Peasantry on the Eve of Emancipation." *Journal of Modern History* 46 (3) 1974: 395-424.

Bolland, O. Nigel. "Systems of Domination after Slavery: The Control of Land and Labor in the British West Indies After 1838." *Comparative Studies in Society and History* 23 (4) 1981: 591-619.

——————————— and Shoman, A. *Land in Belize 1765-1871*. Kingston: University of the West Indies (ISER), 1977.

Breman, J. *Taming the Coolie Beast Plantation Society and the Colonial Order in Southeast Asia* (New York: Oxford University Press, 1989).

Brereton, B. A *History of Modern Trinidad 1783-1962*. London: Heinemann, 1981.

——————— *Race Relations in Colonial Trinidad 1870-1900*. London, Cambridge University, 1979.

——————— "The Birthday of our Race: A Social History of Emancipation Day in Trinidad, 1838-1888." Pp.69-83 in *Trade Government and Society in Caribbean History 1700-1920* ed. B.W. Higman. Mona, Jamaica: Heinemann, 1983.

——————— "The Experience of Indentureship: 1845-1917." Pp.25-38 in *Calcutta to Caroni The East Indians of Trinidad* ed. John La Guerre. London: Longman, 1974.

——————— "The Trinidad Carnival 1870-1900." *Savacou* 11-12, 1975, 46-57.

Burns, Alan. *History of the British West Indies*. London: George Allen and Unwin, 1954.

Caldecott, A. *The Church in the West Indies*. London: Frank Cass, 1970.

Campbell, C. *Cedulants and Capitulants The Politics of the Coloured Opposition in the Slave Society of Trinidad 1783-1838* (Port of Spain, Trinidad: Paria, 1992)

——————— "Ralph Woodford and the Free Coloureds: The Transition from a Conquest Society to a Society of Settlement, Trinidad 1813-1828." *Journal of Caribbean Studies 2* (2-3) 1981: 238-49.

———————"Charles Warner and the Development of Education Policy in Trinidad, 1838-1870," *Journal of Caribbean History* 10-11 (1978): 54-81.

Carmichael, G. H*istory of the West Indian Islands of Trinidad and Tobago 1498-1900*. London: Alvin Redman, 1961.

——————— "Some Notes on Sir Ralph James Woodford, Bt." I*n Caribbean Quarterly 2* (3) 1952: 26-38.

———————"La Reconnaisance Estate, Lopinot Valley, Arouca," *Caribbean Quarterly*, 6 (4) 1960: 279-81.

Carnegie, C.V. ed. *Afro-Caribbean Villages in Historical Perspective*. Kingston: African-Caribbean Institute, 1987.

Carrington, S. The *British West Indies during the American Revolution*. Dordrecht, Holland: Foris, 1988.

Ching-Hwan, Yen. *Coolies and Mandarins China's Protection of Overseas Chinese during the Late Chi'ing Period (1851-1911)*. Singapore: Singapore University Press, 1985.

Craton M. ed. *Roots and Branches Current Directions in SLaves Studies*. Toronto: Pergamon, 1979.

Crowley, D.J. "The Traditional Masques of Carnival." *Caribbean Quarterly*, 4 (3-4) 1956: 194-223.

Cross, M. "Colonialism and Ethnicity: A Comparison and Case Study." In *Ethnic and Racial Studies 1*(1) 1978: 37-59.

——————— *The East Indians of Guyana and Trinidad*. London: Minority Rights Group, (Report No.13) 1972.

——————— and Heuman, G. eds. *Labour in the Caribbean From Emancipation to Independence*. London: Macmillan, 1988.

Cumpston, I.M. *Indians Overseas in British Territories 1834-1854*. London: Dawsons, 1953 and 1969 Clarendon edition.

Curtin, Phillip D. *The Atlantic Slave Trade: A Census*. Madison: University of Wisconsin Press, 1969.

——————————— *Death by Migation Europe's Encounter with the Tropical World in the Nineteenth Century*. Cambridge: Cambridge University Press, 1989.

——————————— *The Rise and Fall of the Plantation Complex Essays in Atlantic History*. Cambridge: Cambridge University Press, 1990;1991.

——————————— "The British Sugar Duties and West Indian Prosperity." Journal of Economic History XIV (2) 1954: 157-64.

Deerr, Noel. *The History of Sugar* (2 volumes). London: Chapman and Hall, 1949; 1950.

Degler, Carl N. "Plantation Society: Old and New Perspectives on Hemispheric History." *Plantation Society in The Americas* 1 (10) 1979: 9-14.

de Verteuil, L.A.A. *Trinidad Its Geography, Natural Resources, Administration, Present Condition, and Prospects*. London: Ward and Lock, 1858.

de Verteuil, Anthony. *The Years of Revolt Trinidad 1881-1888*. Port of Spain: Paria, 1984.

——————————— *Eight East Indian Immigrants*. Port of Spain: Paria, 1989.

——————————— *A History of Diego Martin 1784-1884*. Port of Spain: Paria, 1987.

Dookhan, Isaac. *Post-Emancipation History of the West Indies* London: Collins, 1975.

Dunn, R.S. *Sugar and Slaves The Rise of the Planter Class in the English West Indies, 1624-1713*. Chapel Hill, University of North Carolina Press, 1972.

Eco, U. "The Frames of Comic Freedom." Pp.1-10 in T.A. Seboek ed. *Carnival!* Berlin: Mouton, 1984.

Eltis, D. "Abolitionist Perceptions of Society After Slavery."
Pp.195-213 in *Slavery and British Society 1776-1846* ed. James
Walvin. Baton Rouge: Louisiana State University, 1982.

—— "Traffic in Slaves Between British West Indian Colonies,
1807-1833." *Economic History Review XXV*, 1972:55-64.

Emmer, P.C. ed. *Colonialism and Migration; Indentured Labour
Before and After Slavery.* DorDrecht: Martinus Nijhoff, 1986.

Engerman, S.L. "Some Economic and Demographic Comparisons of Slavery in the United States and the British West Indies."
Economic History Review, Second series. XXIX (2) 1976: 258-75.

————————— "Servants to Slaves to Servants: Contract Labour
and European Expansion." Pp.263-294 in P.C. Emmer ed. *Colonialism and Migration; Indentured Labour Before and After Slavery.*
DorDrecht: Martinus Nijhoff, 1986.

————————— "Some implications of the Abolition of the
Slave Trade." Pp.3-18 in D. Eltis and J. Walvin eds. *The Abolition
of the Atlantic Slave Trade Origins and Effects in Europe, Africa, and
the Americas.* Madison: University of Wisconsin, 1981.

Fraser, L.M. *History of Trinidad 1781-1813.* Volumes 1 and
2. London: Frank Cass, 1891 and 1971 reprint.

Gamble,W.H. Trinidad: *Historical and Descriptive London: Yates
and Alexander, 1866.*

Genovese, E. Roll, Jordan, *Roll The World the Slaves Made.*
New York: Pantheon, 1972;1974.

Gordon, S. *A Century of West Indian Education A Source Book.*
London: Longmans, 1963.

———— "The Keenan Report, 1869 [Part 1]." *Caribbean
Quarterly* 8 (4) 1962: 3-16.

Grant, Reverend Kenneth. *My Missionary Memories*, (Nova
Scotia: Imperial Publishing Company, 1923).

Green, William A. *British Slave Emancipation The Sugar Colonies and the Great Experiment 1830-1865* London: Oxford University Press, 1976.

————————— "Plantation Society and Indentured Labour:
the Jamaican case, 1834-1865." Pp.163-186 in *Colonialism and*

Migration; Indentured Labour Before and After Slavery ed. P.C. Emmer. DorDrecht: Martinus Nijhoff, 1986.

Hall, D. *A Brief History of the West India Committee.* Barbados: Caribbean Universities Press, 1971.

——— "The Flight from the Estates Reconsidered: The British West Indies, 1838-42." *Journal of Caribbean History* (10-11) 1978: 7-24.

——— "Slaves and Slavery in the British West Indies." *Social and Economic Studies.* 11 (4) 1962: 305-18.

Hamid, Idris. *A History of the Presbyterian Church in Trinidad 1868-1968* (San Fernando, Trinidad: St. Andrews Theological College, 1980).

Hamshere, C. *The British in the Caribbean* (Cambridge, Massachusetts: Harvard University Press, 1972) p.158.

Haraksingh, K. "Control and Resistance among Overseas Indian Workers: A Study of Labour on the Sugar Plantations of Trinidad, 1875-1917." *Journal of Caribbean History* (14) 1981: 1-17.

——— "Indian Leadership in the Indenture Period." *Caribbean Issues* 2 (3) 1976: 17-38.

Heavner, R.O. *Economic aspects of Indentured Servitude in Colonial Pennsylvania.* New York: Arno, 1978.

Hennessy, A. ed. *Intellectuals in the Twentieth-Century Caribbean: Volume 2 Unity in Variety: The Hispanic and Francophone Caribbean* (London: MacMillan, 1992) .

Higman, B.W. "The Slave Populations of the British Caribbean: Some Nineteenth Century Variations." Pp.60-70 in S. Proctor ed. *Eighteenth Century Florida and the Caribbean.* Gainesville: University of Florida, 1976.

——— *Slave Populations of the British Caribbean, 1807-1834.* Baltimore: Johns Hopkins University Press, 1984.

Hill, Errol. *The Trinidad Carnival Mandate for a National Theatre.* Austin: University of Texas, 1984.

Hjortshoj, Keith. "Shi'i Identity and the Significance of Muharram in Lucknow,India." Pp. 289-309 in M. Kramer ed., Shi'ism, *Resistance, and Revolution,* Boulder: Westview, 1987.

Ivanov, V.V. "The Semiotic Theory of Carnival as the Inversion of Bipolar Opposites." Pp.11-35 in T.A. Seboek, ed. *Carnival!* Berlin: Mouton, 1984.

Jagan, C. "Indo-Caribbean Political Leadership." Pp. 15-25 in Frank Birbalsingh ed. *Indenture and Exile* (Toronto: York University, 1989).

John. A.M. *The Plantation Slaves of Trinidad, 1783-1816* A Mathematical and Demographic Enquiry. Cambridge: Cambridge University, 1988.

Johnson, H. "'A Modified Form of Slavery': The Credit and Truck Systems in the Bahamas in the Nineteenth and Early Twentieth Centuries." *Comparative Studies in Society and History.* 28(4) 1986: 729-53.

Joseph, E.L. *History of Trinidad.* London: Frank Cass, 1970.

Kingsley, Charles. *At Last A Christmas in the West Indies.* New York: Harper and Brothers, 1871.

Kinser, S. *Carnival, American Style.* Chicago: University of Chicago, 1990.

Klass, M. "East and West Indians [,] Cultural Complexity in Trinidad." *Annals of the New York Academy of Sciences* 83 (5) 1960: 855-861.

Kloosterboer, W. *Involuntary Labour Since the Abolition of Slavery A Survey of Compulsory Labour Throughout the World.* Leiden: E.J. Brill, 1960.

Knaplund, P. *The British Empire 1815-1939.* New York: Harper and Brothers, 1941.

Knight, F.W. "The Colonial Period in Caribbean History." Pp.255-67 in K.O. Laurence ed. *A Selection of Papers presented at the Twelfth Conference of the Association of Caribbean Historians.* Barbados: Association of Caribbean Historians, 1985.

——————— *Slave Society in Cuba During the Nineteenth Century.* Madison: University of Wisconsin, 1970.

Kuczynski, R.R. *Demographic Survey of the British Colonial Empire.* Volume III. London: Oxford University, 1953.

La Guerre, John. ed. *Calcutta to Caroni The East Indians of Trinidad.* London: Longman, 1974.

Lai, W.L. *Indentured Labor, Caribbean Sugar: Chinese and Indian Migrants to the British West Indies, 1838-1918* (Baltimore, Johns Hopkins University, 1993).

Lal, Brij V. Girmitiyas *The Origin of the Fiji Indians Canberra: Journal of Pacific History,* 1983.

——————; D. Munro; E.D. Beechert eds. Plantation Workers, *Resistance and Accommodation* (Honolulu: University of Hawaii Press, 1993).

Lamont, Sir Norman. Burnley of Orange grove *A Public Lecture Delivered under the auspices of the Historical Society of Trinidad and Tobago* on 29 November 1946 Port of Spain, 1947.

Laurence, K.O. "The Development of Medical Services in British Guiana and Trinidad 1841-1873." *Jamaica Historical Review* (4) 1964: 59-67.

—————— "The Evolution of Long-Term Labour Contracts in Trinidad and British Guiana." In *The Caribbean in Transition Papers on Social, Political and Economic Development,* eds. F.M. Andic and T.G. Matthews. Rio Piedras: University of Puerto Rico, 1965.

—————— *Immigration Into the West Indies in the Nineteenth Century.* Barbados: Caribbean Universities, 1971.

—————— "Colonialism in Trinidad and Tobago," *Caribbean Quarterly* 9 (3) 1963), 44-56.

Lobdell, Richard, A. "Patterns of Investment and Sources of Credit in the British West Indian Sugar Industry, 1838-97." *Journal of Caribbean History,* (4) 1972: 31-53.

Lovelace, Earl. *The Dragon Can't Dance.* Harlow, Essex: Longman Group, 1981.

Lowenthal, David. West Indian Societies London: Oxford University Press for the Institute of Race Relations, 1972.

Magid, Alvin. *Urban Nationalism A Study of Political Development in Trinidad.* Gainesville: University of Florida Press, 1988.

Maingot, Anthony P. "Politics and Populist Historiography in the Caribbean: Juan Bosch and Eric Williams." Pp.145-74 in A.

Hennessy ed. *Intellectuals in the Twentieth-Century Caribbean: Volume 2 Unity in Variety: The Hispanic and Francophone Caribbean* (London: MacMillan, 1992).

Marshall, W.K. "A Review of Historical Writing on the Commonwealth Caribbean since c.1940." *Social and Economic Studies*, 24 (1975): 271-287.

——————"Commentary One" on Sidney Mintz's "Slavery and the rise of Peasantries." Pp. 243-8 in M. Craton ed. *Roots and Branches Current Directions in SLaves Studies.* Toronto: Pergamon, 1979.

Martin, R.M. *History of the Colonies of the British Empire in the West Indies, South America, ...and Europe.* London: W.H. Allen and Co., 1843.

Martin, *The British Colonial Library comprising a Popular and Authentic Description of all the Colonies of the British Empire,* Volume IV. London: Henry Bohn, 1844.

Mathieson, W.L. *Great Britain and the Slave Trade 1839-1865.* London: Longmans, Green and Co., 1929.

McNeill, John Thomas. *The Presbyterian Church in Canada 1875-1925.* Nova Scotia: J.T. McNeill, 1925.

Memmi, A. *The Colonizer and Colonized.* Boston: Beacon, 1965.

Merivale, H. Lectures on Colonisation and Colonies Delivered before the University of Oxford in 1839, 1840 and 1841. London: Oxford University, 1928.

Millet, T. *The Chinese in Trinidad* (Port of Spain, Inprint, 1993) pp.1-9.

Millette, J. *The Genesis of Crown Colony Government Trinidad, 1783-1810.* Curepe, Trinidad: Moko, 1970.

Mintz, S.W. *Sweetness and Power The Place of Sugar in Modern History.* New York: Viking, 1985.

—————— *Caribbean Transformations.* Chicago: Aldine, 1974.

——————"Foreword" in R. Guerra y Sanchez's *Sugar and Society in the Caribbean.* New Haven: Yale University, 1964.

—————— "Slavery and the Rise of Peasantries." Pp. 213-42 in M. Craton ed. *Roots and Branches Current Directions in Slaves Studies.* Toronto: Pergamon, 1979.

Moonilal, R. and S. Siewah eds., *Basdeo Panday An Enigma Answered*. Tunapuna, Trinidad: Chakra, 1991.

Mount, G.S. *Presbyterian Missions to Trinidad and Puerto Rico*. Hantsport, Nova Scotia: Lancelot Press, 1983.

Naipaul, V.S. *The Loss of El Dorado A History*. London: Andre Deutsch, 1969.

Nath, D. *A History of Indians in British Guiana* (London: Thomas Nelson and Sons, 1950);

Newson, Linda. *Aboriginal and Spanish Colonial Trinidad A study in Culture Contact*. London: Academic Press, 1976.

Niehoff, A. and J. *East Indians in the West Indies* Milwaukee, Wisconsion: Milwaukee Public Museum, 1960.

Northrup, *Indentured Labor in the Age of Imperialism 1834-1922* (New York: Cambridge University Press, 1995)

Nunley, J. and Bettelheim, J. *Caribbean Festival Arts*. Seattle: Saint Louis Art Museum, 1988.

Ottley, C.R. *Slavery Days in Trinidad A Social History of the Island from 1797-1838*. Trinidad, C.R. Ottley, 1974.

————— "A Brief History." Pp.24-30 in M. Anthony and Andrew Carr eds. *David Frost Introduces Trinidad and Tobago*. London: Andre Deutsch, 1975.

Parry, J.H., Sherlock, P. and Maingot, A. *A Short History of the West Indies*. New York: St.Martin's Press, 1987.

Payne, T. "The Village Movement as a Revolutionary Initiative." Pp.38-45 in J. Loncke ed. *Proceedings of the 150th Anniversary of the Abolition of Slavery*. Georgetown: Guyana Commemoration Commission and UNESCO, 1985.

Pearse, A. "Carnival in Nineteenth Century Trinidad." *Caribbean Quarterly*, 4 (3-4) 1956: 175-93.

Pinnington, J.E. "The Anglican Church in the Catholic Caribbean: The C.M.S. in Trinidad, 1836-44." *Journal of Caribbean History* (1) 1970: 23-40.

Powrie, Barbara E. "The Changing Attitudes of the Coloured Middle Class Towards Carnival." *Caribbean Quarterly* 4 (3-4) 1956: 224-32.

Ragatz, L.J. *The Fall of the Planter Class in the Caribbean, 1763-1833, A Study in Social And Economic History.* New York: Octagon Books, 1971.

Ramesar, Marianne. "Indentured Labour in Trinidad 1880-1917." Pp.57-77 in K. Saunders ed. *Indentured Labour in the British Empire.* London: Croom Helm, 1984.

Ramraj, V.J. "Needs and Directions in Indo-Caribbean Studies." Pp.67-80 in F. Birbalsingh, ed. *Indo Caribbean Resistance* (Toronto: TSAR, 1993).

Richardson, P. "Chinese Indentured Labour in the Transvaal Gold Mining Industry, 1904-1910." Pp.260-90 in K. Saunders, *Indentured Labour In the British Empire.* London: Croom Helm, 1984.

Roberts, B.C. *Labour in the Tropical Territories of the Commonwealth.* Durham: Duke University, 1964.

Roberts, G.W. "Immigration of Africans into the British Caribbean." In *Population Studies*, 7 (3) 1954: 235-62.

——————— Byrne, J. "Summary Statistics on Indenture and Associated Migration Affecting the West Indies, 1834-1918." *Population Studies,* 20 (1) 1966: 125-34.

Root, j.W. *The British West Indies and the Sugar Industry.* Liverpool: J.W. Root, 1899.

Ryan, S.D. *Race and Nationalism in Trinidad and Tobago: A Study of Decolonization in a Multi-Racial Society.* Toronto: University of Toronto Press, 1972.

Saunders, K. ed. *Indentured Labour in the British Empire.* London: Croom Helm, 1984.

Schuler, Monica. *'Alas, Alas, Kongo' A Social History of Indentured African Immigration into Jamaica, 1841-1865.* Baltimore: The Johns Hopkins University Press, 1980.

Seboek, T.A. ed. *Carnival!* Berlin: Mouton, 1984.

Sewell, W.G. *The Ordeal of Free Labor in the British West Indies.* London: Frank Cass, 1861; 1968.

Sheridan, R. *Doctors and Slaves A Medical and Demographic History of Slavery in the British West Indies, 1680-1834.* London and New York: Cambridge University, 1985.

R. Shlomowitz, "On Punishments and Rewards in Coercive Labour Systems," *Slavery and Abolition* 12 (20) September 1991): pp.97-102.

Siewah, S. and Indira Rampersad-Narinesingh eds., *Basdeo Panday Man in the Middle; A Second Volume of Speeches.* Tunapuna, Trinidad: Chakra Publishing House, 1995.

Singaravelou. "Indian Religion in Guadeloupe, French West Indies." *Caribbean Issues,* 11 (3) 1976: 39-51.

Singh, H.P. *The Indian Struggle for Justice and Equality Against Black Racism in Trinidad and Tobago (1956-1962)* [Compiled and introduced by Indian Review Press] Couva, Trinidad: Indian Review Press, 1993.

Singh, Harjinder, "Introduction." In H. Singh ed. *Caste Among Non-Hindus in India.* Jaipur, India: National, 1977.

Singh, Kelvin. *Bloodstained Tombs: The Muharram Massacre 1884* London, MacMillan, 1988.

——————— "The Abolition of Indian Indentureship and Response of the Planter Interests in Trinidad." Journal of Caribbean History 21 (1) 1987: 43-54.

Smith, A. *Wealth of Nations.* New York: Macmillan, 1895.

Sookdeo, A. "Indian West-Indians and Ethnic Processes in Trinidad and Tobago with Some Reference to Indian Fijians." *Journal of Ethnic Studies* 16 (3) 1988: 27-45.

——————— "Authority and Resistance, and Everyday Searches for Dignity." *Minority Voices 7* (2) 1991: 15-25.

Stolcke, Verena. *Coffee Planters, Workers and Wives Class Conflict and Gender Relations on Sao Paulo Plantations, 1850-1980* New York: St. Martin's, 1988.

Tinker, Hugh. *A New System of Slavery: The Export of Indian Labour Overseas 1830-1920.* London: Oxford University, 1974.

——————— "The Origins of Indian Migration to the West Indies." Pp.63-72 in Frank Birbalsingh ed. *Indenture and Exile.* (Toronto: York University, 1989).

Trotman, David. V. *Crime in Trinidad Conflict and Control in a Plantation Society 1838-1900*. Knoxville: University of Tennessee Press, 1986.

——————————— "Women and Crime in Late Nineteenth Century Trinidad." *Caribbean Quarterly* 30 (2-3) 1984: 60-72.

Underhill, E.B. *The West Indies: Their Social and Religious Condition*. Westport: Negro Universities, 1862;1970.

Weller, J.A. *The East Indian Indenture in Trinidad*. Rio Piedras: University of Puerto Rico, 1968.

Williams, E.E. *Capitalism and Slavery*. Chapel Hill: University of North Carolina, 1944.

——————————— *History of the People of Trinidad and Tobago*. New York: F.Praeger, 1962.

——————————— *From Columbus to Castro: The History of the Caribbean 1492-1969*. New York: Harper and Row, 1970.

——————————— "The British West Indian Slave Trade after Abolition in 1807." *Journal of Negro History*, 27, 1942: 175-91.

Wilson, Rev. W.C. *The Madeira Persecutions*. London: The Religious Tract Society, 1856.

Wood, D. *Trinidad in Transition The Years after Slavery*. London: Oxford University Press, 1986.

——————— "Kru Migration to the West Indies." *Journal of Caribbean Studies*, 2 (2-3), 1981: 266-82.

Yarwood, A.T. "The Overseas Indians as a Problem in Indian and Imperial Politics at the End of World War One." *Australian Journal of Politics and History.* XIV (2) 1968: 204-18.

Unpublished Material

Bolland, O. Nigel. "Slave Wages in the Americas: Between Slave Labour and Wage Labour." May 1991 Conference at the Institute of Commonwealth Studies (London).

de Verteuil, A. "Madrasi Emigration to Trinidad, 1846-1916." Paper presented at the 22nd Annual Meeting of Association of Caribbean Historians, St. Augustine, Trinidad. April, 1990.

Martell, Anne. "The Canadian Presbyterian Mission to Trinidad's East Indians 1868-1912," (Unpublished M.A. Thesis in History at Dalhousie University: 1974)

Samaroo, B. "Missionary Methods and Local responses: The Canadian Presbyterians and the East Indians in the Caribbean," p.1. Read at the United Church Archives, Toronto: March 1991.

Sinha, Vineetha. "The Birth of 'Indian Anthropology' vis-a-vis Colonial Encounters and the Construction of 'India' as 'Space' for the 'Subject' of Anthropological Discourse." American Ethnological Meetings (Memphis, Tennessee) April 1992.

Other Sources:

Brierley, J.N. *Trinidad: Then and Now. 1874-1912*. Port of Spain: J.N. Brierley, 1912.

Carmichael, A.C. *Domestic Manners and Social Condition of the White, Coloured and Negro Population of the West Indies*. (Volumes 1 and 2) New York: Negro Universities Press, 1969 reprint from 1833.

Cochin, A. *Results of Emancipation*. Translated by Mary L. Booth. Boston: Walker, Wise and Company, 1864.

Coleridge, H.N. *Six Months in the West Indies in 1825*. London: John Murray, 1871.

Comins, Surgeon-Major D.W.D. *Note on Emigration from India to Trinidad*. Calcutta: Bengal Secretariat Press, 1893.

Day, Charles. *Five Years' Residence in the West Indies*, I. London: Colburn and Company, 1852.

Innes, John. *Letter to The Lord Glenelg Containing a Report from Personal Observation, on the Working of the New System in the British West India Colonies*. London: Longman and Co., 1835.

Scoble, J. *A Brief Exposure of the Deplorable Condition of the Hill Coolies.* London: Harvey and Darton, 1840.

Caribbean Presbyterian, The Volume 1 No. 1 (1958), U.C. Archives, Toronto.

Diaries of Abbe Armand Masse 1878-1883. (4 volumes) Translated by M.L. de Verteuil. Port of Spain: M.L. de Verteuil, 1988.

East Meets West in Trinidad (Prepared by the Mission Council of Trinidad, United Church of Canada: Published by the Committee on Young People's Missionary Education. United Church Archives, Toronto.

Egbert M. Madoo Memorial, in The Minutes of the Mission Council, 2 October 1900. United Church Archives, Toronto.

Eversley, T. Fitz-Evan. *The Trinidad Reviewer for the Year 1900* Volume 2. London: Lombard & Co., 1900

Handbook of Trinidad and Tobago (Port of Spain: Government Printing Office, 1924.

Historical Society of Trinidad and Tobago Publications [Cited as "999 Documents" by Eric Williams.]

Historical Statistics of the United States, 1789-1945. Washington, D.C.: Bureau of the Census, 1949.

Mahabir, N.K. [Collector and Compiler] *Personal Accounts of East Indians in Trinidad and Tobago During Indentureship (1845-1917).* Tacarigua, Trinidad: Calaloux Publications, 1985.

Morton, S. *John Morton of Trinidad.* Toronto: Westminster, 1916.

Negro Slavery; or a view of some of the more prominent features of that state of society, as it exists in the United States of America and in the colonies of the West Indies, especially in Jamaica. New York: Negro Universities Press, 1969 reprint of an 1823 edition   [author may be W. Wilberforce].

Notes on Conditions in Trinidad and Tobago. London: Royal Commonwealth Society, 1974

[Philip, J.B.] "A Free Mulatto", *An Address to the Right Honorable Earl Bathurst ... relative to the claims of the Coloured Population of Trinidad* (London, 1824),

Trinidad and Tobago Statistical Pocket Digest, 1985

Presbyterian Yearbook, 1884-85, "Appendix xcix: Report on Foreign Missions." (United Church Archives).

Trinidad Express Newspapers Ltd. *Trinidad Under Siege The Muslimeen Uprising 6 Days of Terror*. Port of Spain: Trinidad Express, 1990.

END NOTES

[1] David Northrup, *Indentured Labor in the Age of Imperialism 1834-1922* (New York: Cambridge University Press, 1995) Preface p.ix. He says the non-European migrants' motives and mortality rates are closer to those obtaining during European servitude.

[2] Hugh Tinker, "The Origins of Indian Migration to the West Indies." Pp.63-72 in Frank Birbalsingh ed. *Indenture and Exile* (Toronto: York University, 1989). Tinker disagrees with the accepted names and dates of the arrival of the first ship from Calcutta; the names *Futty Rozack*, *Futty Mobarik* and *Futty Sultan* refer to victory, "fateh" meaning "victorious."

[3] We use "debt-peonage" to convey that Indians owed the plantations part of their earnings for food given, per regulations, to those in their first year of indenture. More often, Indians owed employers a debt of unworked "time."

[4] Cyril Hamshere, *The British in the Caribbean* (Cambridge, Massachusetts: Harvard University Press, 1972) p.158. More telling in this regard is what Anthony P. Maingot describes in his essay, "Politics and Populist Historiography in the Caribbean: Juan Bosch and Eric Williams." Pp.145-74 in Hennessy, A. ed. *Intellectuals in the Twentieth-Century Caribbean: Volume 2 Unity in Variety: The Hispanic and Francophone Caribbean* (London: MacMillan, 1992) See essays, especially Victor J. Ramraj, "Needs and Directions in Indo-Caribbean Studies," which challenges the historiography for its "tokenism" instead of serious studies of Indians and other minorities. Pp.67-80 in *Indo Caribbean Resistance* (Toronto: TSAR, 1993). And on the Chinese minority, Trevor M. Millet, *The Chinese in Trinidad* (Port of Spain, Inprint, 1993) pp.1-9.

[5] E.L. Joseph, *History of Trinidad* (London: Frank Cass, 1970)

p.233. Joseph writes that the British Indian ship, *Fortitude* brought "Tartars... or Chinese" from Macao. The gender imbalance of 192 men to 1 woman led to all but 23 to repatriate.

[6]   Baltimore: Johns Hopkins University Press, 1993.

[7]   New York: Cambridge University Press, 1995. Northrup refers to the US role in uncovering US-based employers who traded in "bonded" sweat-shop workers from Asia in the 1990s!

[8]   Eric E. Williams, *From Columbus to Castro: The History of the Caribbean 1492-1969* (New York: Harper and Row, 1970). A trained historian and also Prime Minister of the Republic of Trinidad and Tobago for almost 30 years, Williams chose to write separate chapters on "Asian Immigration" and "The Ordeal of Free Labour."

[9]   Our objective is not to show that indenture was similar to slavery; almost nothing will be gained by that effort. But the efforts in China, and the struggles of Gandhi in South Africa, and the Rev. C.F. Andrews and others in India itself for the abolition of indenture, suggest that it was a form of national shame, not free labor. (Northrup, *Indentured Labor*, pp.142-45).

That this labor fuelled anti-colonialism is equally important.

[10]   Northrup, *Indentured Labor*, p.6.

[11]   The process "operates in every-day contexts but tends to be especially compelling when the historian is also an active politician or statesman ...." Anthony P. Maingot, "Politics and Populist Historiography in the Caribbean: Juan Bosch and Eric Williams." Pp.145-74 in A. Hennessy ed. *Intellectuals in the Twentieth-Century Caribbean: Volume 2 Unity in Variety: The Hispanic and Francophone Caribbean* (London: MacMillan, 1992).

[12]   Lai, *Indentured Labor, Caribbean Sugar*, pp.155-56. "Even more ironically, the end of indenture came as a result of Indian-inspired nationalist agitation within India itself ...It did not come from the initiatives of London officialdom or London-based social activist organizations (like the earlier abolition movement).

[13]   This author is glad that a diaspora of Indians took place; it does not contradict our quest to know the details. We will use the

impersonal "plantations" for the forces arrayed against Trinidad's laborers. This is not to deny agency, for planters did try to preserve and maintain profits from slavery days, but we wish to emphasize that ultimately, Indians were generally weak negotiators with powerful forces, but they certainly negotiated, again through their festivals (Chapter Five). We prefer "trade" where sources speak of "the coolie trade."

[14] Had we chosen a Marxist approach, the heroism of ordinary villagers and Indians shipped off from their motherland, would have been confounded with such notions as "false consciousness."

[15] Donald Wood, *Trinidad in Transition The Years After Slavery* (London: Oxford University Press, 1968) pp.231-32. Wood says the Tacarigua Orphanage alone taught Indians the rudiments of how to live amidst "an almost unapproachable society."

[16] Lai, *Indentured Labor, Caribbean Sugar*, p.154.

[17] Northrup, *Indentured Labor*, p.6. It is striking that he who acknowledges Shlomowitz as much as he does Tinker, does not use Shlomowitz's work which correlates longer indentures with higher mortality; and facts that Indians and other indenteds went to places where malaria, hookworm, tuberculosis and pneumonia were introduced by Africans and Europeans. Indian indenteds in Malaya had "a relative lack of immunity" against their underlying killer, malaria. For Trinidad, note that malaria and hookworm have secondary symptoms (debility; anaemia) and secondary infections (dysentery). R. Shlomowitz and Lance Brennan, "Mortality and Indian Labour in Malaya, 1877-1933" in *The Indian Economic and Social History Review* 29 (1) 1992, pp.57-75.

[18] Northrup's *Indentured Labor* (in discussing the Caribbean) refers largely to Guyana not Trinidad and other territories. We firmly believe that our case-study is atypical and yet valid, for there is no typical truth in history. More importantly, the solid chapters on "repatriation" and "abolition of indenture" in G.S. Arora, *Indian Emigration* (New Delhi: Puja, 1991) directly challenge Northrup's interpretations.

OK

[19] R. Shlomowitz, "On Punishments and Rewards in Coercive Labour Systems," *Slavery and Abolition* 12 (20) September 1991): pp.97-102.

[20] P. Knaplund, *The British Empire 1815-1939* (New York: Harper and Brothers, 1941) pp.144-7.

[21] Kingsley, *At Last A Christmas*, pp.145-6 and David Trotman, *Crime in Trinidad Conflict and Control in a Plantation Society 1838-1900* (Knoxville: University of Tennessee, 1986) p.266.

[22] Harjinder Singh ed., *Caste Among Non-Hindus in India* (Jaipur, India: National, 1977). See Editor's Introduction.

[23] The "Dhangurs" are specifically recalled by J. Scoble, *A Brief Exposure of the Deplorable Condition of the Hill Coolies*, (London: Harvey and Darton, 1840) p.5. John Gladstone, who owned plantations in Guyana, privately arranged for laborers from India (beginning in 1836), received "Hill coolies" or *Dhangurs*, unassimilated non-Hindus from the hills of Bengal who usually worked for settled communities as porters of various kinds. Later, Hindus, Muslims and Christians were induced to leave, but the misnomer, "coolie or Koli" stuck, only too conveniently for bigots or those with a superficial understanding of Indian social structure, *varna*, or again, the misnomer, "caste."

[24] Lal, *Girmitiyas The Origin of the Fiji Indians*, p.97. He argues that while abuse of Indians outraged people in India, leading to calls to end labor migration, "it was the news of the molestation and abuse of Indian women" which "outraged them most."

[25] Kelvin Singh, in "The Abolition of Indian Indentureship and Response of the Planter Interests in Trinidad," *Journal of Caribbean History* 21 (1) 1987, 43-54. Singh also shows that administrators like the Secretary of State for India, Austin Chamberlain, planned an Inter-Departmental Committee with India, Fiji and the West Indies so that non-indentured laborers would continue to those colonies which still needed them, even while concurring with the Viceroy of India to end "a system of forced labour entailing much misery and degradation and differing but little from a form of slavery." M.K. Gandhi rejected this deal.

[26] B.C. Roberts, *Labour in the Tropical Territories of the Commonwealth* (Durham: Duke University, 1964) pp.100-101,204. In Natal, M.K. Gandhi had successfully agitated the abolition of labor migration in 1911, three years before returning to India.

[27] Eric Williams, *History of the People of Trinidad and Tobago* (New York, Praeger, 1962) p.109. We detected a clear distinction between the early, radical writings of Eric Williams and his later, more populist works. Overall, we are indebted to the early Williams for his unique scholarly contribution.

[28] L. Newson, *Aboriginal and Spanish Colonial Trinidad A Study in Culture Contact* (London: Academic Press, 1976) pp.29-37.

[29] K.O. Laurence, *Immigration into the West Indies in the Nineteenth Century*, (Jamaica: Caribbean Universities, 1971) pp.36-39. Chinese immigration foundered because of China's insistence on free return passages, Britain's insistence on its minimum ratio of males:females, and abuses in recruitment.

[30] V.S. Naipaul, *The Loss of El Dorado A History* (London: Andre Deutsch, 1969), Chapter 9, especially pp.270-80.

[31] *Historical Society of Trinidad and Tobago Publications* (British Library, London), Publication 791: "An account of the Great Fire in Port of Spain, 1808." (Hereafter *HSTPubl#*).

[32] [J.B. Philip] "A Free Mulatto", *An Address to the Right Honorable Earl Bathurst ... relative to the claims of the Coloured Population of Trinidad* (London, 1824), p.136.

[33] J. Millette, *The Genesis of Crown Colony Government Trinidad 1783-1810*, (Curepe, Trinidad: Moko, 1970) pp.7; 16.

[34] L. Newson, *Aboriginal and Spanish Trinidad*, pp.195;197.

[35] Newson, *Aboriginal and Spanish Trinidad*, p.199; Table 1.4.

[36] A.M. John, *The Plantation Slaves of Trinidad 1783-1816 A Mathematical and Demographic Enquiry* (Cambridge: Cambridge University, 1988) pp.101-8.

[37] Abolitionists often made reference to Jamaica, but rarely to Trinidad. Vide W. Wilberforce, *Negro Slavery; or a view of some of the more prominent features of that state of society, as it exists in the*

United States of America and in the Colonies of the West Indies, especially in Jamaica (New York: Negro Universities Press, 1969; 1823), pp.35-9.

[38] Wilberforce in *Negro Slavery* points to sugar harvests in Jamaica, when able-bodied slaves were divided into two groups, each slave working "six days and three nights in the week." Between Saturday night and Monday, work ended for a maximum of 20 hours. In Trinidad, each slave who worked on Monday night in crop, did not work nights again till Thursday, according to A.C. Carmichael, *Domestic Manners and Social Condition of the White, Coloured and Negro Population of the West Indies* Volumes 1 and 2 (New York: Negro Universities Press, 1833).

[39] Eric Williams, "Race Relations In Caribbean Society," pp.54-60 in Vera Rubin ed., *Caribbean Studies: A Symposium* (Mona: Institute of Social and Economic Research, 1957).

[40] B. Brereton, *A History of Modern Trinidad 1783-1962* (Port of Spain: Heinemann, 1981) pp.54-5.

[41] John, *The Plantation Slaves*, p.55.

[42] C.R. Ottley, "A Brief History," in M. Anthony and A. Carr eds., *David Frost Introduces Trinidad and Tobago* (London: Andre Deutsch, 1975). Ottley says by 1797 (conquest), Trinidad had "no fewer than 468 plantations"; only a third (or 159 estates totalling 86,268 acres) were planted in sugar.

[43] C.R. Ottley, *Slavery Days in Trinidad A Social History of the Island from 1797-1838* (Trinidad, C.R. Ottley, 1974) pp.40-1; 66. For "mildness" of Trinidad slavery see E.L. Joseph, *History of Trinidad* (London: Frank Cass, 1970) pp.27-8; Naipaul, *The Loss of El Dorado*, pp.108-9; Carmichael, *Domestic Manners*, pp.181-213.

[44] Carl Campbell, "Ralph Woodford and the Free Coloureds: The Transition from a Conquest Society to a Society of Settlement, Trinidad 1813-1828," *Journal of Caribbean Studies* 2 (2-3) 1981, 238-49.

[45] R.S. Dunn, *Sugar and Slaves The Rise of the Planter Class in the English West Indies, 1624-1713* (Chapel Hill, University of North

Carolina, 1972) pp.226-9 for how quickly slave numbers grew once sugar was introduced (versus the earlier tobacco era) in Barbados and Jamaica. Spanish Trinidad could neither maintain their towns nor cultivate the land (lacking capital and labor), according to Newson, *Aboriginal and Spanish Trinidad*, pp.118-23.

[46] E. Williams, *History of the People of Trinidad and Tobago* (New York: F.A. Praeger, 1962) p.65.

[47] "Growth" may be more appropriate than "development" for this discussion. Newson's *Aboriginal and Spanish Trinidad*, pp.204-13 shows that Spanish Trinidad produced 1,588,000 pesos of commercial crops - 40.45% sugar; 32.87% cotton; 19.52% coffee and 7.15% cocoa - along with 272,400 pesos in food crops (maize, plantains, manioc, etc). Other items exported in small quantities were timber, coconuts, turtles and rice.

[48] Joseph, *History of Trinidad*, pp.226-8.

[49] It is illustrative of different levels of integration both during and after the Spanish era in Trinidad that Nihell, an Irish Catholic, had immigrated under the 1783 Cedula; his knowledge of Spanish laws led to his appointment as Chief Justice by the departing British general, Abercromby. Gertrude Carmichael, *History of the West Indian Islands of Trinidad and Tobago 1498-1900* (London: Alvin Redman, 1961), p.43.

[50] St. Hillaire Beggorat, at times referred to as the leader of the French Republicans, was the only member retained of the pre-invasion Council; his descendant, a popular historian of Trinidad writes, but only so Governor Picton "could see him and more easily control him." Anthony de Verteuil, *A History of Diego Martin 1784-1884* (Port of Spain: Paria, 1987) pp.43-7. The others on the Council appear to be all of British (English?) origin.

[51] C.O. 298 #3, 25 March 1808: pp.158-9. Cotton continued to be Trinidad's most valuable export as under Spanish rule, even though a 1790 disease redounded to sugar's advantage.

[52] *HSTPubl #791.*

[53] G. Carmichael, *History of the Islands* p.94; M. Anthony, *Profile Trinidad A Historical Survey from the Discovery to 1900* (London: MacMillan Caribbean, 1975) pp.78-80.

[54] C.O. 298 #3, 25 March 1808: p.159. Joseph, *History of Trinidad*, p.236 lamented that "Few of these colonies grew enough of provisions to supply wants ...find[ing] it more advantageous to purchase provisions from the United States."

[55] Joseph, *History of Trinidad*, pp.234-5. In this instance, "property" included one slave.

[56] The Alcaldes in Ordinary were the two magistrates, elected by the town board or *cabildo*. They administered justice, and the first of these officers retired at year's end to be succeeded by his (junior) colleague. After three years out of office, one might become a candidate again.

[57] C.O.298 Trinidad#3, 26 March 1808. Barrios or ward divisions, with their freeholders, elected Alcaldes de Barrio who helped maintain peace and administer local justice.

[58] For more on the legacies of the Cabildo, see J. Millette, *The Genesis of Crown Colony Government*, pp.37-41.

[59] Joseph, *History of Trinidad*, pp.237-8; Gen. Picton donated L4,000 and Hislop, L1,000 towards alleviating the human suffering. Of the Parliamentary relief, says Joseph, "none of the sufferers by the fire, I believe, got a shilling...."

[60] C. Campbell, "Ralph Woodford and the Free Coloureds: The Transition from a Conquest Society to a Society of Settlement, Trinidad 1813-1828." *Journal of Caribbean Studies*, 2 (2-3) 1981, 238-49. He argues that lack of capital was the "most crucial weakness," for future economic development.

[61] *Parliamentary Papers*, Vol.31, 1831-32. In *HSTPubl* #759.

[62] G. Beckford, *Persistent Poverty Underdevelopment in Plantation Economies of the Third World* (New York, Oxford University, 1983).

[63] P.D. Curtin, *The Atlantic Slave Trade A Census* (Madison: University of Wisconsin, 1969) p.57. An implicit criticism of Curtin's vague terminology comes from Barry Higman, "it is difficult to define what Curtin means by 'full production'" with reference

to Barbados. Higman, "The Slave Populations of the British Caribbean: Some Nineteenth Century Variations," pp.60-70 in S. Proctor ed. *Eighteenth Century Florida and the Caribbean* (Gainesville: University of Florida, 1976).

[64] G. Carmichael, *History of the Islands*, p.94.

[65] Naipaul, *The Loss of El Dorado*, p.281.

[66] Naipaul, *The Loss of El Dorado*, pp.243-5; 278-9.

[67] Joseph, *History of Trinidad*, pp.238-43.

[68] *HSTPubl* #1003.

[69] Ottley, *Slavery Days*, pp.114-15.

[70] G. Carmichael, "La Reconnaisance Estate, Lopinot Valley, Arouca," *Caribbean Quarterly* 6 (4) 1960, 279-81. Comte de Lopinot had served with the British army before 1789; he was eventually granted land in the forests of Trinidad, whence he and his slaves cut their way to, and planted in cocoa. After his death in 1819, "so endeared [was he] to his negroes and was so much beloved by them that for twenty years after [1819] they observed an annual holiday in his memory."

[71] A.C. Carmichael, *Domestic Manners*, Preface.

[72] Ottley, *Slavery Days in Trinidad*, pp.40-2.

[73] Carmichael, *Domestic Manners* Vol.1 pp.157; 181-6; 216.

[74] L.J. Ragatz, *The Fall of the Planter Class in the Caribbean, 1763-1833, A Study in Social And Economic History* (New York: Octagon Books, 1971), pp.386-7.

[75] Carmichael, *Domestic Manners*, Vol.II pp.18-19; 325.

[76] R. Sheridan, *Doctors and Slaves A Medical and Demographic History of Slavery in the British West Indies, 1680-1834* (London: Cambridge University, 1985) pp.49, 272. For the 1800 Code, see Carmichael, *History of the Islands*, pp.379-83.

[77] E. Genovese, *Roll, Jordan, Roll The World the Slaves Made* (New York: Pantheon, 1972;1974), especially Part 2; pp.133-48.

[78] Douglas Hall, "Slaves and Slavery in the British West Indies," *Social and Economic Studies* 11 (4) 1962, 305-18.

[79] O. Nigel Bolland, "Slave Wages in the Americas: Between Slave Labour and Wage Labour," p.23. Presented at the May 1991

"From Chattel to Wage Slavery" Conference at the Institute of Commonwealth Studies (London). Quoted with author's permission.

[80] Carmichael's *Domestic Manners*, Volume II p.213, mentions the setting up of a savings bank for "negroes ...which the white population did not even possess." The slaves did not want to keep their money there for exactly that reason!

[81] John, *The Plantation Slaves*, p.18 and chapter 6, especially p.106. F.W. Knight, *Slave Society in Cuba During the Nineteenth Century* (Madison: University of Wisconsin, 1970) says "sugar and slavery have had a familiar historical association from Cyprus... to Cuba," p.194; N. Deerr, *The History of Sugar* Volumes 1 and 2 (London: Chapman and Hall, [1949] 1950) p.259.

[82] B.W. Higman, *Slave Populations of the British Caribbean, 1807-1834* (Baltimore and London: Johns Hopkins, 1984) p.59.

[83] Campbell, "Ralph Woodford," *Journal of Caribbean Studies* 2 (2-3) 1981, p.239 shows that land was granted by Woodford to those who planted provisions and raised livestock, "not staple crop or export" to be cultivated. G. Carmichael, *History of the Islands*, pp.53-4 argues that the Colonial Office, in deference to the abolitionists, did not want to encourage sugar, but Picton's report declared that sugar and coffee were the most profitable crops if labor *and* capital were matched; "Cocoa ...[also had] a fine reputation and could be cultivated by white people," including poor whites from Barbados.

[84] Higman, *Slave Populations*, pp.59-60 including Figure 3.3.

[85] H.N. Coleridge, *Six Months in the West Indies in 1825* (London: John Murray, 1871), p.64.

[86] *HSTPubl* #260.

[87] Martin, *The West Indies* (Volume 1) p.208.

[88] S. Carrington, *The British West Indies during the American Revolution* (DorDrecht, Holland: Foris, 1988), p.128. He posits that it was Barbados which first made the demand, "No taxation without representation."

[89] Higman, *Slave Populations*, p.44

[90] Higman, *Slave Populations*, p.45

[91] R. Sheridan, "Mortality and Medical Treatment of Slaves in the British West Indies," pp.282-95 in S. Engerman and E. Genovese eds. *Race and Slavery in the Western Hemisphere: Quantitative Studies* (Stanford University, 1975), pp.287-88.

[92] B. Brereton, *A History of Modern Trinidad 1783-1962* (London: Heinemann, 1981) pp.54-5.

[93] Newson, *Aboriginal and Spanish Trinidad*, p.200.

[94] These are statistics for 1813 per Registration Returns according to Brereton, *A History of Modern Trinidad*, p.55.

[95] H.O.B. Wooding, "The Constitutional History of Trinidad and Tobago," *Caribbean Quarterly* 6 (2-3) 1960, 143-59.

[96] Picton Code, Carmichael, *History of the Islands*, p.379ff.

[97] John, *The Plantation Slaves*, p.107. John must be lauded for the valuable statistical clarity he brings to many "grey areas of Trinidad's slavery experience; however, it is rather surprising that he does not make use - critical or otherwise -of the Carmichael volumes, which are in his bibliography.

[98] Millette, *Genesis of Crown Colony*, p.63 acknowledges the Code "as generous and humane," but points to the lack of a clause for manumission as a "very significant omission." We have already seen that this did not prevent a minimum of 130 slaves being freed yearly between 1816-28.

[99] Sheridan, *Doctors and Slaves*, p.273.

[100] The case known as "Campbell v. Hall" decided that once Britain granted legislative powers to a colony, it could not thereafter use its legal prerogatives over that colony.

[101] [Philip], *An Address*, p.27.

[102] J. Sanderson, *An Appeal to the Imperial Parliament upon the Claims of the Ceded Colony of Trinidad, to be Governed by a Legislature and Judicature, Founded upon Principles Sanctioned by Colonial Precedents and Long Usage* (London, 1812), p.21.

[103] D.J. Murray, *The West Indies and the Development of Colonial Government 1801-1834* (London: Oxford University, 1965) pp.71-2.

[104] Also, L. M. Fraser, *History of Trinidad* Volume 2 (London: Frank Cass, [1891] 1971). Fraser contends that "in the history of Trinidad from 1797 to 1840, there are but two prominent figures, Picton and Sir Ralph Woodford...." (p.359).

[105] Campbell, "Ralph Woodford and the Free Coloureds," *Journal of Caribbean Studies* 2 (2-3) 1981, p.241.

[106] D. Wood, *Trinidad in Transition The Years After Slavery* (London: Oxford University, 1968), pp.31-1.

[107] Campbell, "Ralph Woodford and the Free Coloureds," *Journal of Caribbean Studies* 2 (2-3) 1981, 245-6.

[108] C.O. 295/37 #113: Woodford to Bathurst, 5 August 1815.

[109] K.O. Laurence in "The Settlement of Free Negroes in Trinidad Before Emancipation," *Caribbean Quarterly* 9 (1-2) 1963, 26-52.

[110] Laurence, "The Settlement of Negroes," *Caribbean Quarterly* 9 (1-2) 1963, p.29.

[111] Ottley, *Slavery Days,* pp.76-7.

[112] The West Indies (Institute of Commonwealth Studies Collection, n.d.) *Sundry Pamphlets, Volume XI,* p.13.

[113] F. Bayley, *Four Years' Residence in the West Indies, During the Years 1826, 7, 8, and 9* (London: William Kidd, 1833) p.211.

[114] Ottley, *Slavery Days,* p.141.

[115] Trinidad Express, *Trinidad Under Siege: The Muslimeen Revolt 6 Days of Terror* (Port of Spain: Express Ltd., 1990).

[116] *Parliamentary Papers, Volume XIII* (July 1842): "Report of the Select Committee on West India Colonies." Testimony on 28 April. Hereafter, *PP Vol.XIII* (1842 Comm.) as Notes, "1842 Select Committee" or "1842 Report" in the text.

[117] Hugh Tinker, "The Origins of Indian Migration to the West Indies." Pp.63-72 in Frank Birbalsingh ed. *Indenture and Exile* (Toronto: York University, 1989).

[118] This is possibly why occasional suspension of the trade accompanied outrage at abuses in the Caribbean and Mauritius (1838-44) but evidence of ill-treatment of indentured Indians in

the French colonies led to the termination of that privilege in the 1880s. By contrast, an 1884 massacre of Indians in Trinidad led to damage control and a innocuous Commission of Inquiry. There were Inquiries into the abuse of indented Indians again for British Guiana (1871), British Natal (1872) and Mauritius (1875).

[119] This is a premise in Judith Ann Weller's *The East Indian Indenture in Trinidad* (Rio Piedras: University of Puerto Rico, 1968). Slaves did not run away from their "homes" after 1838, as Douglas Hall demonstrated in "The Flight from the Estates Reconsidered: The British West Indies, 1838-42." *Journal of Caribbean History*, Volumes 10-11 (1978) 7-24.

[120] A. Memmi *The Colonizer and the Colonized* (Boston: Beacon Books, 1965) for stereotypes of the lazy black and brown peoples of the world. These will be cited in Chapter 4/3.

[121] Jean Besson discusses examples of post-slavery free villages in Jamaica, and refers to developments in Trinidad and Giuana, in "Family Land as a model for Martha Brae's New History: Culture Building in an Afro-Caribbean Village," pp.100-32 in C.V. Carnegie ed. *Afro-Caribbean Villages in Historical Perspective*. Kingston: African-Caribbean Institute, 1987. See also the Bolland-Green debate in my Introduction.

[122] J.W. Root, *The British West Indies and the Sugar Industry* (Liverpool: J.W. Root, 1899), pp.136-40. This account shows how, even in the 1890s, managers sought to reduce wages below the minimum of 25 cents a day. One manager told Root, "the coolie could live on four or five cents a day ...were his remuneration reduced to eighteen cents from the legal twenty-five [just set in 1872, the Coolie] would still be overpaid."

[123] If a planter's evidence is accurate (Note 120), a "struggle" in May 1841 over wage reduction was won by the workers, who maintained their income at 2s. 2d. a task.

[124] David Northrup, *Indentured Labor in the Age of Imperialism, 1838-1922* (New York: Cambridge University, 1995) p.106.

[125] J.H. Stark, *Guide Book and History of Trinidad* (Boston: J.H. Stark, 1897), p.20. Stark was one of the earliest writers to

observe that in those colonies where the land to population ratio was in favor of land, as in Trinidad with its "almost limitless field for squatting," the former slaves would find occupations outside of the plantations. O. Nigel Bolland advises against using the ratio as a magical formula.

[126] In Appendix C, population density is seen to have increased steadily after 1844, from 32 persons per square mile to 59 per square mile in 1871, at the same time almost doubling the population from 59,815 to 109,638.

[127] J.U.J. Asiegbu, *Slavery and the Politics of Liberation 1787-1861 A Study of Liberated African Emigration and British Anti-Slavery Policy* (New York: Africana, 1969), pp.34-42; W.L. Mathieson, *Great Britain and the Slave Trade 1839-1865* (London: Longmans, Green and Company, 1929), p.1.

[128] A land-for-passages policy aimed at converting Trinidad's part of the costs into small land grants, was discarded by 1880. In 1869, there were just 12 who accepted land instead of going home and 22 in 1870. In 1871 the offer was improved by allowing Indians to take the option in the eighth or ninth year of their indentures and also splitting the grant into L5 in cash and five acres in land. Arora, *Indian Emigration*, p.206-207.

[129] Northrup, *Indentured Labor*, p.30. On the same page Northrup says, "The indentured labor trade depended as much on the West's 'informal' empire of financial and commercial networks as it did on the formal empire of colonies." We also note that British South Africa recruited both Indian and Chinese indenteds concurrently in the period after the Anglo-Boer War, 1899-1902.

[130] D. Northrup, *Indentured labor in the Age of Imperialism, 1834-1922* (New York: Cambridge University, 1995) pp.66-70.

[131] Asiegbu says outmoded agricultural methods, absenteeism among planters and mismanagement also made for declines. "Perhaps even more painful to the planters than the Act of 1834 was the failure of the mother country to secure total international abolition." *Slavery and Liberation*, pp.34-37.

[132] P.D. Curtin, *The Rise and Fall of the Plantation Complex Essays in Atlantic History* (Cambridge: Cambridge University Press, 1990) pp.178-179; Northrup, *Indentured Labor*, p.29.

[133] See views of Trinidad's governors (Notes 97-100).

[134] Curtin says colonies like Barbados appeared to be overpopulated, but "others ...like Trinidad" and Guiana, "lacked population for further development," even as several colonies had achieved self-sustaining slave populations by 1805. *Rise and Fall of Plantation*, pp.174-75; Northrup, *Indentured Labor*, p.104-106.

[135] Asiegbu, *Slavery and Liberation*, p.36; E. Williams, *From Columbus to Castro: The History of the Caribbean 1492-1969* (New York: Harper and Row, 1970) pp.328-29 recalls Lord Howick, a prime mover for emancipation, anticipated ex-slaves buying land with their high wages as threatening to the labor supply: 'Accordingly it is to the imposition of a considerable tax upon land that I chiefly look for the means of enabling the planter to continue his business....'

[136] *PP Vol. XIII* (1842 Comm.). Testimony of W.H. Burnley, and his estate statistics. Production figures will follow.

[137] Surgeon-Major D.W.D. Comins, *Note on Emigration from India to Trinidad* With Diary, Appendices and Census of East Indian Population by H.J. Clark (Calcutta: Bengal Secretariat Press, 1893) p.i. of Comins' Appendix A. By 1849, 5,162 Indians had arrived, and 14,338 during 1852-61. Appendix B of this study.

[138] P. Curtin argues that the planters' problems were only indirectly related to labor or the removal of protection; the reasons he cites for the decline are lack of technical innovation owing to the small-scale basis of production, problems of "social readjustment and reorganization of the labor system" after emancipation, and European beet sugar competition after c.1870. "The British Sugar Duties and West Indian Prosperity," *Journal of Economic History* XIV (2) 1954, 157-164.

[139] R.A. Lobdell, "Patterns of Investment and Sources of Credit in the British West Indian Sugar Industry, 1838-97." *Journal of Caribbean History*, 4 (1972) 31-53 (notably p.42).

[140] Output on Burnley's estates, even if exceptional - but there is no reason to believe they were - shows that good profits were made under the new regime.

[141] Stanley to Peel (27 November 1843) *Peel Papers* [British Library]. See also Chapter Three.

[142] W.A. Green, "Plantation Society and Indentured Labour: The Jamaican Case, 1834-1865," pp.163-186 in P. Emmer ed. *Colonialism and Migration; Indentured Labour Before and After Slavery* (DorDrecht: Martinus Nijhoff, 1986), p.166.

[143] Monica Schuler, *'Alas, Alas, Kongo' A Social History of Indentured African Immigration into Jamaica, 1841-1865.* (Baltimore: Johns Hopkins University, 1980).

[144] Appendix 2.2 and Report of the 1842 Select Committee. Below, we shall see that Britain took over the initiative both for African and Indian indentured migration.

[145] On 27 November 1843, Lord Stanley had written about the "very favourable accounts" received of Indian workers in Mauritius, which "have brought upon me still more urgent and pressing entreaties from the West Indians for a relaxation of the prohibition in their favour...." Stanley felt he would have to oblige them "if we take any step for reducing the amount of protection now enjoyed by the West Indians, without at the same time increasing their facilities for obtaining labour." Stanley to Peel: 27 November 1843, *Peel Papers.*

[146] Hume in his *Political Discourses* said, "Everything in the world is purchased with labour." This was particularly true of post-1833 Trinidad. In *Wealth of Nations* (New York: Macmillan, 1895) Adam Smith says, "The value of any commodity, therefore, to the person who possesses it, and who means not to use or consume it himself, but to exchange it for other commodities, is equal to the quantity of labour which it enables him to purchase or command. Labour, therefore, is the real measure of the exchangeable value of all commodities." On Mauritius' advantages, see I. M. Cumpston, *Indians Overseas in British Territories 1834-1854* (London: Dawsons, 1969), pp.11-15.

[147] K.O. Laurence, *Immigration into the West Indies in the Nineteenth Century*, (Jamaica: Caribbean Universities, 1971) pp.36-39 says this migration foundered (1843-59) because of China's insistence on free repatriation, London's insistence on its male:female ratios, and recruitment abuses.

[148] "No, no, said he, it is enough to have desolated Africa, without introducing this pest into Asia too." In *Hansard's Parliamentary Debates* Third Series Volume XLI (1837-1838): "Importation of Hindoos into Guiana," 6 March 1838.

[149] *PP Vol. XIII* (1842 Comm.): Testimony of 10 June. Planters could have turned to the Colonial Bank with its branches in the West Indies (founded in 1836), but the bank expressly forbade loans on the security of lands, houses or tenements, precluding loans to sugar estates. In Lobdell, "Patterns of Investment" in *Journal of Caribbean History* 4 (1972), 31-53.

[150] J. Scoble, *A Brief Exposure of the Deplorable Condition of the Hill Coolies in British Guiana and Mauritius* (London: Harvey and Darton, 1840) points out that in 1834 already, John Gladstone (Guiana planter) thought of alternative laborers from India to "use as a set-off" against his former slaves. In 1838, Trinidad's Governor wrote the Colonial Secretary, "The introduction of Labourers from other places would evidently assist towards curing th[e] disinclination to work." C.O. 295/122 *Trinidad* #120: Hill to Glenelg.

[151] Laborers from USA, from Sierra Leone, from West Indian and Portuguese territories were ultimately more capable of holding their own against the planters than were East Indians. Elementary props of the system were not provided for Indians even after Governor Henry McLeod wrote London, "the great difficulty we have and shall have to encounter is, the want of some Government officer possessing a perfect knowledge of their character, language and customs." *Parliamentary Papers Volume 31, Part II* "Papers relative to the Emigration of Laborers, Trinidad," Despatch from McLeod to Stanley, 15 July 1845. Indians were the ideal, non-English speaking workers who were minimally equipped to draw attention

to abuses endured within the free labor regime (but which the Portuguese were to able expose).

[152] C.O. 295/129 *Trinidad#1*: Mein to Governor MacGregor of Barbados. 10 January 1840.

[153] *PP Vol. XIII* (1842 Comm.) Testimony on 10 June 1842.

[154] *PP Vol. XIII* (1842 Comm.) "Report of the Committee."

[155] *Reports on the State of Her Majesty's Colonial Possessions,* (Trinidad, 18 May 1852) Despatch: Governor Harris to Sir John Pakington.

[156] G.W. Roberts and J. Byrne, "Summary Statistics on Indenture and Associated Migration Affecting the West Indies, 1834-1918," *Population Studies,* 20 (1) 1966, 125-34. See Tables 1 and 2.

("Immigrants" would be the total minus deaths *and* repatiration).

[157] Lobdell, "Patterns of Investment," *Journal of Caribbean History* 4 (1972) pp.41-42.

[158] Kelvin Singh, "The Abolition of Indian Indentureship and Response of the Planter Interests in Trinidad," *Journal of Caribbean History* 21 (1) 1987, 43-54.

[159] Modified from David V. Trotman, *Crime in Trinidad Conflict and Control in a Plantation Society 1838-1900* (Knoxville: University of Tennessee, 1986) p.292.

[160] E. Williams, *Capitalism and Slavery* (Chapel Hill: University of North Carolina, 1944; 1966), Chapter 1, especially pp.7-19. Alan Burns, *History of the British West Indies* (London: George Allen and Unwin, 1954) pp.662-663.

[161] C.O. 295/130 *Trinidad#120*: McLeod to Russell, 29 May 1840.

[162] B. Brereton, "The Experience of Indentureship: 1845-1917," pp.25-38 in John La Guerre ed. *Calcutta to Caroni The East Indians of Trinidad* (London: Longman, 1974) p.25. Brereton does acknowledge that various experiments were tried in Trinidad; our objection remains that Indian labor is portrayed as the only and inevitable solution for Trinidad.

[163] *PP Vol. XIII* (1842 Comm.): Testimony on 10 June 1842.

[164] L.A.A. de Verteuil, *Trinidad: Its Geography, Natural Resources, Adminstration, Present Condition, and Prospects* (London: Ward and Lock, 1858) p.178.

[165] Despite a long history of labor migration from China to neighboring territories before the 1800s, the early Q'ing (Ch'ing or Manchu) dynasty made it a treasonous act, punishable by death.

Northrup, *Indentured Labor*, p.52 says that early Caribbean labor recruitment took place among the Chinese of Southeast Asia.

[166] David Northrup, *Indentured Labor*, p.51-52.

[167] W. Kloosterboer, *Involuntary Labour since the Abolition of Slavery A survey of Compulsory Labour Throughout the World* (Leiden: E.J. Brill, 1960) p.1.

[168] *PP Vol. XIII* (1842 Comm.), Testimony on 10 June.

[169] Lamont, Norman. *Burnley of Orange Grove A Public Lecture Delivered under the Auspices of the Historical Society of Trinidad and Tobago on 29 November 1946* (Port of Spain, 1947).

[170] Lamont, *Burnley of Orange Grove*, p.12.

[171] H. Merivale, *Lectures on Colonisation and Colonies Delivered before the University of Oxford in 1839, 1840 and 1841* (London: Oxford University, 1928), p.574. He promoted immigration in these lectures: "One favourite bugbear is, the fear of introducing a new system of slavery under the guise of regulations for the newly imported free labourers; surely a most chimeral fear, when the eyes of Government and of the public are so jealously fixed on the subject ... The danger of injustice to the employer is, just at present, the greatest [sic] of the two." pp.317-319.

[172] C.O. 884/1 *West Indian No.6.* "Memoranda on the Progress of the Free System in the West India Colonies in 1840."

[173] *PP Vol. XIII* (1842 Comm.), pp.93ff.

[174] C.O.295/136 *Trinidad#60.* McLeod to Stanley, 28 May 1842.

[175] *PP Vol. XIII* (1842 Comm.), pp.273ff.

[176] C.O. 295/136. McLeod to Stanley, 28 May 1842.

[177] C.O. 295/136. McLeod to Stanley, 28 May 1842.

[178] *PP Vol. XIII* (1842 Comm.), Evidence of 10 June 1842.

[179] *Parliamentary Papers. Accounts and Papers Vol. XXXI* (1845). Section 4 of 25 sections: "Colonies - Session of 4 February - 9 August 1845," pp.96-8.

[180] While their race and cultural baggage made Indians easily distinguishable when they absconded from horrid plantations, some were enterprising enough to escape to Venezuela.

[181] Lobdell, "Patterns of Investment and Sources of Credit," *Journal of Caribbean History*, 4 (1972) pp.52-53.

[182] Both Lobdell and Curtin suggest 1870 is the crucial date, when beet sugar made up a third of world sugar output.

[183] *PP Vol. XIII* (1842 Comm.): Evidence of Robert Bushe.

[184] *Duplicate Despatches*, No. 22 of 1834, as printed in *HSTPubl* #252 (12 February 1834).

[185] *Duplicate Despatches*, Miscellaneous No. 4, as printed in *HSTPubl* #253 (20 July 1834).

[186] The case was made that the Portuguese were not "uncivilized" immigrants and therefore it was difficult to enforce contracts upon them anyway. See K.O. Laurence, "The Evolution of Long-Term Labour Contracts in Trinidad and British Guiana 1834-1863," in *Jamaica Historical Review* 5 (1) 1965, 9-27.

[187] Original Please! .... //// ???? "[I]t appears to me that, in the first place, the immigrants must pass through an initiatory process; they are not, neither Africans nor Coolies, fit to be placed in a position which the labourers of civilised countries may at once occupy. They must be treated like children - and wayward ones, too - the former from the utterly savage state in which they arrive; the latter, from their habits and religion." In E. Williams, *History of the People of Trinidad and Tobago* (New York: F.A. Praeger, 1962; 1964) p.111.

[188] W.A. Green, *British Slave Emancipation The Sugar Colonies and the Great Experiment 1830-1865* (London: Oxford University, 1976), p.277.

[189] *Duplicate Despatches* (#24 of 1834, with 2 enclosures): Sir George Hill to the Hon. E.G. Stanley. 9 March 1834.

[190] A "Circular" from Governor Hill to Commandants of the Quarters charged them with returning these Africans to employers if they should leave their "present domicile" before the "expiration of the six months." *Duplicate Despatches* #24 of 1834, Enclosure: 28 February 1834.

[191] *Duplicate Despatches*: 28 February 1834 (from George Hill).

[192] C.O. 296/11 *Trinidad#26*: Spring-Rice to Hill (2 November 1834). And Asiegbu, *Slavery and Liberation*, pp.42-43.

[193] Laurence, "The Evolution of Long-Term Labour Contracts," *Jamaica Historical Review* 5 (1) 1965, 9-27.

[194] As early as December 1837, Trinidad passed "An Act for the Suppression of Vagrancy, and for the Punishment of Idle and Disorderly persons, Rogues, and Vagabonds, and Incorrigible Rogues." To the planters' chagrin, London disallowed this act on 10 November 1838. *Parliamentary Papers Vol. XLV* 1847-8, p.204.

[195] C.O. 296/12 *Trinidad#22*: Glenelg to Hill (15 July 1835).

[196] *Parliamentary Papers Vol. LII* (Demerara, 22 December 1836): Smyth to Glenelg. Including Enclosure 2 in No.3.

[197] *Parliamentary Papers Vol. LII*, No.163: Glenelg to Smyth (31 October 1836).

[198] Laurence, "The Evolution of Long-Term Labour Contracts," *Jamaica Historical Review* 5 (1) 1965, p.10.

[199] *ZHC-1, No. 1398*: "Accounts and Papers, 6 (1842): Lord John Russell to McLeod, 9 June 1840 (p.414).

[200] Green, *British Slave Emancipation*, p.265.

[201] Green, *British Slave Emancipation*, p.266.

[202] *Reports on the State of Her Majesty's Colonial Possessions*, (Sierra Leone. 18 August 1851), pp.187-188. [Institute of Commonwealth Studies Library, London].

[203] *Reports on the State of Her Majesty's Colonial Possessions*, (Trinidad. 18 May 1852). In the 1851 report to Sir John Pakington, Harris said 8,010 Africans had arrived.

[204] *Reports on the State of Her Majesty's Colonial Possessions. Trinidad*, Harris' despatch to London, enclosing Blue Books for 1851 (Signed, 18 May 1852).

[205] The highest foreign-born percentage for any single year was that for 1881 (46.38 per cent). These estimates do not factor in those who returned "home" to India, but excludes 441 persons listed as "not described" in Appendix 2.3.

[206] *Memorandum by the Acting Committee of the West India Planters and Merchants* Transmitted to Her Majesty's Government on 25 February 1853, [signed: A. Colville, Chairman in *Papers of the West India Committee*].

[207] Schuler, "*Alas, Alas, Kongo,*" p.9.

[208] Asiegbu, *Slavery and Liberation*, pp.34-7.

[209] Augustin Cochin, *Results of Emancipation*. Translated by M.L. Booth (Boston: Walker, Wise and Company, 1864), p.330.

[210] Cochin, *Results of Emancipation*, pp.327-328.

[211] C.O. 295/121 *Trinidad#66*: Governor Hill to the Secretary for the Colonies, Glenelg (28 June 1838).

[212] C.O. 295/121. Hill to Glenelg. 28 June 1838.

[213] The "Council" is the Legislative Council, which comprised official and unofficial members, all nominees until 1831.

[214] C.O. 295/121 *Trinidad#2686*: Lt.-Governor Hill to Lord Glenelg (26 July 1838).

[215] *PP Vol. XIII* (1842 Comm.) Testimony of Robert Bushe.

[216] C.O. 295/125 *Trinidad#36*: Col. J.A. Mein to Secretary of State (18 May 1839).

[217] C.O. 295/125 *Trinidad#36*: Col. J.A. Mein to Secretary of State (18 May 1839).

[218] C.O. 295/125 *Trinidad#36*: Mein to Secretary of State (18 May 1839).

[219] Comins, *Note on Immigration*, p.46

[220] E. Williams, *Capitalism and Slavery* (Chapel Hill: University of North Carolina, 1944), pp.152-153. Williams says that in 1807 and in 1833, the West Indies had over-produced sugar, which he linked, perhaps deterministically, with Abolition and Freedom: "Overproduction in 1807 demanded abolition; overproduction in 1833 demanded emancipation."

[221] *PP Vol. XIII* (1842 Comm.): Testimony of W.H. Burnley.

[222] C.O.295/121 *Trinidad#80*: Hill to Glenelg (10 August 1838).

[223] *Trinidad Standard and West India Journal*, 19 February 1839.

[224] *Trinidad Standard and West India Journal*, 19 February 1839.

[225] Noel Deerr, *The History of Sugar* (London: Chapman and Hall, 1949; 1950) Volume 2, pp.430; 442-443.

[226] C.O.295/122 *Trinidad#120*: Hill to Glenelg (11 Dec. 1838).

[227] C.O.295/122 *Trinidad#120*: Hill to Glenelg, (11 Dec. 1838).

[228] C.O.295/122 *Trinidad#120*: Hill To Glenelg, (11 Dec. 1838.

[229] *Reports on the State of Her Majesty's Colonial Possessions*. Despatch from Harris to Colonial Secretary, with Blue Books for 1851 (Signed, 18 May 1852). This rivalry is discussed in Wood, *Trinidad in Transition*, pp.65-66.

[230] D. Hall, *A Brief History of the West India Committee* (Barbados: Caribbean Universities press, 1971) pp. 16-17. Hall notes the shift within the West India body, during the later 18th century, the predominance of planters giving way to a dominance by merchants as more estates were lost to merchant-creditors after 1807; "leadership was coming to rest with those who combined in themselves both the mercantile and the proprietory interests." Burnley was just such an example.

[231] D. Wood, *Trinidad in Transition The Years After Slavery* (London: Oxford University, 1968) pp.60 and 67.

[232] Lamont, *Burnley of Orange Grove*, p.8.

[233] *Report of Messrs. Peck and Price, who were appointed at a meeting of the Free Colored People of Baltimore, held on the 25th November, 1839, Delegates to Visit British Guiana, and the Island of Trinidad; for the purpose of ascertaining the Advantages to be Derived by Colored People Migrating to those Places*. Baltimore: Woods and Crane, 1840.

[234] Hall, *A Brief History*, p.18. For a comparison with the other Asian emigration, see Yen Ching-Hwan, *Coolies and Mandarins*

China's Protection of Overseas Chinese during the Late Ch'ing Period (1851-1911) (Singapore: Singapore University, 1985) pp.44-47 for how the British ignored abuses in this trade from Amoy as much of its commercial expansion was due to "supplying coolies."

[235] Linguistic Deconstruction might have something to say about the planters use of *power* to describe the rights of African and Asian workers, including festivals (Chapter Five).

[236] J. Blum writes that for about two-thirds of Europeans in 1770 (or 100 million peasants) "through the accident of their birth into [that class], the society in which they lived denied them certain freedoms and privileges enjoyed by those [upon whom they were] compelled to be dependent and subservient to ...." In "The Condition of the European Peasantry on the Eve of Emancipation." *Journal of Modern History* 46 (3) 1974, 395-424.

[237] W.G. Sewell. *The Ordeal of Free Labor in the British West Indies.* (London: Frank Cass, 1861; 1968) p.111. He defended ex-slaves from the charge of vagabondism: "Unquestionably there is a certain amount of idleness and vagabondism among the Creole laborers of Trinidad, but I see no evidence that [these] exist in a larger proportion among them than would exist among any other class of laborers similarly situated." On indenture: "It was not started for the aggrandizement of the planter, but to stimulate his prostrate energies, to benefit [C]oolie as much as Creole [Upon arrival] not only families, but people from the same district are kept together; their wants are immediately cared for, and, the prospects of work and wages being certain, their condition is far more comfortable and encouraging than that of the mass of Irish immigrants who arrive every week in New York."

[238] I found that the two higher "castes" (usually a small number) were distributed among 18 of 20 estates to which these immigrants were sent. *General Registers:*(20 August 1873) *Syria*; ship registers are held by Trinidad's Archives.

[239] *PP Vol. XIII* (1842 Comm.): Testimony on 28 April 1842.

[240] Carmichael, *History of the Islands*, pp.211-12.

[241] Both Burnley and Bushe argued that rent-free houses were an added expense, some of which were new construction. In some cases of competition over workers, some planters went "to greater expense than others in erecting houses ... of American timber, 20 feet long by 12 feet wide, consisting of two rooms of 10 feet by 12 ... above 200 dollars [each]." The 1842 Select Committee asked Bushe, "Have you ever tried a system of payment of rent by your labourers?" The answer was negative. Wage decreases were effected, which might be construed as an indirect rent. *PP Vol. XIII* (1842 Comm.).

[242] Deerr, *History of Sugar*, p.362.

[243] Carmichael, *History of the Islands*, p.211.

[244] *Parliamentary Papers* Vol.7 (1848): "Report of the Select Committee on Sugar and Coffee Planting." M.J. Higgins, p.153ff.

[245] Williams, *History of the People*, p.109. In one of his more objective moments, Williams said: "One can only wonder today how it was possible for any country that had abolished slavery on the ground that it was inhuman to justify Indian indenture with its 25 cents a day wage and its jails."

[246] For instance Merivale's *Lectures*, pp.317-319, where he refers to this, as well as the fear of injustice to the planters which was "now" greater than toward the laborers.

[247] Malcolm Cross, "The Political Representation of Organized Labour in Trinidad and Guyana: A Comparative Puzzle," pp. 285-308 in M. Cross and G. Heuman eds. *Labour in the Caribbean From Emancipation to Independence*. London: Macmillan Caribbean, 1988.

[248] *State of Her Majesty's Colonial Possessions, 1851*: "Sierra Leone," Governor MacDonald to Earl Grey, pp.157-191.

[249] *Parliamentary Papers, Vol. LXVII* (1852-53): Governor Harris to Earl Grey (7 January 1851).

[250] The phrase belongs to Lord Brougham; in 1838 he used it in the House of Lords to describe the ambiguities of the apprenticeship period which freed slaves had to live through since

1833. In *Hansard's Parliamentary Debates, Third series (Volume XLI, 1837-38)*: 6 March 1838 (p.420).

[251] *State of Her Majesty's Colonial Possessions. 1851*: "Sierra Leone," Governor MacDonald to Earl Grey, pp.157-191; especially pp.187ff. (Bound Documents at Institute of Commonwealth Studies).

[252] Roberts and Byrne, "Summary Statistics," *Population Studies* 20 (1) 1966, 125-34.

[253] Williams, *From Columbus to Castro*, p.350.

[254] Williams, *From Columbus to Castro*, p.346.

[255] It is noteworthy that a cobbler and dealer in leather may enjoy relatively high esteem in Western society; yet the ascriptive status from India is often recalled by non-Indian writers, even as they generally adhere to the philosophy of *achieved* status. Hindus regard leather as unclean only because it is obtained through killing cows and animals.

[256] Cow-keepers are regarded as a clean, Sudra caste in India, and one of the best known epic heroes, Sri Krishna, the exponent of the *Bhagavad Gita*, spent his youth as a cowherd.

[257] Appendix B and Comins *Note on Emigration*, p.37.

[258] The total number of immigrants on the *Syria* was 307.

[259] However, 26 persons of the "caste" *Jat* are in fact Khatriyas or "warriors"; seven *Gosaine and Athit* are Brahmins, as is the last entry, *Awasti*. Based on conversations with Indian nationals (Silver Spring, MD. on 22 September 1991): Messrs. R. Beladakere, Alok Gupta and L. Singh.

[260] Comins, *Note on Emigration*, p.24.

[261] Brij V. Lal, *Girmitiyas The Origins of the Fiji Indians* (Canberra: The Journal of Pacific History, 1983) pp.1-2.

[262] Northrup, *Indentured Labor*, p.142-44.

[263] K.O. Laurence, "The Development of Medical Services in British Guiana and Trinidad 1841-1873," *Jamaican Historical Review* 4 (1964), 59-67. Only after an Ordinance of 1865 demanded medical facilities be provided, did some estates begin the service; 13 estates gave up indenture, instead!

²⁶⁴ When Trinidad was drawing its (Indian) Immigration Ordinance, Lt. Governor MacLeod sought and received the wage scale adopted in Guiana from its Governor. See C.O. 295/144: MacLeod to Lord Stanley, 18 October 1844.

²⁶⁵ J. Scoble's *A Brief Exposure of the Deplorable Condition* cited an August 1839 article in the Calcutta paper *Friend of India*, and suggested that promises to prevent horrid episodes similar to African slavery were hollow, and the "cooley trade" will make all "tread the same circle." These fears were well-founded because another Scoble-like effort had to be made in 1870 (by Edward Jenkins in *The Coolie His Rights and Wrongs*) without even a temporary suspension. Plantations had to be supported.

²⁶⁶ *Hansard's Parliamentary Debates*, Third series (XLI) 1837-38: pp.416-476. (Brougham in House of Lords, 6 March 1838.)

²⁶⁷ *Hansard's Parliamentary Debates*, Third series (XLI) 1837-38: Brougham's speech, pp.418, 423-25, 430-431.

²⁶⁸ Comins, *Note on Emigration*, Appendix A, p.29.

²⁶⁹ Comins, *Note on Emigration*, p.i of Appendix A.

²⁷⁰ J.A. Weller, *The East Indian Indenture in Trinidad* (Rio Piedras, University of Puerto Rico, 1968) describes how East Indians who escaped the plantations and who knew they could be apprehended by non-Indians, fled across the sea to Venezuela.

²⁷¹ H. Clarke to Hugh W. Austin, 28 October 1862. Letterbook 2, No. 49, Edith Clarke Papers. as quoted in D. Lowenthal, *West Indian Societies*, pp.62-63.

²⁷² J.W. Root noted Guiana's slow population growth. Almost half of the indented Indians repatriated but, "under the law of natural increase, they would have doubled or trebled themselves." Up to 1895 in Trinidad, 16,024 Indians left upon completion of their contracts. *British West Indies*, pp.135-41.

²⁷³ Laurence, "The Evolution of Long-Term Labour Contracts," *Jamaica Historical Review* 5 (1) 1965, p.10.

²⁷⁴ *HSTPubl* #254.

²⁷⁵ Carmichael, *History of the Islands*, pp.189-190.

²⁷⁶ Carmichael, *History of the Islands*, p.212.

[277] C.O. 295/126, *Trinidad*#81. J.A. Mein to Governor MacGregor (sent on to Lord Russell), 20 December 1839.

[278] C.O. 295/126, *Trinidad*#81. Mein to MacGregor.

[279] *Historical Statistics of the United States, 1789-1945*, (Washington, D.C.: Bureau of the Census, 1949) pp.33-4.

[280] Tables 2.1 and 2.2; Appendix C on foreign-born.

[281] Ching-Hwan, *Coolies and Mandarins* notes the similarity between the slave trade and Chinese migration, pp.87ff; D. Northrup, *Indentured Labor*, concludes that in places such as Peru, Chinese suffered some of the worst abuses. See also, Walton Look Lai, *Indentured Labor, Caribbean Sugar: Chinese and Indian Migrants to the British West Indies, 1838-1918* (Baltimore: Johns Hopkins University, 1993).

[282] If anything, Harris fought hard with the Colonial Office both to tie Indians with indentures and tighten labor laws.

[283] C.O. 295/120 (12 January 1838): Petition of 12 Mandingo slaves forwarded to London by Governor Hill. Witness, Edward Schack. (The petition was not granted.)

[284] Carmichael, *History of the Islands*, pp.188-89.

[285] More Portuguese (32,000) ended up in Guiana, but they may have been predominantly Catholic, because K.O. Laurence writes that they "were the objects of violent attack by the Negroes in 1848 and again in 1856 and 1889. The root cause seems to have been Negro jealousy of Portuguese success and privileges, excited in 1856 by an anti-Catholic agitator." *Immigration into the West Indies* p.18.

[286] Rev. W. C. Wilson, *The Madeira Persecutions* (London: The Religious Tract Society, 1856) pp.130-133.

[287] E.B. Underhill, *The West Indies: Their Social and Religious Condition* (Westport: Negro Universities, 1862) p.19.

[288] Wilson, *The Madeira Persecutions*, pp.145-47.

[289] Wilson, *Madeira Persecutions*, p.149.

[290] Roberts and Byrne, Table 3 in "Summary Statistics," *Population Studies* 20 (1) 1966, p.129.

[291] *Papers Relating to Her Majesty's Colonial Possessions* Trinidad #6: Despatch from Bushe to Kimberley, 14 August 1882.

[292] Laurence, "The Evolution of Long-Term Contracts," *Jamaica Historical Review* 5 (1) 1965, p.10.

[293] Isaac Dookhan, *Post-Emancipation History of the West Indies* (London: Collins, 1975) p.57.

[294] G.S. Arora, *Indian Emigration* (New Delhi: Puja Publishers, 1991) pp.142-43.

[295] Arora, *Indian Emigration*, p.162.

[296] On 26 April 1848, the *Trinidad Spectator* had criticized Indian migration for the low male:female ratio, inadequate medical provision, irregular payment of wages, and "the inhuman manner in which they [migrants] were treated." Whether in Mauritius or in Trinidad, planters had tried to restrict labor migration to males; Britain did not demand an equal gender ratio, but adamantly insisted on allowing females/families to migrate.

[297] Arora, *Indian Emigration*, p.169.

[298] D. Northrup's recent *Indentured Labor in the Age of Imperialism, 1834-1922* (New York: Cambridge University, 1995) is exceptional in locating indenture within the imperial economy, but displays a bias that indenture became less abusive over time. He omits data used in G.S. Arora's *Indian Emigration* (New Delhi: Puja, 1991) on sub-topics which discuss the ongoing controversies over "repatriation rights;" the impact of beet sugar competition (1870ff) and weaknesses in official mortality data.

[299] W.A. Green, *British Slave Emancipation The Sugar Colonies and the Great Experiment 1830-1865* (London: Oxford University Press, 1976), p.281-83; also Northrup, *Indentured Labor*, p.106 admits that despite "governmental efforts" to *not* have indenteds treated as "slaves, the inescapable fact was that their lives were controlled by employers who had recently been slave owners and protected by local officials who were closely allied with this class."

[300] See Note 16, below, for Indian reactions when changes to rules were explained to them in India by Indians; Arora, *Indian Emigration*, pp.243ff. cites examples of abuses as late as 1913-14.

Inspector Natho Singh of Alipur saved four of 12 "emigrants" who were abductees. Dr Sharma of the London Missionary Society and M.C. Brahman gave evidence about Guiana and Trinidad: "Many immigrants who never heard of jail became convicts overnight due to such petty faults" as "reporting to work at 4 a.m. [minus a] doctor's certificate."

[301] Arora, *Indian Emigration*, p.144 quotes Dr. Henry Mitchell, one of Trinidad's Protectors of Immigrants: referring to this "humiliation with which a free Indian was greeted on the road: 'Slave, where is your free pass?', he wrote to the Colonial Secretary, in April 1873: 'Let a similar Regulation be applied to expected immigrants under indenture from Barbados, and its nature will be at once revealed.' But these officers were few and far between."

[302] Perhaps this restriction, officially to save the coolie from "ruinous" habits, implicitly agreed with one Indian perspective about Indians who "became vagrants and wandered about secretly, hoping to find some way out, of returning to India." In Arora, *Indian Emigration*, p.113.

[303] The Agent-General of Immigration, or Protector, oversaw the welfare of indented Indians *as well as free Indians*, and was required to visit the estates at least twice a year.

[304] J.A. Weller, *The East Indian Indenture in Trinidad* (Rio Piedras, Puerto Rico: Institute of Caribbean Studies, 1968) p.59 cites the Petit Morne Estate; G.S. Arora, *Indian Emigration*, pp.115ff, mentions cases of ships from India embarking liberated slaves in Africa for common destinations with Indians. "Tyburnia" with 24 fatalities (7.81%) reached Trinidad on 4 March 1860, had picked up 78 "liberated African male adults" at St. Helena.

[305] C.O. 295/153: Major Fagan's Report (29 August 1846). [This document is part of Original Correspondence files in the Kew Gardens Archives near Richmond, UK].

[306] David V. Trotman, *Crime in Trinidad Conflict and Control in a Plantation Society 1838-1900* (Knoxville: University of Tennessee Press, 1986) p.185.

[307] As late as 1884 "small parties" of new indenteds "deserted from plantation Aurora," only to give the general explanation "that they had been informed that after a few days' journey through the forest they would arrive at a mountain on the farther side of which a road was to be found leading to Calcutta." In Dwarka Nath, *A History of Indians in British Guiana* (London: Thomas Nelson and Sons, 1950) p.90. For Trinidad, see Arora, *Indian Emigration*, p.113.

[308] Arora, *Indian Emigration*, p.199. The author goes on to show that those leaving Trinidad after their first indentures took about L5,000 back to India, but outside of that gross statistic, "'very few' had saved enough individually for their own passages. 'That fact once known, would deprive [Indians] of sustaining hope of returning home ... and convert willing labourers working for a future into moody discontented vagrants.'"

[309] Arora, *Indian Emigration*, pp.198-211.

[310] J.A. Weller, *The East Indian Indenture in Trinidad* (Rio Piedras, Puerto Rico, Institute of Caribbean Studies, 1968) p.60 noted "most ...barracks" were leaky, damp and dark, while water was muddy and unfiltered at Woodford Lodge in 1914, while on the McBean estate, water was unavailable on Sundays; Arora, *Indian Emigration*, pp.156-57 says that "only after 1914 [were] latrines provided," because of the belief Indians used the bushes, and also because very few Indians would accept the job of cleaning.

[311] Northrup, *Indentured Labor*, pp.107-108; p.34.

[312] Arora. *Indian Emigration*, p.143-182. The rules set out initially in 1845 (See Note 69) would earn an average male worker $2.40 per month; before and after the Immigration Amendment Ordinance No.5 of 1872 fixed wages at 25 cents a day for 9-hour days, Indians were receiving 20 cents or less, by a strategy of increasing tasks. J.H. Trollope, an Immigration officer, noted in his Report for 1870-71, that Indians were (in violation of the law) being paid less than free workers 'residing on the same plantation or in the neighborhood.' He thought it 'pitiable that in such a productive country, and among such a frugal race, so many coolies

should start their second year's apprenticeship saddled with a considerable debt for the first year's rations.' Even in 1913, Commissioners McNeill and Chiman Lal investigating grievances on behalf of the Government of India, calculated that a male laborer earned enough for himself but when 'family responsibilities ...were taken into consideration, the savings would appear to be more nominal than real.' Mangal Chand Brahman returned from Trinidad to tell the Presidency Magistrate of Calcutta on 16 July 1914 that he and 'several others' earned about '8 cents a day with utmost endeavour [and] that Mangha, a cooly from Kathiawur committed suicide owing to such treatment.'

[313] R.M. Martin, *History of the Colonies of the British Empire in the West Indies, South America, ...and Europe* (London: W.H. Allen and Co., 1843) p.30.

[314] C.O.295/121 *Trinidad*#80: Hill to Glenelg, 10 August 1838.

[315] Arora, *Indian Emigration*, p.143.

[316] *Trinidad Standard and West India Journal*, 19 February 1839.

[317] *Papers Relating to Her Majesty's Colonial Possessions* Trinidad #6 (138): Longden to Earl of Kimberley, 22 July 1871.

[318] *Papers Relating to Her Majesty's Colonial Possessions* Trinidad #6 (138) Governor Longden to Earl of Kimberley.

[319] *The Trinidad News*, 7 July 1874, p.3 [Colindale Library].

[320] *Council Papers* (Trinidad) No.39 of 1874.

[321] *Papers Relating to Her Majesty's Colonial Possessions*: Trinidad. Irving to Carnarvon, 24 July 1875.

[322] *Council Papers*. (Trinidad) No.33 of 1871, p.6.

[323] David V. Trotman, "Women and Crime in Late Nineteenth Century Trinidad," *Caribbean Quarterly* 30 (2-3) 1984, 60-72.

[324] For 1870 and 1872-3, we find an upward trend in sending "recalcitrant" workers to jail: "natives" of India moved to 48.6 per cent of prisoners, or 979 out of the total (2,012). A high proportion of the Chinese population of 1,400 (10.5 per cent) were imprisoned in 1870. 62 Europeans, 22 Venezuelans six Australians and three "North Americans" were also imprisoned. In *Papers Relating to Her*

Majesty's Colonial Possessions Trinidad. Longden to Kimberley, 22 July 1870.

[325] Blue Book for 1880 in *Papers Relating to Her Majesty's Colonial Possessions* Trinidad #6. Governor Freeling to Earl of Kimberley, 8 September 1881 (p.155).

[326] *Papers Relating to Her Majesty's Colonial Possessions* Trinidad #6: Despatch from Bushe to Kimberley, 14 August 1882.

[327] Blue Book for 1881, in *Papers Relating to Her Majesty's Colonial Possessions* Trinidad #6. Administrator J. Scott Bushe to Earl of Kimberley, 14 August 1882 (p.103).

[328] Blue Book for 1886, in *Papers Relating to Her Majesty's Colonial Possessions* Trinidad #4. Robinson to Holland, 30 June 1887 (p.72).

[329] *Papers Relating to Her Majesty's Colonial Possessions*: Trinidad. Irving to Carnarvon, 24 July 1875. [330] T.F. Eversley, *The Trinidad Reviewer for the Year 1900* Volume 2 (London: Lombard, Court and Sussex, 1900) pp.148-9.

[331] Trotman, *Crime in Trinidad*, Introduction (pp.3-12).

[332] Governor Irving observed that "10, 12, or 15 previous convictions are by no means uncommon." *Papers Relating to Her Majesty's Colonial Possessions* Trinidad: Irving to Carnarvon, 24 July 1875. Trotman, *Crime in Trinidad*, pp.68-102. Yet another difficulty with official data relates to incompleteness, contradictions, and choice of reporting dates. Trotman's figures are at times unhelpful because prisoners confined on 29 September of each year jar with analyses of the committals for the same years (Tables A1 and A2). Neither do his figures always "add up", as per tables A10-A12, where total police strength in 1871 is given at 204 but the location of the force shows a total of 245. Table A13 gives police strength in 1895 as 537 (same as that for 1897 per Table A10), but the total adds up to 529.

[333] B.C. Roberts, *Labour in the Tropical Territories of the Commonwealth* (Durham: Duke University, 1964) p.xiii.

[334] I.M. Cumpston, *Indians Overseas in British Territories 1834-1854* (London: Dawsons, [1953] 1969) p.6. Even in neighboring

countries, Indians were not a presence until well after emancipation (1838); "in 1838 there were only nineteen British Indians in Rangoon [Burma]." Although traders have been in contact with the East African and Mediterranean worlds for over two millennia, this was a seasonal movement only.

[335] The author attended this two-day conference at the Institute during a research trip to Britain in 1991.

[336] S. Engerman, "Servants to Slaves to Servants: Contract Labour and European Expansion," pp.263-94 in P.C. Emmer ed. *Colonialism and Migration; Indentured Labour Before and After Slavery* (DorDrecht: Martinus Nijhoff, 1986).

[337] The sex ratios alone, of women to men immigrants ranged from minuscule proportions to no better than 25 per cent of males, late in the century; and uxoricide for the "crime" of infidelity was, in large part, due to this imbalance. Trotman, "Women and Crime," *Caribbean Quarterly* 30 (2-3) 1984, 60-72.

[338] Cumpston, *Indians Overseas*, p.21.

[339] J.A. Weller, *The East Indian Indenture in Trinidad* (Rio Piedras: Institute for Caribbean Studies, 1968) p.59. The distribution was a room for families of four, or shared by three single men. Barracks were 100 feet long, cut into 10 rooms. Also see Arora, *Indian Emigration*, pp.154-57.

[340] HC 1 (1842) No.1398 [Public Record Office], pp.429-30. The doctor apparently gave evidence at Burnley's planter-oriented enquiry into Trinidad's economic troubles after 1838.

[341] C.O. 295/153. Report on the Investigation into the Abuses of British Indians at the Clydesdale Cottage Estate, before J. Fagan and H.N. Huggins (24 August 1846).

[342] Arora, *Indian Emigration*, pp.145-46.

[343] Gladstone, the Colonial Secretary, did not consider African or Indian laborers capable of defending their rights since written contracts were unfamiliar to them. C.O. 318/169: Gladstone in his interaction with the West India Committee (25 February; 26 May; 29 June 1846). However, Lord Harris used paternalistic reasons for insisting that contracts were essential. D.W.D. Comins,

Note on Emigration from India to Trinidad (Calcutta: Bengal Secretariat Press, 1893), p.7.

[344] Eric Williams, *From Columbus to Castro: The History of the Caribbean 1492-1969* (New York: Harper and Row, 1970) p.351.

[345] Even this must not be assumed, for, during the early days of Indian emigration to Mauritius, a law was deemed necessary to outlaw selling "coolies" from one planter to another. Act XXXII of 1837 (20 November) had a novel clause "...intended to prevent the transfer of coolies as chattels from one employer to another", an abuse which had been publicized by the Governor of Mauritius, "but to which the chief police magistrate of Bombay had particularly called attention." *Parliamentary Papers* Volume XLVIII, (1874): "Note on Emigration from India by J. Geoghegan."

[346] S. Engerman, "Servants to Slaves to Servants: Contract Labour and European Expansion," pp.263-94 in P.C. Emmer ed. *Colonialism and Migration; Indentured Labour Before and After Slavery* (DorDrecht: Martinus Nijhoff, 1986).

[347] H. Tinker, *A New System of Slavery: The Export of Indian Labour Overseas 1830-1920* (London: Oxford University, 1974) pp.1-19.

[348] Those who petitioned against Indian labor had referred to this possibility: "[W]e beseech you to ...communicate with the Governor of Demerara ...to learn whether their inveterate superstition, particularly with regard to food, permit[s] them to be happy in a strange [situation and] land." C.O. 295/144 (15 July 1845): Thomas Hinde to McLeod.

[349] C.O. 300/34. The Medical Book [Surgeon's diary] of *Poitiers*, 1847.

[350] *Parliamentary Papers* Volume XLIV (1847-48). Part 6, "West Indies and Mauritius," Enclosures and No.1, p.5.

[351] Arora, *Indian Emigration*, pp.110-13.

[352] Arora, *Indian Emigration*, pp.112-14.

[353] Trotman, *Crime in Trinidad*, p.58.

[354] Governor McLeod attempted to redirect European immigrants elsewhere because they suffered high mortality, became

"vagrants" and a "burthen to the Community in the shape of beggars, or as suffering from disease." He was therefore "shocked" when on 15 May 1840, "another ship," *The Louise* from Havre arrived "having on board 190 German and French people." He tried unsuccessfully to have them "return to France." C.O. 295/ 130 (29 May 1840), Trinidad #20: McLeod to Lord John Russell. McLeod showed unusual concern for the Indians too.

[355] Arora, *Indian Emigration*, p.114.

[356] Arora, *Indian Emigration*, pp.114-18.

[357] *Source*: *State Papers Colonial*, 38/1 (1871), p.114. From documents in the Public Record Office (London, UK).

[358] *State Papers Colonial* 38/1 Public Record Office, 1871.

[359] J.W. Root, *The British West Indies and the Sugar Industry* (Liverpool: J.W. Root, 1899), p.135.

[360] E.E. Williams, *History of the People*, p.109.

[361] Stanley to Peel (27 November 1843) *Peel Papers* [British Library].

[362] C.O.295/144: McLeod to Stanley, as printed in *Historical Society of Trinidad and Tobago* Publication #952. Hereafter *HSTP*

[363] C.O.295/144: McLeod to Stanley, *HSTPubl* #952.

[364] A *Sirdar* was the Indian leader of a work group.

[365] Arora, *Indian Emigration*, p.150. "In 1864-65, the recruiters for Trinidad offered Rs.18-12-0 for adults and women, Rs.9-6-0 for children ...[without] a chance of fulfillment."

[366] C.O.295/144: McLeod to Stanley, *HSTPubl* #952.

[367] The exaggeration of Rs.5 (five rupees) were mild in comparison to Rs.18 promised adult men *and women* and the Rs.9 to children during 1864-65. Arora, *Indian Emigration*, p.150. The minimum wage of 25 cents per day were realized only if Indians completed six tasks weekly, thereby "'reducing the wages of the indented man by five cents.'" The stronger men could earn 25c.

[368] C.O.295/144: McLeod to Stanley, *HSTP* #952.

[369] Comins, *Note on Emigration*, p.1.

[370] Graeme S. Mount, *Presbyterian Missions to Trinidad and Puerto Rico* (Hantsport, Nova Scotia: Lancelot Press, 1983) p.83.

Shortcomings in Indian culture were, admittedly, manifested in the subcultures the immigrants exported to Trinidad; Europeans and Americans played a part in reinforcing Indian foibles.

[371] Mount, *Presbyterian Missions to Trinidad*, p.83.

[372] C.O. 295/144: McLeod to Stanley, 18 October 1844.

[373] Carl Campbell, *Cedulants and Capitulants The Politics of the Coloured Opposition in the Slave Society of Trinidad 1783-1838* (Port of Spain, Trinidad: Paria, 1992) p.237 writes that "the image of themselves was dominated by the conviction that they were a specially favoured group" because of the conditions of Spain's capitulation in 1797. Although the British might have seen them as "subversive," they were conservative and loyal. In March 1832, 428 Port of Spain and "elite" coloureds signed a "petition of loyalty" to distance themselves from the amelioration measures prior to slave emancipation in 1834.

[374] C.O. 295/144: Petition against East Indian immigration, addressed to Lt.-Governor McLeod and the Council of Government on 15 July 1845.

[375] Mount, *Presbyterian Missions*, pp. 234-235.

[376] Quoted by M. Ramesar, "Indentured Labour in Trinidad 1880-1917." Pp.57-77 in K. Saunders ed. *Indentured Labour in the British Empire* (London: Croom Helm, 1984) p.69.

[377] C.O. 295/144: Thomas Hinde *et al* to McLeod and the Council of Government, 15 July 1845.

[378] *Parliamentary Papers* Volume XLVIII, (1874): "Note on Emigration from India by J. Geoghegan," p.434; Mount, *Presbyterian Missions to Trinidad*, p.262.

[379] K.O. Laurence, *Immigration Into the West Indies in the Nineteenth Century* (Barbados: Caribbean Universities, 1971) pp.50-51.

[380] K.O. Laurence, "The Development of Medical Services in British Guiana and Trinidad 1841-1873," *Jamaica Historical Review* 4 (1966), 59-67.

[381] In sending details requested about provisions for the destitute, McLeod wrote Lord Stanley, "there is no provision, by

law or otherwise, for widows and fatherless children, or deserted wives and children," as well as a lack of a lunatic asylum. Although the "high rate of wages" allowed many laborers to take care of extended families, McLeod admitted that the hospital and leper establishment were "insufficient to meet the wants of the colony." C.O. 295/147 (Volume 2): August-December 1845.

382 The *Port of Spain Gazette*, 18 January 1850, referred to the positive reader reaction to its article on "Legislation for the Poorer Class." It commented further, "[H]ardly one of our acquaintances whom we have since conversed with, but has instanced to us some case within his own knowledge of great hardship."

383 Mount, *Presbyterian Missions to Trinidad*, p.232.

384 Weller, *The East Indian Indenture*, p.61.

385 Laurence, *Immigration into the West Indies*, p.50.

386 C.O.295/153 Volume 4 (#2201): Major Fagan's Report, 29 August 1846. *Rajpoot* is part of the warrior "caste."

387 C.O.295/153 Volume 4. (#2201): Major Fagan's Report.

388 C.O. 295/153 Volume 4 (#2201): Harris to Grey in Despatch 75. 5 October 1846.

389 Laurence, *Immigration into the West Indies*, p.53.

390 C.O.295/153: Walkinshaw's letter to White, 21 August 1846.

391 E.E. Williams, *History of the People of Trinidad and Tobago* (New York: F.Praeger, 1962) p.105. Eight years later, Williams argues that the contract was enough to save the Indian from slave-like conditions: not coincidentally, that publication *From Columbus to Castro* was dedicated to the PNM, his predominantly Afro-Trinidadian political party, the People's National Movement.

392 C.O. 295/153: Harris to Grey, 5 October 1846.

393 Lai, *Indentured Labor, Caribbean Sugar*, p.160.

394 The letter was sent anonymously to Lord George Bentinck, but when the controversy erupted in Trinidad, Major Fagan did not deny that he was the author. His views were circulated through the April 1848 issue of the *Colonial Magazine* in London.

395 The plantation was the Ganteaume sugar Estate in Mayaro.

[396]   Editorial in the newspaper (which was connected with planter interests), *Port-of-Spain Gazette* (26 May 1848).

[397]   *Trinidad Spectator*, 26 April 1848.

[398]   W.A. Green, *British Slave Emancipation The Sugar Colonies and the Great Experiment 1830-1865* (London: Oxford University, 1976), p.280.

[399]   Arora, *Indian Emigration*, p.144.

[400]   Arthur and Juanita Niehoff, *East Indians in the West Indies* (Milwaukee, Wisconsin: Milwaukee Museum, 1960) p.77.

[401]   P.J. Keenan, "Report on the State of Education in Trinidad," *Parliamentary Papers* Volume L (1870), p.701. Hereafter, Keenan Report, with page or paragraph numbers.

[402]   Carl Campbell, *Colony and Nation A Short History of Education in Trinidad and Tobago* (Mona, Jamaica: Ian Randle Publishers, 1992), p.12. He espoused the view "from the 1940s to his death."

[403]   Endowed and charity schools had existed in England since the 1700s, and the Factory Acts, Reformatory Acts and Industrial Schools Acts had begun the process of formalizing education. It is well-known that literacy levels had risen in England and Wales in the first two-thirds of the eighteenth-century, an estimate by Lawrence Stone putting literacy at 56 percent between 1700 and 1775. The Elementary Education Act of 1870 removed the exceptions so that "the nation's children had to attend school for a minimum of five years." M. Sanderson, *Education, Economic Change and Society in England 1780-1870* (London: MacMillan, 1983); J.S. Hurt, *Elementary Schooling and the Working Classes 1860-1918* (London: Routledge and Kegan Paul, 1979).

[404]   Campbell, *Colony and Nation*, pp.43 and 5-8, respectively.

[405]   This is the basic argument put forth by David V. Trotman, *Crime in Trinidad Conflict and Control in a Plantation Society 1838-1900* (Knoxville: University of Tennessee Press, 1986); Campbell, *Colony and Nation*, p.7. See also Governor Harris' view that Trinidad relied too much upon the Law (Note #127, below).

⁴⁰⁶ The Canadian here was John Morton. D. Wood argues that until then - but at least since 1857 - an orphanage was "the only means to disseminate European ways" to Indians "in an almost unapproachable society." *Trinidad in Transition The Years After Slavery* (London: Oxford University, 1968) p.231.

⁴⁰⁷ There is a belief among thinkers (eg. Guizot) that every school opened, closes a jail. D. Wood, *Trinidad in Transition The Years After Slavery* (Oxford: Oxford University, 1968) p.214.

⁴⁰⁸ Hugh Tinker, *A New System of Slavery: The Export of Indian Labour Overseas 1830-1920* (London: Oxford University, 1974) p.254 argues that the Emigration clauses (1858; 1875) amounted to the "Magna Carta of the liberties of Indians" conceding "'Privileges no whit inferior to those of any other class [of] ...subjects.'"

⁴⁰⁹ Campbell, *Colony and Nation*, pp.8-9; 17-19.

⁴¹⁰ Keenan Report, Paragraph 22.

⁴¹¹ *Port of Spain Gazette* 13 July 1859; *Trinidad Sentinel* 6 August 1857; *Trinidad Review* 28 February 1884, are anti-Carnival in mood and substance. Protestant generally frowned on Carnival.

⁴¹² Keenan Report, Paragraph 162.

⁴¹³ *Parliamentary Papers* Volume 28 "C" (1846): Carapichaima District, 30 June 1845. This was reported a month after the arrival of the first Indians.

⁴¹⁴ *Parliamentary Papers* Volume XXXIV (1839), pp.460-61.

⁴¹⁵ Under "Exercise for Girls," the *Chronicle* (11 November 1864) described a worrisome development: "The two-and-two walk is the sole and single form of exercise that appears ever to have presented itself to being necessary, or even desirable. Can we wonder, then, that the hollow chest and twisted spine are so sadly frequent, or that the habit of long-continued sitting should act so fatally upon the healthful and symmetrical development of the whole body? Is it strange that few grow to womanhood either healthy or graceful?"

⁴¹⁶ C. Kingsley, *At Last A Christmas in the West Indies* (New York: Harper and Brothers, 1871) p.424-7 says that while English

races were attended by "the most degraded beings," in Trinidad everything symbolized "very good humours." The black and "coloured man ...was smart, shiny, happy ...The coolies seemed as merry as the negroes; even about the face of the Chinese there flickered, at times, a feeble ray of interest."

[417] Fairs and races were enthusiastically covered in the press, as for instance, *Trinidad Review*: 13 March 1884, 10 April and 17 April 1884; and *Trinidad News* (25 July 1874) complained about "the absence of any permanent place of amusement," in the colony.

[418] L.A.A. de Verteuil, *Trinidad: Its Geography, Natural resources, Administration, Present Condition, and Prospects* (London: Ward and Lock, 1858) p.197.

[419] K.J. Grant, *My Missionary Memories* (Nova Scotia: Imperial Publishing Company, 1923) p.56.

[420] Criticisms would include: teaching children how to dress and enunciate words like Englishmen and women, when they spent so few hours at school. Catholics objected to use of the Anglican Bible.

[421] The use of "coolie" for all Hindus, has been mentioned; there was the assumed antipathy between coolie and creole.

[422] For details, see A. Memmi, *The Colonizer and the Colonized* (Boston: Beacon Books, 1965) pp.81-151, and Orlando Patterson, *The Sociology of Slavery* (Jamaica: Sangster, 1967) p.174.

[423] Rev. R.H. Moore to Governor William Robinson, Quoted By D.W.D Comins, *Note on Emigration From India to Trinidad* (Calcutta: Bengal Secretariat Press, 1893) pp.33-34.

[424] Objections were raised against an educational system described as "British National," and "National System of England," by the Catholics, in the first instance.

[425] C.O. 295/130 (Trinidad), 15 June 1840.

[426] Wood, *Trinidad in Transition*, p.105.

[427] B. Brereton, *History of Modern Trinidad 1783-1962* (London: Cambridge University, 1979) p.138.

[428] Grant, *My Missionary Memoirs*, pp.53-54.

[429] *Parliamentary Papers* Vol. XXXIV (1839): Latrobe Report (pp. 1-6). Also Wood, *Trinidad in Transition*, p.214.

[430] de Verteuil, *Trinidad: Its Geography*, p.193.

[431] Coloured teachers were also employed in Presbyterian schools

for Indian children, according to Rev. Grant, *My Missionary Memories* p.84; Comins, *Note on Emigration*, pp.34-35. Wood, *Trinidad in Transition* p.232, says primary school was all that was required of would-be teachers, but Indian teachers were produced only after their own education by Canadian in the 1870s.

[432] Keenan Report, Paragraphs 42, 43, 44.

[433] Keenan Report, Paragraph 68, p.674.

[434] B. Brereton, *Race Relations in Colonial Trinidad 1870-1900* (London: Cambridge University, 1979) p.69 discusses how the Normal, and Boys' and Girls' Model (teacher training) schools were "one of the few instances where white, coloured and black children could be found together." Soon afterwards, the Attorney-General felt it vital to announce "that the government had no intention of using the Model Schools as a vehicle for social mobility." When the Queen's Collegiate School opened in 1859 "some white boys were" transferred to it to prevent inter-mixing.

[435] de Verteuil, *Trinidad: Its Geography*, p.193.

[436] de Verteuil, *Trinidad: Its Geography*, pp.173-74. Charles Warner was Attorney-General between 1845 and 1870. Carl Campbell has written about his role in "Charles Warner and the Development of Education Policy in Trinidad, 1838-1870," *Journal of Caribbean History* (10-11) 1978, 54-81.

[437] C.O. 295/130: McLeod to Lord John Russell, 1 May 1840.

[438] C.O. 295/130: McLeod to Lord John Russell, 1 May 1840.

[439] *Parliamentary Papers* Volume XXXIV (1839), p.461.

[440] de Verteuil, *Trinidad: Its Geography*, p.195.

[441] C.O. 300/50 [P.R.O. 3184941]: Blue Book (1838) p.178.

[442] C.O. 300/50: Blue Book for 1838, p.178.

[443] Wood, *Trinidad in Transition*, p.213.

⁴⁴⁴ Parliament had sponsored Latrobe's Investigation and briefly, school funding, but began to reduce support in 1841.

⁴⁴⁵ S. Gordon, *A Century of West Indian Education A Source Book* (London: Longmans, 1963) pp.36-38.

⁴⁴⁶ de Verteuil, *Trinidad: Its Geography*, pp.173-174.

⁴⁴⁷ Quoted by J.E. Pinnington, "Anglican Problems of Adaptation in the Catholic Caribbean - the CMS in Trinidad 1836-1844." *Journal of Caribbean History* 1 (1970) p.29.

⁴⁴⁸ Blue Book for 1838 (Trinidad).

⁴⁴⁹ Modified from data in Blue Books, Trinidad (1838).

⁴⁵⁰ C.O. 295/130, Trinidad #10: McLeod to Russell, 1 May 1840.

⁴⁵¹ C.O. 295/130, Trinidad #10: McLeod to Russell.

⁴⁵² C.O. 295/130, Trinidad #10: McLeod to Russell.

⁴⁵³ C.O. 295/144: McLeod to Stanley, 18 October 1844.

⁴⁵⁴ C.O. 295/130, Trinidad #26: McLeod to Russell, 8 June 1840.

⁴⁵⁵ B. Blout, "Land Politics in Trinidad 1838-1850." *Journal of Caribbean History* 9 (1977), 43-59.

⁴⁵⁶ C.O. 295/130, Trinidad #26: McLeod to Russell.

⁴⁵⁷ C.O. 295/134: McLeod to Russell, 13 October 1841.

⁴⁵⁸ C.O. 295/134: McLeod to Russell, 13 October 1841.

⁴⁵⁹ C.O. 295/1118: Lord Stanley to McLeod, 8 January 1842.

⁴⁶⁰ C.O. 295/1118: Lord Stanley to McLeod, 8 January 1842.

⁴⁶¹ *Parliamentary Papers* Vol 28 (4): "Accounts and Papers, Colonies; 22 January - 28 August 1846." McLeod's despatch.

⁴⁶² *Parliamentary Papers* Volume 28 (4): "Accounts and Papers, Colonies; 22 January-28 August 1846." McLeod's Despatch.

⁴⁶³ Harris himself told Secretary Gladstone that he would offer his views on education by expounding on the "rules lately passed by [McLeod] my predecessor." *Parliamentary Papers* Volume 39 (1847): "No. 35, Copy of the despatch dated 31 July 1846."

⁴⁶⁴ *Parliamentary Papers* Volume 28 (4): "Accounts and Papers, Colonies; 22 January-28 August 1846." Enclosure 1 in No. 1.

[465] *Trinidad Review* (6 March 1884) had an article on Trinidad's governors, in which Arthur Gordon (1866-70) won praise: "[T]he balance of advantage is largely in Sir Arthur Gordon's favour in comparison of his brief term of office with the prolonged term of residence here either of Sir Ralph Woodford or Lord Harris."

[466] *State Papers Colonial* 38/1 (1871) Public Record Office, p.114; Wood, *Trinidad in Transition*, p.219.

[467] *Parliamentary Papers*, Volume 39 (1847): Enclosure in No.2 (1 July 1846), p.101.

[468] Quoted in Keenan Report, Paragraph 23.

[469] Quoted in Keenan Report, p.102.

[470] *Parliamentary Papers* Volume 39 (1847), p.102.

[471] *Parliamentary Papers* Volume 39 (1847): Harris to Grey.

[472] Keenan Report, Paragraph 26.

[473] Keenan Report, Paragraph 21.

[474] During my research on Indian South Africans the term "Gentoos" also came up; I used it interchangeably with "Hindoos." I speculate it may originate in conflating "gentiles" and "Hindoos."

[475] While Hindus and Muslims were often called "heathens" in the documents, especially in newspapers and in Canadian parlance, it is not clear these "heathens" were only Muslims and Hindus.

[476] Keenan Report, p.101.

[477] Campbell, *Colony and Nation*, p.14.

[478] *Parliamentary Papers* (1847): Harris to Grey, p.104.

[479] Keenan Report, Paragraph 11.

[480] *Parliamentary Papers* (1847): Harris to Grey, p.104.

[481] Keenan Report, Paragraph 8.

[482] Keenan Report, Paragraph 177, p.726.

[483] Keenan Report, especially the Appendix.

[484] Keenan Report, Paragraph 138.

[485] Wood, *Trinidad in Transition*, pp.231-32. The need for the orphanage meant that children had been alone on board ships and that immigrant parents died en route to Trinidad. In 1876, says

Wood, the Tacarigua Orphanage became a Church of England industrial school open to destitute children of all races.

[486] The Tacarigua orphanage taught 42 Indian orphans, twice the number being educated at ward schools (seen by Keenan).

[487] Keenan Report, Paragraph 141.

[488] Keenan Report, p.703.

[489] Keenan Report, *Parliamentary Papers* (1870) Appendix, p.748. Others had noted poverty also played a role in whether Indian children could afford "school" clothes.

[490] Keenan wrote, "For instance, it occupied me upon one occasion nearly 13 hours to perform the island journey between Mayaro and the Lothian estate, a distance of only 30 miles; the 'trace' for nearly the whole length of the way being through a virgin forest." Keenan Report, *Parliamentary Papers* Volume L.

[491] Keenan Report, Paragraph 89, p.685.

[492] Keenan Report, Paragraphs 32-39.

[493] Grant, *Missionary Memories*, p.89.

[494] Keenan Report, Paragraphs 49 and 50.

[495] *Chronicle* (3 June 1870) published the Ordinance (6 of 1870) which ended support for the Queen's Collegiate School in favor on the new all-Trinidadian "'The Royal College of Trinidad,'and the yearly sum of L3,000, now appropriated from the general revenues." The article also carried extracts from Governor Gordon's speech on the opening of the Royal College which expressed the hope that a sound secondary education "will be secured to Protestants and Roman Catholics alike, without the slightest compromise of their respective principles."

[496] Anthony de Verteuil, *Eight East Indian Immigrants* (Port of Spain: Paria, 1989) p.63.

[497] Mount, *Presbyterian Missions*, p.81.

[498] *East Meets West in Trinidad* (Prepared by the Mission Council of Trinidad, United Church of Canada: Published by the Committee on Young People's Missionary Education), p.17. United Church Archives, Toronto.

[499] *East Meets West in Trinidad*, pp.36-37.

[500] Grant, *Missionary Memories*, p.79.

[501] His wife, Sarah Morton, recalled in 1918 "the number baptised was not remarkable." *Trinidad Guardian*, 31 March 1918. She testifies to the Indian habit of honoring all religious persons, especially those of non-Indian religions: "the people were very friendly from the first, bringing [Morton] little presents of corn and fruit." They were friendly, but *not* in search of a new religious repertoire, except those few who came to the church with knowledge of English like Clarence Soodeen and Lal Singh Baharie.

[502] I. Hamid, *A History of the Presbyterian Church in Trinidad 1868-1968* (San Fernando, Trinidad: St. Andrews Theological College, 1980) pp. 59-60; S.E. Morton, *John Morton of Trinidad* (Toronto: Westminster Co., 1916) pp.57-58.

[503] Gordon, *Century of West Indian Education*, p.81.

[504] S.E. Morton, *John Morton of Trinidad*, p.58.

[505] Grant, *Missionary Memories*, p.80.

[506] During fieldwork (1990), Dr. K. Boodhoo informed me that Presbyterian hymns rendered in Hindi and with *tabla* and *bhaja* accompaniment, is a popular pastime for all Indians.

[507] Mount, *Presbyterian Missions*, p.119, says that Indians went to church to listen to organ music or to be entertained by the preacher's performances, though they didn't understand a word.

[508] Both S. Morton and Grant acknowledge their Church began at a propitious moment because a year after their arrival, Keenan was to recommend state-aid to church schools. While Indo-Trinidadians told me (in Trinidad, 1990) that they always appreciated the work of the Canadian Presbyterians, they avoided becoming converts.

[509] Mount says that the Presbyterians wanted Indians to speak, dress and walk like Canadians, along with becoming Christian.

[510] Mount, *Presbyterian Missions*, p.84.

[511] She was talking about her late husband being able to "rightly interpret the needs of the strange people" for the governor. Reported in *Trinidad Guardian*, 31 March 1918.

[512] *The Caribbean Presbyterian*, 1 (1) 1958, U.C. Archives.

[513] Anthony de Verteuil, *Eight East Indian Immigrants*, p.63.

[514] *Trinidad Council Papers*, (#68) 29 September 1883.

[515] The impact of the depression cannot be discounted, for schools usually also received aid from the planter/plantation.

[516] Trinidad Council Paper: No. 68, 29 Sept 1883. Education Office, L. Guppy's "Report on Public Education in Trinidad."

[517] *Palladium*, 4 (183), 24 April 1880.

[518] *Palladium*, 4 (183), 24 April 1880.

[519] Grant, *Missionary Memories*, p.78.

[520] Hamid, *History of the Presbyterian Church*, pp.48-49.

[521] Egbert M. Madoo Memorial, in The Minutes of the Mission Council, 2 October 1900. United Church Archives, Toronto.

[522] B. Samaroo, "Missionary Methods and Local responses: The Canadian Presbyterians and the East Indians in the Caribbean," p.1. Read at the United Church Archives, Toronto: March 1991.

[523] A. Martell, "The Canadian Presbyterian Mission to Trinidad's East Indians 1868-1912," (Unpublished M.A. thesis in History at Dalhousie University: 1974), pp.vi;128. Hamid shows how Morton opposed the start of the Theological College in 1890 although Grant had already collected donations in Canada for it; in 1892 Morton agreed and became the first principal of the college. "Morton could be sharp in his visions; but he could be equally sharp in his contradictions," says Hamid, *History of the Presbyterian Church*, p.111.

[524] *Presbyterian Yearbook, 1884-85*, "Appendix xcix: Report on Foreign Missions." p.ciii. (United Church Archives).

[525] Naparima College for Boys, the first high school, was petitioned by Indians of all groups (with Grant's assistance). Hamid, *History of the Presbyterian Church*, p.78.

[526] Grant, *Missionary Memories*, p.82.

[527] *Royal Franchise Commission*, Testimony of Grant, p.41.

[528] Keenan Report, *Parliamentary Papers* (1870), p.747. Parents "evinced a great anxiety to have their children educated."

[529] The Report was printed a year after the Inquiry.

[530] He offered land to indenture-free Indians so that the colony might, inter alia, save the cost of repatriation. This policy lasted until 1880 when depression made Indian repatriation cost-effective. See *Trinidad Council Paper* (#20/1884) which noted that 9,750 Indians (4,897 children) benefitted from the offer.

[531] *Royal Franchise Commission*, Testimony of Grant, p.41.

[532] C.O. 295/152: Harris to Grey, 21 December 1846.

[533] Trotman, *Crime in Trinidad*, p.215.

[534] Trotman's ancillary hypothesis is that law was the means of socializing non-Europeans.

[535] Shopkeeping was the most common way of improving one's position among Indians - it required little education - since their ventures were in Indian-dominated villages. For greater social mobility, a secondary school education was vital.

[536] Lord Harris asserted that apart from expense, a plan of education in Trinidad would be challenged by "the carelessness of the parents as to making their children attend school...." *Parliamentary Papers* Volume 39 (1847): "Immigration of Labourers into the West India Colonies and the Mauritius. State of the Labouring Population."

[537] S. Gordon's important source book, *A Century of West Indian Education*, lacks footnotes and a bibliography. In an illustrative quotation from a related article "The Keenan Report, 1869 [Part 1]" in *Caribbean Quarterly* 8 (4) 1962, Gordon provides an instance of selective and damaging quotation. She begins with a quotation from the Keenan Report: "The adult coolie is by no means free from serious moral defects," but omits the crucial few lines which say, "Examples are not unfrequent, even in England, of the family tone and discipline being improved by lessons brought home from school by little children." One becomes convinced that what is left out of quotations is often CRUCIALLY important; Gordon's omitting one sentence renders Indians again as an outlandish group in Trinidad.

[538] It is noteworthy that Governor Henry McLeod of Trinidad was an exception. This chapter acknowledges him as Trinidad's

first Education Governor, who was humane and more foresighted about social mobility and needs of the masses. Campbell's *Colony and Nation*, p.12 dismisses McLeod as one who, like the Solicitor General, was an "anglophile." They "thought alike" on arresting the growth of "Catholic" schools and promoting the Mico charity schools "responsive to government control."

[539] John Nunley and Judith Bettelheim, *Caribbean Festival Arts* (Seattle: Saint Louis Art Museum, 1988) p.119.

[540] S. W. Mintz, Foreword to R. Guerra y Sanchez' *Sugar and Society in the Caribbean* (New Haven: Yale, 1964) p.xiv.

[541] Carl Degler, "Plantation Society: Old and New Perspectives on Hemispheric History," *Plantation Society in the Americas* 1 (1) 1979, 9-14.

[542] S. Engerman, "Some implications of the Abolition of the Slave Trade." Pp.3-18 in D. Eltis and J. Walvin eds. *The Abolition of the Atlantic Slave Trade Origins and Effects in Europe, Africa, and the Americas* (Madison: University of Wisconsin, 1981).

[543] White men made these decisions. Even Churches ignored the input of women, which is discussed at the end of Chapter Five.

[544] Andrew Pearse, "Carnival in Nineteenth Century Trinidad," *Caribbean Quarterly* 4 (3-4) 1956, 175-93. Pearse believes that the unemployed, the equivalent of the lumpen-proletariat, took "vicarious delight both covert and overt" in rejecting the norms of the "superstructure."

[545] African indenteds who came after Emancipation brought Rada and Shango practices to Trinidad, which the elites frowned upon, and "Obeah," was punished with imprisonment and flogging. D. Trotman, *Crime in Trinidad Conflict and Control in a Plantation Society 1838-1900* (Knoxville: University of Tennessee, 1986) pp.223-29. Some Africanisms had survived slavery, too.

[546] Andre's letter, which appeared in the *Times* (London) dated 8 November 1884, had been forwarded by C.H. Allen of the Anti-Slavery Society.

[547] Earl Lovelace, *The Dragon Can't Dance* (Harlow, Essex: Longman, 1981) p.121.

[548] T. Payne, "The Village Movement as a Revolutionary Initiative," pp.38-45 in J. Loncke ed. *Proceedings of the 150th Anniversary of the Abolition of Slavery*, (Georgetown: Guyana Commemoration Commission and UNESCO, 1985), p.45.

[549] I am grateful to Professors Mintz and Jean Besson for their efforts to have me develop an anthropological angle to my work. Besson has argued the role of free villages (and traditional land tenure) in continued peasant resistance to plantations. See for instance her "Family Land as a model for Martha Brae's New History: Culture Building in an Afro-Caribbean Village," pp. 100-132 in C.V. Carnegie ed. *Afro-Caribbean Villages in Historical Perspective* (Kingston: Institute of Jamaica, 1987).

[550] I. Ahmed, "The Shia-Sunni Dispute in Lucknow, 1905-1980," pp.335-50 in M. Israel and N. Wagle, eds. *Islamic Society and Culture*, (New Delhi: Manohar, 1983) p.336. Ahmed argues that not only Hindus and Muslims, but the opposing Muslim sects too, celebrated Hosay jointly until recent decades. The root of the rift lies in a 1905 dispensation wherein Britain encouraged communalism by allocating local electoral votes on religious, sectional lines.

[551] Among those with whom Kinser appears to disagree are Max Gluckman, E. Leach and Da Matta. S. Kinser, *Carnival, American Style* (Chicago: University of Chicago, 1990) pp.xv; 3.

[552] "Report on the Recent Coolie Disturbances in Trinidad." Sir W.L. Norman to Secretary Earl of Derby, *British Sessional Papers* Command Paper 4366 of 1885. Hereafter, *British Papers* Cmd.4366.

[553] Charles Day, *Five Years' Residence in the West Indies* Volume 1 (London: Colburn and Company, 1852) pp.313-16.

[554] V.V. Ivanov, "The Semiotic Theory of Carnival as the Inversion of Bipolar Opposites," pp.11-35 in T.A. Seboek, ed. *Carnival!*, (Berlin: Mouton, 1984) p.11.

[555] Umberto Eco, "The Frames of Comic Freedom," pp.1-10 in T.A. Seboek ed.) *Carnival!*

[556] Errol Hill, *The Trinidad Carnival Mandate for a National Theater*, (Austin: University of Texas, 1984) pp.23-24.

[557] Pearse, "Carnival," *Caribbean Quarterly* 4 (3-4) 1956, pp.191-2.

[558] D.J. Crowley, "The Traditional Masques of Carnival," *Caribbean Quarterly* 4 (3-4) 1956, 194-223.

[559] M.L. de Verteuil (translator), *The Diaries of Abbe Armand Masse 1878-1883* Volume 4, (Port of Spain: de Verteuil, 1988) pp.143-9.

[560] Hill, *Trinidad Carnival*, pp.10-17.

[561] *Diaries of Abbe Masse*, p.146.

[562] *Diaries of Abbe Masse*, pp.146-47.

[563] I use "massification" to indicate that the masses were now dominant in Carnival; consequently, non-elite themes came to dominate the celebrations and masquerades.

[564] L.M. Fraser, Registrar of the Supreme Court of Trinidad, as quoted by R.G.C. Hamilton in C.O. 884/4 (Public Record Office).

[565] I. Ahmed, "The Shia-Sunni Dispute in Lucknow," in Israel and Wagle, eds. *Islamic Society and Culture*, p.336.

[566] G. Carmichael, *History of the West Indian Islands of Trinidad and Tobago 1498-1900* (London: Alvin Redman, 1961) pp.273-74 says that permission for Hosay was granted in "1863 [by] Queen Victoria... so long as [Trinidad had] Indian residents." This may point to the first official Hosay and is not a refutation of Nunley and Bettelheim's study which posits, "[A]s early as the 1850s, the ...Muhurram brought Muslims, Hindus, Afro-Jamaicans, Afro-Trinidadians, Afro-Guyanese, and Afro-Surinamese together in ways that suggest a developing solidarity." *Caribbean Festival Arts*, p.121.

[567] Nunley and Bettelheim, *Caribbean Festival Arts*, p.127.

[568] Nunley and Bettelheim, *Caribbean Festival Arts* pp.119-20.

[569] Kelvin Singh, *Bloodstained Tombs: The Muharram Massacre 1884* (London: MacMillan, 1988).

[570] Apart from the fieldwork of John Nunley and Judith Bettelheim, I conducted interviews with Hosay participants in Trinidad in 1990 (See Interview with Mr. Harry, 30 June 1990).

[571] Carmichael, *History of the Islands*, p.273-4.

[572] *San Fernando Gazette*, 10 December 1881.

[573] C.O. 295/289 (Trinidad No. 6460).

[574] B.E. Powrie, "The Changing Attitudes of the Coloured Middle Class Towards Carnival," *Caribbean Quarterly* 4 (3-4) 1956, 224-230.

[575] *Port of Spain Gazette*, 22 January 1833.

[576] Letter to the *Port of Spain Gazette*, as quoted in Pearse, "Carnival," in *Caribbean Quarterly* 4 (3-4) 1956, 175-93.

[577] C.O. 884/4, "The Hamilton Report" [Carnival 1881], p.6.

[578] A "great change," after Emancipation, "which has taken place within this Colony," was "the want of spirit ... [and the] deficiency of elegant bustle, which was to be seen during the Carnival week in olden times." Pearse, "Carnival," *Caribbean Quarterly* 4 (3-4) 1956.

[579] Powrie, "Changing Attitudes," *Caribbean Quarterly* 4 (3-4) 1956, pp.224-230.

[580] C.O. 884/4. The Hamilton Report, p.5.

[581] C.O. 884/4, The Hamilton Report, p.5.

[582] C.O. 884/4, The Hamilton Report, p.5.

[583] Donald Wood, *Trinidad in Transition The Years After Slavery* (London: Oxford University, 1968) pp.145-52.

[584] B. Brereton, "The Birthday of our Race: A Social History of Emancipation Day in Trinidad, 1838-1888," pp.69-83 in B.W. Higman ed. *Trade Government and Society in Caribbean History 1700-1920* (Mona, Jamaica: Heinemann, 1983).

[585] Until the 1870s, the opposition to Carnival took the form mainly of press criticism and elite withdrawal from the fete.

[586] At about this time too, owing to the "Mutiny" in India, there were difficulties in procuring indented workers.

[587] Bridget Brereton, *Race Relations in Colonial Trinidad 1870-1900* (London: Cambridge University, 1979), p.169.

[588] Brereton, *Race Relations*, pp.166-67.

[589] *New Era*, 19 March 1877.

[590] Brereton, "The Birthday of our Race," in *Trade Government and Society*, pp.75;77-83.

[591] Nunley and Bettelheim, *Caribbean Festival Arts*, pp.10-37.

[592] Crowley, "Traditional Masques," *Caribbean Quarterly* 4(3-4) 1956, p.74 discusses the "'pretty' devil band" or, because of the preference of Indians for this masque, - "Coolie Devils." Was this a way for Indians to assume more "strength" than they had in real life?

[593] Pearse, "Carnival," *Caribbean Quarterly* 4(3-4)1956, p.192.

[594] Nunley and Bettelheim, *Caribbean Festival Arts*, p.112.

[595] J.N. Brierley, *Trinidad: Then and Now. 1874-1912*, (Port of Spain: J.N. Brierley, 1912) pp.323-326.

[596] Bridget Brereton, "The Trinidad Carnival 1870-1900." *Savacou* 11-12, 1975, 46-57.

[597] K. Haraksingh, "Control and Resistance among Overseas Indian Workers: A Study of Labor on the Sugar Plantations of Trinidad, 1875-1917," *Journal of Caribbean History* (14) 1981, 1-17.

[598] *Port of Spain Gazette*, 13 July 1959 (original emphases).

[599] *Trinidad Sentinel*, 6 August 1857.

[600] C.O. 884/4, Hamilton Report, p.18. This phrase was used here, and in local papers. It is odd that Hamilton thought it important to write this single paragraph calling for restrictions against Hosay, although he was investigating an 1881 Carnival riot.

[601] Keith Hjortshoj, "Shi'i Identity and the Significance of Muharram in Lucknow, India," pp.289-309 in M. Kramer ed. *Shi'ism, Resistance, and Revolution* (Boulder: Westview, 1987).

[602] Ordinance #9 of 1882 quoted by Q. Hogg, Acting Chairman of the West India Committee, in the *Times*, 2 December 1884.

[603] *British Papers* Cmd.4366: Drennan and Scott testimonies.

[604] Wood, *Trinidad in Transition*, pp.151-52.

[605] Nunley and Bettelheim, *Caribbean Festival Arts*, p.127; Brereton, *Race Relations*, p.191.

[606] J.A. Weller, *The East Indian Indenture in Trinidad* (Rio Piedras, University of Puerto Rico, 1968) pp.49-54. On the injustice of planters "adding" days to expired indenture contracts, allegedly due to Indians' negligence, see criticism of the Protector's failures in *New Era*, 22 March 1880.

[607] *Royal Franchise Commission*, Testimony of K.J. Grant, p.41.

[608] *Royal Franchise Commission*, p.9. There were controversies concerning other sectors of the population, for instance the effort to get signatories "to the Reform Petition," from the "Fifth Company Village," as in the article "Mohomet going to the Mountain," in *Public Opinion*, 20 March 1888.

[609] *British Papers* Cmd.4366, "The Norman Report into Disturbances at the Muhurram Festival," (1885).

[610] *Diaries of Abbe Masse 1878-1883*, pp.113-14.

[611] The Ordinance itself was ratified and dated three weeks before the 30 October Hosay; there could not have been enough time to allow for Britain's ratification *and* its contents explained to the simple workers in Trinidad. Unless of course, the plantocracy had premeditated an attack on Hosay with or without Colonial Office notification.

[612] Interview: Mr. Harry in Tunapuna, Trinidad. 30 June 1990.

[613] K. Haraksingh, "Indian Leadership in the Indenture Period," *Caribbean Issues* 2 (3) 1976, 17-38.

[614] H. Tinker, *A New System of Slavery: The Export of Indian Labour Overseas 1830-1920* (London: Oxford University, 1974) p.227.

[615] *Times* (of London), 28 November 1884.

[616] One enduring impression left upon me by my interviews with Indo-Trinidadians (6/1990) was the almost universal recollection of Hosay 1884, even though the massacre itself is a century old.

[617] Singh, *Bloodstained Tombs*, pp.22-23.

[618] C.H. Allen's cover letter in *Times*, 28 November 1884, p.10.

[619] *Times*, 28 November 1884: "An English Observer."

[620] *British Papers* Cmd.4366, pp.596-604: Testimonies of B. Sing and Dulloo.

[621] *Times*, 28 November 1884.

[622] *Times*, 2 December 1884, p.4.

[623] *British Papers* Cmd. 4366: "Correspondence respecting the Recent Disturbances in Trinidad at the Muhurram Festival, with the Report by Sir H.W. Norman," pp.531-636.

[624] Enclosure 3 in 6, Acting Colonial Secretary W. Pyne to Captain Baker, 23 October 1884. *British Papers* Cmd.4366, p.543.

[625] *British Papers* Cmd. 4366, p.579.

[626] Ordinance #9 of 1882, quoted in full by Hogg in *Times*, 2 December 1884, p.4.

[627] *Port of Spain Gazette*, 7 May 1884.

[628] Quoted in *British Papers* Cmd. 4366, p.561.

[629] *British Papers* Cmd.4366, p.561.

[630] These were the concluding remarks in Hamilton's Report on the carnival riots of 1881. C.O. 884/4, Hamilton Report.

[631] Mikhail Bakhtin, *Rabelais and his World* (Cambridge: Massachusetts Institute of Technology, 1968) p.257.

[632] I.M. Cumpston, *Indians Overseas in British Territories 1834-1854* (London: Dawsons, 1953 and 1969) p.122.

[633] W.H. Gamble, *Trinidad: Historical and Descriptive* (London: Yates and Alexander, 1866) pp.30-31.

[634] *British Papers* Cmd. 4366, p.580.

[635] *British Papers* Cmd.4366, Earl of Derby to F. Scott Bushe.

[636] *British Papers* Cmd.4366, Testimony of W.R. Pyne.

[637] C.O. 295/134, Trinidad #92: McLeod to Russell, 13 October 1841.

[638] S.D. Ryan, *Race and Nationalism in Trinidad and Tobago: A Study of Decolonization in a Multi-Racial Society* (Toronto: University of Toronto, 1972) p.17.

[639] Trotman, *Crime in Trinidad*, pp.30-31.

[640] *New Era*, 22 March 1880.

[641] *British Papers* Cmd.4366, Norman's Report, p.635.

[642] *British Papers* Cmd.4366, H. Pasea's testimony.

[643] de Verteuil, *The Years of Revolt*, p.125.

[644] *Diaries of Abbe Masse*, p.114.

[645] *Handbook of Trinidad and Tobago* (Port of Spain: Government Printing Office, 1924) p.190 presents a List of Governors; Barlee and Sir A.E. Havelock *only* are named during 1884 and 1885, with William Robinson taking over during 1885.

[646] *British Papers* Cmd.4366, Pasea's Testimony, Freeling was ostracized after disciplining the police; in my research, I found a convoluted communication about Freeling's plea for "Leave."

[647] *British Papers* Cmd.4366, Pasea's Testimony, p.606.

[648] Native Indians totalled 36,020; Trinidad-born children numbered 12,809. See Despatch in *Papers Relating to Her Majesty's Colonial Possessions* Trinidad#6 (14 August 1882).

[649] An historian-in-training at Johns Hopkins University - D.V. Trotman - and an Afro-Trinidadian himself, titled his useful post-slavery work: *Crime in Trinidad Conflict and Control in a Plantation Society 1838-1900*.

[650] A. Caldecott, *The Church in the West Indies* (London: Frank Cass, 1970) pp.206-07.

[651] Singh, *Bloodstained Tombs*, p.16.

[652] Hjortshoj, "The Shi'a-Sunni Dispute in Lucknow." In Kramer ed. *Shi'ism, Resistance and Revolution* pp.289-309.

[653] In Comins, *Note on Emigration*, p.7.

[654] H.N. Coleridge, *Six Months in the West Indies in 1825* (London: John Murray, 1871), p.64.

[655] Major Fagan (Trinidad Magistrate 1846-48) in C.O. 295/158: Harris to Grey, 7 December 1847.

[656] Williams, *History of the People*, p.109.

[657] K.O. Laurence, *Immigration into the West Indies in the Nineteenth Century* (Jamaica: Caribbean Universities, 1971) pp.36-

39. Laurence writes that this intermittent migration "failed" due to China's insistence on free return passages, a minimum ratio of males:females, and abuses in recruitment.

[658]   Baltimore: Johns Hopkins University Press, 1993.

[659]   Trevor Millet, *The Chinese in Trinidad* (Port of Spain: Inprint, 1993) pp.1-9.

[660]   Comins, Surgeon-Major D.W.D. *Note on Emigration from India to Trinidad* (Calcutta: Bengal Secretariat Press, 1893) p.7.

[661]   Carl Campbell, *Cedulants and Capitulants The Politics of the Coloured Opposition in the Slave Society of Trinidad 1783-1838* (Port of Spain: Paria, 1992).

[662]   J.U.G. Asiegbu, *Slavery and the Politics of Liberation 1787-1861 A Study of Liberated African Migration and British Anti-Slavery Policy* (New York: Africana, 1969) pp.328-9.

[663]   P.D. Curtin, "The British Sugar Duties and West Indian Prosperity," *Journal of Economic History* XIV (2) 1954, 157-64.

[664]   *Trinidad Spectator,* 26 April 1848.

[665]   *Trinidad Spectator,* 3 May 1848.

[666]   W.A. Green, *British Slave Emancipation The Sugar Colonies and the Great Experiment 1830-1865* (London: Oxford University, 1976), p.280.

[667]   *Royal Franchise Commission,* 2 February 1888 Meeting in the Council Hall, Government House (Port of Spain) p.9.

[668]   Green, *British Slave Emancipation,* pp.281-83.

[669]   Anthony de Verteuil, *The Years of Revolt 1881-1888.* (Port of Spain: Paria, 1984) p.23.

[670]   David V. Trotman, *Crime in Trinidad Conflict and Control in a Plantation Society 1838-1900* (Knoxville: University of Tennessee, 1986) pp.30-31.

[671]   Other areas were San Fernando with 1.28 percent; Couva and Chaguanas 10.43 percent; Tacarigua 8.29; Savannah Grande 6.24; St. Anns and Diego Martin 5.56; Montserrat 5.07; Arima 3.04; Cedros 1.60; Mayaro, Toco and Blanchisuesse .21 percent - thus making up 54.68 percent of the Indians.

672 Anne Martell, "The Canadian Presbyterian Mission to Trinidad's East Indian Population, 1868-1912," Master's Thesis (Dalhousie University, Department of History, 1976) pp.76-77.

673 Letters had begun to appear in the press, for instance, that to the editor of the *San Fernando Gazette*, where "Indo-Trinidadian" is substituted for "coolies." By 1898 Indians were publishing *The Indian Kohinoor Gazette* both in English and Hindi. B. Brereton, *Race Relations in Colonial Trinidad 1870-1900* (London: Cambridge University, 1979) p.191.

674 T. Fitz-Evan Eversley, *The Trinidad Reviewer for the Year 1900* Volume 2 (London: Lombard and Company, 1900) p.89.

675 *Papers Relating to Her Majesty's Colonial Possessions* Trinidad No.4: Robinson to Holland, 30 June 1887. The same despatch mentions the "extremely heavy" costs of maintaining 992 miles of roads, only 204 of which are worthy of the name. Since 1879 an annual sum of L34,000 was set aside for roadworks (p.59).

676 In the last years of the century, there was an 88 per cent increase in small farmer numbers, "almost equally divided between Indian and African proprietors." This and the better economy in Trinidad, vis a vis its neighbors, prevented racial hostility, according to M. Cross, "Colonialism and Ethnicity: A Comparison and Case Study," *Ethnic and Racial Studies* 1 (1) 1978, 37-59.

Printed in the United States
4611

9 781401 017682